NEAR-DEATH
EXPERIENCES
the rest of the story

NEAR-DEATH
EXPERIENCES
the rest of the story

WHAT THEY TEACH US ABOUT LIVING, DYING, AND OUR TRUE PURPOSE

P.M.H. ATWATER

HAMPTON ROADS

Cover design by Barb Fisher, www.levanfisherdesign.com
Cover photographs © Getty Images/PhotoAlto/Odilon Dimier and Shuttersock/kaktuzoid
Interior design by Dutton & Sherman Design

Hampton Roads Publishing Company, Inc.
Charlottesville, VA 22906
www.hrpub.com

Library of Congress Cataloging-in-Publication Data available on request.

ISBN 978-1-57174-651-1

10 9 8 7 6 5 4 3 2 1

Printed on acid-free paper in Canada

TCP

DEDICATION

I dedicate this book to the powers of darkness and light. Without both, Creation's story would not exist, nor would we. The swings of Creation's pendulum between these two great polarities enable growth to occur. I witnessed this truth when I died. Researching that edge—the one between life and death—clarified what I had witnessed.

The bigness of forever lies in the eyes of near-death experiencers. I've had the privilege of looking through thousands of them, including my own. Now, it's your turn.

CONTENTS

WHAT THIS BOOK IS

Raymond E. Moody, Jr., M.D., started it. In 1975, his book *Life After Life*[1] took off. I mean like a rocket ship. And it has yet to stop turning heads worldwide. Imagine it: a medical doctor discussing patients' stories of entering another realm, an afterlife, at the point of death or when they nearly died, and then describing a pattern to the stories that seemed to indicate that what they spoke of might really be true. The hoopla that resulted was, well, off the charts.

Scientists in other countries objected strenuously. They couldn't match Moody's claims. Ignoring prior work, some of it dating back to the seventeen hundreds and featuring essentially the same patterning as modern cases, their objections held that there were "too many variables" for comparisons between what they found and what Moody claimed. Kenneth Ring changed that when he published *Life at Death*,[2] a scientific study that verified Moody's work, five years later.

I entered the scene in 1978, quietly researching near-death states and amassing a great deal of data. I would have never known about others had it not been for a phone call from Kenneth Ring. Quite by accident he had run across a small, self-published book of mine entitled *I Died Three Times in 1977*[3] in Hartford, Connecticut. How it got there nobody knows. At his invitation, I journeyed to his "neck of the woods" to meet my peer group. The year was 1981.

My peers turned out to be physicians, psychologists, psychiatrists, and scientists who spoke a "language" I was unfamiliar with. They practiced a type of research that seemed inappropriate for the work at hand. Experience had long taught me that transformational shifts in consciousness and the wide sweep of exceptions that can occur because of them were outside the range of double-blind studies with a control group (the "scientific method"). I felt that my work was just as valid as anyone else's—90 to 95 percent of what is learned in medicine comes from personnel listening to patients, and over 70 percent of the medical procedures used, even today, resulted from trained observers such as myself who cross-checked and tested what they found. Never once did I just ask questions of people—I observed, watched, and studied them—as behaviors and body language often say more than words do.

My previous experience spanned the sixties and most of the seventies, when I was experimenting with and studying altered states of consciousness, mysticism, psychic phenomena, and the transformational process. Nearly three thousand people were involved in the various talks, classes, experiments, and all manner of projects I sponsored—eventually through "Inner Forum," a nonprofit metaphysical corporation I created in Boise, Idaho.[4] I couldn't learn enough, fast enough.

Those were heady days, and then I died. Not once, but three times in three months. What I went through is another story. What I did about it is this story. During my third episode, what I came to call The Voice Like None Other spoke. It said: "Test revelation. You are to do the research. One book for each death." I was shown what that meant and what was to be in each book. Books two and three were named, but not book one. When I could breathe again, every cell and bone filled with the Presence of that Voice, and a passion and fierce determination began to grow inside me. I knew at that moment that somehow I had to put what happened to me on a "shelf" in my mind. I needed to become totally objective. After my body reasonably healed, I moved to Virginia and got a job that had me living out of a suitcase and working on-site during large computerized telephone installations. I traveled half the United States and found experiencers at every turn. I have penned many books on what I discovered, many more than the original three I was asked to write.

So what is this book?

Call it my "last hurrah," as I retire from active fieldwork in 2010.

Counting my previous work back in Idaho, this book contains the summation of forty-three years of research involving nearly seven thousand adults and children.

Chapters 1 through 15 center on near-death states, and are solidly grounded in actual stories. Some of it may sound familiar to you if you've read any of my previous work, but most of it will not. That's because I finally say things I never dared to say before. (Researchers have to be careful, you know.)

Everything pivots with chapter 16. It is there that we jump from the familiar into the unfamiliar, the type of material that recognizes that near-death states are *not* some type of anomaly, but rather, part of the larger genre of transformations of consciousness.

Consistently over the years I have noticed something else going on with transformative states besides an expansion of faculties and consciousness—what some might call a spiritual awakening or breakthrough. I first described this in a paper I wrote called "Brain Shift: A Theoretical Model Using Research on Near-Death States to Explore the Transformation of Consciousness (Phases I and II)." In essence, this book is Phase III of what became the Brain Shift/Spirit Shift model.

Why a Phase III? Because what I noticed is this: *transformations of consciousness are a biological imperative for the advancement and evolution of the human species.* You can actually track the Brain Shift part through sensitivity/synchronicity, the limbic system, temporal lobes, and deep structures. You can do the same thing with the Spirit Shift that occurs through evidence of a "second birth," the biological imperative, a new model of existence, and a new Christology.

It's all here, what I believe to be proof that near-death research needs to step up to the next level, and the next level after that. The transformative process guarantees that we as humans fulfill our destiny . . . but the way this works is far more surprising than what any guru, master teacher, or scientist could ever say.

None of this works quite like it seems, as you will soon see.

OPENING STATEMENT

The physicist Wolfgang Pauli once decreed that a new science is needed to explore the objective side of human consciousness and the subjective side of matter. *Not* mysticism, but a science willing to incorporate objective *and* subjective avenues to discovery while recognizing the legitimacy of personal experience. This new science is now emerging, despite the objections of those who have forgotten how to question and search from fields afar.

Seemingly unrelated ideas now overlap, as one discovery cross-fertilizes another. Today, we are making connections few ever believed possible—in medical breakthroughs, in the study of consciousness, in the esoteric teachings of "mystery," and within the realms of our own hearts and minds.

I am honored to be part of this revolution, along with hundreds of thousands of others who refuse, as I do, to accept attempts to standardize the unknown.

ACKNOWLEDGMENTS

The phrase "thank you" can never express my deepest and most sincere gratitude to the following people, without whose aid I could never have accomplished the goal set before me:

Kenneth L. Johnston
William G. Reimer
Elisabeth Kübler-Ross
Wally Johnston
David McKnight
Terry Young Atwater
Kenneth Ring

As years passed, this group expanded to include:

Tam Mossman
Nancy Bush
Leslee Morabito
Pat Fenske
Bruce Greyson
Diane Corcoran
Stephanie Wiltse

CHAPTER ONE

GROUNDWORK:
THE NEAR-DEATH EXPERIENCE

"Research is the highest form of adoration."

—Pierre Teilhard de Chardin

People forget that the vast majority of near-death experiences emerge from situations of violence or trauma. A typical experiencer contends with body damage (sometimes severe) and the immediacy of recognizing that "here" (where they are now) is not the same as "there" (where they once were). No matter how ecstatic or terrifying the experience may be, what comes next is usually confusing, maybe angry, as most of us didn't want to come back. We wanted to stay where we were.

The phenomenon captures public attention as none other. It is soul-stirring in the way it reminds even the most staid that home, our true home, is not a joke. It exists, and it is real.

"Off-limit" signs disappear when you engage in research. Starkly different versions of reality emerge . . . about abortion, suicide, life after death, flow states, brain development, the dead coming back, otherworldly realms, spiritual lights, good and evil, drugs, energy fields, the soul, Deity, biological imperatives, animals, ghosts, religious/mystical traditions, psychic ability, children, evolutionary change, and much more. What was once sacred and taboo vanishes.

No skeptic, medical or otherwise, has ever investigated the entire phenomenon—the near-death experience *and* its aftereffects—to any appreciable degree or with a research base large enough for informed comment. A number of near-death researchers have "rushed to judgment," without recognizing that it is the aftereffects, both physiological and psychological, that validate the phenomenon—not the other way around. You cannot study one without the other.

As for me, I have spent most of thirty-three years working full-time in the field of near-death studies, not as an academician or scientist but as a cop's kid raised in a police station and taught as a youngster to never believe everything a person tells you—to ask questions, search further, watch, listen, and challenge your own findings. Whatever appears as truth seldom is.[5] Actually, I was a spunky kid who was getting into trouble long before Dad ever became my dad (he adopted me when I was in the third grade, after he married my mom).

I have every intention of saying things throughout the pages of this book that I have never allowed myself to say before. Now that some of my observations have been verified in clinical studies, and my work has passed "the test of time," I feel a certain ease I have never felt before.[6] That ease, however, could simply be a sign of age—I have passed the seventy-three mark.

Having admitted that much, let me warn you that this book digs deep and covers a lot of territory. It is definitely not for the fainthearted or for those who just want to be entertained. I've geared it for courageous, curious folk who demand more from their questions than pat answers. I begin piecemeal with lots of "headers," each section building upon the last, like "maps and models" spread out for viewing. The fact is that the near-death experience reveals more about life than it does death, and what it reveals is stunning! So, let's get started.

COMMONLY ACCEPTED DEFINITION OF A NEAR-DEATH EXPERIENCE

Let's clarify the subject. Yes, I have my preferences on what to offer here, but so does every other researcher in the field of near-death studies. Virtually no two definitions are alike, which drives medical types crazy. So, for the sake of consistency, I offer this definition, originally developed by the International Association for Near-Death Studies (IANDS):[7]

> The near-death experience is an intense awareness, sense, or experience of otherworldiness, whether pleasant or unpleasant, that happens to people who are at the edge of death. It is of such magnitude that most experiencers are deeply affected, many to the point of making significant changes in their lives because of what happened to them. Aftereffects often last lifelong and can intensify over time.

WHAT IS MEANT BY DEATH

Who among us can be certain if all near-death experiencers were fully dead? Many revived or were resuscitated after clinical death; some were close to death; others, in a split second of utter fear, were convinced they were going to die but didn't (called a "fear" death). Because of this abstraction, what is meant by the "final verdict" and how a physician or emergency worker makes such a determination are called into question. Over time, though, death criteria has radically changed. Back in "merry old England," for instance, when locals ran out of places to bury people, they dug up coffins, took bones to a bone-house, and reused the grave. Once these coffins were opened, one out of twenty-five was found with scratch marks on the inside, proof that people had been buried alive. From then on a string was tied to the wrist of the corpse with the other end secured to a bell above ground. Someone would sit out in the graveyard each night to listen for bell sounds and hopefully, save a life. The slang phrases "graveyard shift," "saved by the bell," and "dead ringer" all trace back to this practice.

We've come a long way since that time in history in developing criteria more dependable than "bell ringing" to be certain the dead are truly dead. But a surprise finding in 2007 abruptly challenged what we thought we had learned.

We've known for some time that five minutes without oxygen is fatal to brain cells. Yet dying itself takes longer to occur because cell death isn't an event, it's a process. An exception is with humans who are exposed to extreme cold or who drown in icy water. It is possible for them to benefit from hypothermia, a survival response that automatically lowers body temperature enough to slow cell death, sometimes for up to thirty minutes or more.

The 2007 discovery? *Brain cells can actually live for hours after vital signs cease.* Patients die not because of lack of oxygen, but because oxygen was resumed too fast during what were thought to be lifesaving procedures (a reversal of the scratched-coffin terror). Standard emergency room protocols, as it has turned out, are exactly backwards.[8] A revolution in resuscitation techniques is now under way.

WHAT IS TYPICAL TO NEAR-DEATH STATES

There is little argument among researchers that, on average, most near-death experiencers, adults *and* children, go without vital signs (pulse, breath, brain waves) for between five and twenty minutes. Amazing as this may seem, considering how quickly brain damage can occur after cessation of vital signs, even more amazing is that usually there is little or no brain damage afterward; rather, there is brain enhancement. You heard me right: Individuals return to life smarter than before. Sometimes this enhancement can be quite dramatic, especially with young kids. In my own work, I discovered so many who had revived in a morgue—maybe an hour, maybe six hours after having "died"—that I no longer came to regard this as unusual. I admit a bias here. Being a three-time experiencer myself, it would take a lot to impress me as concerns "the dead come back," yet impressed I was when I met a man who had revived while being cut open during autopsy after a full three days of being a corpse in a freezer vault.[9]

I doubt that the new resuscitation techniques from the 2007 discovery about brain cells will affect near-death research, as the bulk of cases take place outside hospital environments and the immediacy of emergency treatment. Still, the finding is very important. It proves that what appears to be brain death is not synonymous with cell death. Maybe we ought to entice angels to serve as "cell ringers" with this one (no pun intended).

CURRENT STATISTICS

Data has been downscaled in the last several years to reflect a more conservative approach to statistics (since the majority of surveys done were not scientific). At this writing, countries worldwide that engage in near-death research report that between 4 to 5 percent of their general population has had a near-death experience (this includes the United States). Global estimates jump to between 12 to 21 percent when focused on those receiving critical care when the phenomenon occurs. What we're talking about here are huge numbers—hundreds of millions of people—of every age, size, ethnicity, social status, belief, and intelligence level imaginable.[10]

Unfortunately, none of the statisticians have ever used a separate category to track child experiencers, so we have no overall data on them. The closest to a clinical estimate for the young comes from Melvin Morse, M.D., in his book, *Closer to the Light*. Morse estimates that 70 percent of children have had a near-death experience. Although his figures show that children are much more prone to the experience than adults during a health crisis, further study is still needed. Why some people undergo the experience and others do not is not understood.[11]

THE CLASSICAL MODEL

Raymond Moody's original work identified fifteen elements of the near-death experience. He noted how these formed what appeared to be a scenario (content pattern). Moody's list:

- Ineffability, beyond the limits of any language to describe

- Hearing yourself pronounced dead

- Feelings of peace and quiet

- Hearing unusual noises

- Seeing a dark tunnel

- Finding yourself outside your body

- Meeting "spiritual beings"

- A very bright light experienced as a "being of light"

- A panoramic life review

- Sensing a border or limit to where you can go

- Coming back into your body

- Frustrating attempts to tell others about what happened to you

- Subtle "broadening and deepening" of your life afterward

- Elimination of the fear of death

- Corroboration of events witnessed while out of your body

Two years later, after hundreds more interviews, Moody added four more elements to his list of common components to what experiencers claim to have encountered:

- A realm where all knowledge exists

- Cities of light

- A realm of bewildered spirits

- Supernatural rescues

SAME PHENOMENON—DIFFERENT ANGLE

I had never heard of Raymond Moody or his book until Kenneth Ring told me about them and the field of study that had ensued, three years after I had begun my work. Also unknown to me was that other people were doing the same thing I was. My only introduction to even the term "near-death experience" was through Elisabeth Kübler-Ross, who I met at O'Hare Airport near Chicago in 1978.[12] Her plane to Europe was late, so the two of us huddled like school girls on a bench for over an hour. I told her about my own three near-death episodes, and she told me about the phenomenon. She never said a thing about Moody.

Elisabeth called me a "near-death survivor" and validated what had happened to me. I will be forever in her debt for that. Yet what she said gave rise to more questions than answers in my mind. A couple months later, after moving from my home state of Idaho to Washington, D.C., a group of experiencers gathered 'round after a talk I had given and the next thing I knew I was studying them, listening deeply, with a determination for objectivity which I strive for to this day.

Naturally I came to look at the near-death phenomenon, both the experience and its aftereffects, in a different manner than the cohorts I had yet to meet. And therein lies the conflict that later became "a very big deal."

CHAPTER TWO

THE SCOPE OF WHAT I DID

"If one regards oneself as a skeptic, it is a good plan to have occasional doubts about one's skepticism."

—SIGMUND FREUD

As of this writing, my sessions with experiencers of near-death states (at times simple interviews) number nearly four thousand adults and children. This figure does not include the sessions I had with significant others: parents, spouses, children of experiencers, relatives, health-care providers, neighbors, coworkers, friends. I lost count of this segment of my research base long ago, although an estimate in the range of around five hundred people would be reasonable. The bulk of my findings were obtained between the years of 1978 to 2004, after which the search for meaning took precedence (although some fieldwork continued). The majority of these additional cases were from child experiencers who are now adults. These people sought me out after the publication of *Children of the New Millennium*, and later *The New Children and Near-Death Experiences*.[13]

THE SESSIONS I HELD

Knowing that personal bias could jeopardize anything I did, I put my own experiences on a "back shelf" in my mind and played dumb a lot. What I mean is that I asked as many open-ended and unstructured questions as possible, trying not to reveal either my identity or intent. If I did say who I was, experiencers would counter with, "Well, you know how it is." I'd stand my ground if this occurred: "Maybe yes, maybe no, but tell me anyway. Give me details and don't leave a thing out." Mostly, though, I used simple phrases like "oh really" or "tell me more" or that wonderful all-purpose lead of "and . . . ?"

I found that voice intonation and inflection, along with easy, nonthreatening body language, netted more information than "arranged" questions. All I had to do was "leave the door open," and the experiencer would willingly "walk through," as if utterly relieved. There's nothing like a nonjudgmental, sincerely interested listener. I did alter my style somewhat with children, though, and in this manner: no parents allowed, same eye-level contact at all times (with little ones that meant I was on my belly), changed body postures to elicit response, replacing note-taking with a gentle sincerity and steady focus, encouraging feelings as well as memories, opening myself to sense the "wave" of consciousness they "ride" so I could see through their eyes. I had sessions with parents, too, as I wanted to explore what they noticed and any opinions they had. This was important, as children can and sometimes do slant their stories to fit the *emotional expectations of their parents*.

I have used a total of three questionnaires for the purpose of cross-checking previous observations. I developed the first in 1981. It compared random selections from my work with an equal number from the archives of IANDS. No difference in experiencers' answers—all love and forgiveness, as if everything in their life was now perfect—even though I knew folks in my batch were undergoing serious challenges.

None of them, not in the archives of IANDS nor with people I had personally met, recognized the overall impact of their experience or how they had changed because of it. This exercise was proof-positive to me that depending solely on such answers (no matter how cleverly worded a questionnaire might be) is wrong and will distort research findings. Questionnaires can augment, but they can never be a substitute for fieldwork.

My second questionnaire was done in 1994 to test the range of the electrical sensitivity that experiencers reported as part of their aftereffects.[14] The third, in 1999, was designed to further investigate what happened to child experiencers once they reached adulthood. I designed it to "push buttons," and indeed it did, to the extent that some refused to cooperate, saying the information was too personal. One man apologized the following year, after he had overcome his anger long enough to fill it out, and discovered in doing so how he had been hiding things he had not wanted to admit. "What a revelation," he exclaimed. "Answering this thing changed me almost as much as my near-death experience."

STATISTICS FROM MY RESEARCH BASE

All of my findings have been cross-checked at least four times with different people in different parts of the country and with those of other cultures, at differing times. It was as if I was "driven" to explore everything from 360 degrees. The statistics that follow are based on actual sessions:

3,000 adult experiencers

- 80 percent White (from U.S., Canada, England, Belgium, France, Mexico, Egypt, Saudi Arabia, Russia, Georgia, Ukraine—no further breakdowns)

- 20 percent Black (15% African American; 5% Kenya, Haiti, Canada)

277 child experiencers

- 60 percent White (from U.S., Canada, France, England, Ukraine— no further breakdowns)

- 23 percent Latino—U.S., Mexico, Argentina, Colombia

- 12 percent Black—U.S., Canada

- 5 percent Asian—Malaysia, China

NOTE: I rejected an additional 15 percent because the session with the child was compromised by adult interference (adult explaining/interpreting for the child). I found that fascination with "out-of-the-mouths-of-babes" reports can mislead more readily than enlighten.

Percentages of how I connected with these people:

- 60 percent through synchronicity—seven were blind since birth, not certain about two others

- 30 percent through talks I gave and advertisements and announcements I placed in magazines, newspapers, and newsletters

- 10 percent from questionnaire participants who had agreed to take part in my research

The synchronicity of how I met the majority of experiencers is uncanny, if not bizarre. Nearly every day some would pop into my life, sometimes groups of them at a time. Examples: I was sitting at a table in a truck stop near Macon, Georgia, when a giant of a man pulled up a chair opposite me and proceed to describe his near-death experience. In a motel in eastern Kentucky, I was teaching the crew how to use a new computerized phone system. Half of them, one at a time, cornered me later to tell me about their own or a loved one's near-death experience. I hailed a cab in Washington, D.C., and the Haitian cabbie took one look at me, then yelled, "You died like I did. I can tell you about what happened to me and you won't laugh." Unplanned, spontaneous, constant! I finally decided I must have been wearing a "sign" on my back that said "Tell me about your near-death experience." No names. We were drawn together.

HOW TRUE WERE THE STORIES I HEARD

One adult female experiencer lied to me and I didn't catch it. Her daughter contacted me in December of 2007 and admitted that it was she who was the actual experiencer, not her mother. Apparently, her mother craved attention and was willing to lie to get it. The daughter had wrestled with whether or not to go public about this, and then her mother died. She told me about the incident, just to set the record straight, but would not identify her mother.

I do not know if other fraudulent claims have slipped past my notice. Usually, exaggerated or invented stories are easy to recognize, but not always. During the early years of my work, research was straightforward, including third-party verifications. This assured accuracy. Everything changed after Betty Eadie's book *Embraced by the Light*[15] and Dannion Brinkley's *Saved by the Light*[16] became bestsellers (both are experiencers). Individuals wanting to "protect their rights" suddenly withdrew; others called me on the phone and threatened a lawsuit if I used anything of theirs; liars became more blatant, even to the point of one woman taking a published case of mine, changing the names, and spreading it around as hers. Occasionally I was slapped, spit at, or cursed by angry experiencers if I objected. Once media spotlights began to fade, though, this type of negative behavior faded, too.

During 2008 and 2009, conditions changed again—as a direct result of pressure from television talk shows and publishing houses. Talk shows now feature what I call "the stereotypical experience" (person on surgical table dies, is resuscitated or revives, amazes everyone with what is seen and heard while dead, lots of medical verification). Fact: only a small percentage of investigated cases fit this scenario. What about the rest? Since when does "stereotypical" encompass the drama and extremes of what is really typical? Publishers want the "big picture"—what was revealed to the experiencer— and nothing about the *how* or about the near-death state itself. The resulting sensational "one-size-fits-all" and "I-know-everything"–type tomes are shaky at best. One individual went so far as to hire a lawyer and threaten lawsuits against anyone who might tell the truth about a book that was written and the so-called "experiencer" who wrote it.

We have been told since "the near-death phenomenon" first hit the scene in 1975 that experiencers become honest, loving, spiritual paragons after their experiences. Well, many do. The rest improve greatly. Still, there's a shadow side, and we need to admit that.

The narratives that experiencers give help to establish the veracity of near-death experiences—they hold up over time. The stories are as clear, coherent, and vivid as the day originally told, even if twenty years or more have passed. If anything did fade, seldom is it of any significance. This is almost unheard of in memory trials.

There are a few complicating factors when dealing with experiencers that appear to challenge the honesty factor, but really don't. *The majority tend to hold back until they trust you.* Perhaps this is because of the fear of being labeled crazy. Whatever the reason, it is fairly common for narrative stories to be delivered in bits and pieces and spread out over a few months or a year or so.

And then there's "downloading." Few experiencers can process the revelations that surface during their episode. You hear comments such as: "I felt like I would explode if the information didn't stop coming," or "I can't handle this—too much too fast," or "I just can't remember it all." And, indeed, most of the deeper materials that often flood in during an episode, "the revelations," are lost.

Yet, some experiencers report downloading afterward as if what was lost is now coming back. This can occur in dribs and drabs or be quite extensive and go on for years. What I am describing here is *not* an embellishment, per se. Rather, it often signals that the experiencer has developed another form of sensitivity to "otherworldly realities" and has become like a "channel." This "extra" material does not affect the individual's original narrative—thus no embellishment. But it does expand on what is commonplace afterward (a topic for discussion later).

PATTERNS IN DYING

During my research of the phenomenon, I discovered a pattern to the way death visited most of the experiencers, and it went like this: A little over half the men I contacted died because of heart-related ailments, while another 25 percent were involved in violence or accidents. A whopping 70 percent of the women experienced their episode during childbirth, miscarriage, or a hysterectomy.

It doesn't take a psychologist to interpret this pattern. Men in industrialized societies such as ours are not encouraged to express their "hearts" or emotions openly. What are drummed into their heads since boyhood are aggressive behaviors that value strength and power. Anything else is considered a sign of weakness. It should come as no surprise, then, that so many men suffer from heart stress, commit acts of violence, or are involved in accidents. By repressing or holding in emotions, they build up pressure that must be released—internally or externally—sooner or later.

The process of pregnancy and childbirth has always been linked to a time of major transformation for women, carrying with it the possibility of trauma for woman or child. Although childbirth and related conditions accounted for countless deaths in years past, women today still "die" in the sense that the birth of a child demands both the surrender and the rebirth of the mother. Death, whether literal or symbolic, remains an integral component to birth.

Length of near-death scenarios followed a "design" as well. Most of the people I worked with whose episodes were brief and consisted of few elements were usually the types of people who seemed to need a little "nudge" of some kind toward making a change in their life. Conversely, most of those whose experience was long, complex, and quite involved seemed in need of more far-reaching, major changes in basic attitudes and lifestyle. Length of the episode, then, seemed to depend more on the strength of changes that would be the most beneficial to the individual than on happenstance or chance.

There were personality patterns, too. I noticed that people who had more fixed belief systems and inflexible attitudes about life often returned thinking their experience was a religious conversion, or felt a need to somehow evangelize about what they had learned from it. It was almost as if they traded one belief system for another, no matter how altered or unique that new system might be. But those who were more flexible and curious, more open to begin with, often returned so bewildered and confused that they seemed bereft of any belief system at all. This group usually had the most work to do redefining life and its meaning, yet they were the least likely to evangelize. They seemed to spend more time remaking themselves than trying to remake everyone else.

There was one pattern and only one pattern I found present in every single case I came across, and that was that during the near-death scenario, experiencers had the opportunity to come face to face with whatever existed and was fully integrated within their deepest selves. Very few of us are in touch with what we really believe at our deepest level. What we say we believe and what we *really* believe are usually quite different.

If you are honest about near-death episodes and keep them in context with the life of each experiencer, you will discover what I did: that scenarios complement, on some level, the inner reality of those who experience them. Always! Including with children. For a child brings forward into his or her birth the sum total of whatever existed before conception as well as whatever was absorbed during gestation in the mother's womb. Children's stories are simple and direct; adults' are colored from years of living. But it's the same phenomenon with the same patterns.

Let's not miss this point: the near-death phenomenon is now and has always been the subject, not just an "experience" so many want to prove or disprove. As a phenomenon, definable edges elude our best efforts to affix cause.

CHAPTER THREE

A NEW MODEL

"The studies are very significant in that we have a group of people with no brain function . . . who have well-structured, lucid thought processes with reasoning and memory forma-tion at a time when their brains are shown not to function."

—SAM PARNIA, M.D.

A question I have asked of fellow researchers since my first trip to Storrs, Connecticut, in 1981, is . . . why do you compare your cases to the "clas-sical model" when it isn't that classical? The field was not that broad in scope to begin with, nor ethnically diverse. Hellish scenarios were missed; children's came later. Cultural differences, language constraints, and researcher bias were mostly glossed over. Thus, the model that resulted came from a limited base.

Certainly times were different then. Undue pressure from media hype, lack of funding, professional attacks—all took their toll. In spite of this, ini-tial findings were impressive. Still, you can challenge that model, and I do. I believe it is skewed. The entire phenomenon (experience, aftereffects, im-plications) comprises a complex dynamic that cannot be easily defined or understood . . . by anyone.

FOUR TYPES OF NEAR-DEATH EXPERIENCES

In my work, I discovered four distinctive patterns to the experience itself. Here they are. The incident-rate figures I present are based on 3,000 adult and 277 child experiencers.

Initial experience—sometimes called the "non" experience.

Involves one, maybe two or three elements, such as a loving nothingness, the living dark, a friendly voice/visitation, a brief out-of-body experience, or a manifestation of some kind. Usually experienced by those who need the least amount of shake-up in their lives at that point in time. Often, this becomes a "seed" experience or an introduction to other ways of perceiving and recognizing reality. Rarely is any other element present. (*76 percent of children, 20 percent of adults.*)

Unpleasant or hellish experience—sometimes referred to as "distressing."

Encounter with a threatening void, stark limbo, or hellish purgatory, or scenes of a startling and unexpected indifference (like being shunned), even "hauntings" from one's own past or having to face "unfinished business." Usually experienced by those who seem to have deeply suppressed or repressed guilt, fear, and anger, and/or those who expect some kind of punishment or discomfort after death. Life reviews common. Some have life previews. (*3 percent of children, 15 percent of adults.*)

Pleasant or heavenly experience—sometimes referred to as "radiant."

Involves heaven-like scenarios of loving family reunions with those who have died previously, reassuring religious figures or light beings, validation that life counts, affirmative and inspiring dialogue, lovely landscapes. Usually experienced by those who most need to know how loved they are and how important life is, and how every effort has a purpose in the overall scheme of things. Life reviews common. Some have life previews. (*19 percent of children, 47 percent of adults.*)

Transcendent experience—sometimes called the "collective universality."

Encounter with otherworldly dimensions and scenes beyond the individual's frame of reference; sometimes includes revelations of greater truths. Seldom personal in content. Usually experienced by those who are ready for a "mind-stretching" challenge and/or individuals who are apt to utilize (to whatever degree) the truths that are revealed to them. Life reviews rare. Collective previews common—the world's future, evolutionary changes, etc. (*2 percent of children, 18 percent of adults.*)

Although one type of experience can roll into another (e.g., hellish then heavenly), for the majority, each of these patterns constitutes the entirety of a given episode. Of note: the classical model was developed by adults for adults to cover the adult experience. It is not that useful, in my opinion, with children.

Do not affix "positive" or "negative" labels to any of these experience types.

Positive and negative are judgmental terms that do not necessarily apply to near-death states or to the aftereffects that follow. Case in point: I gave a talk about the phenomenon in a large hall. It was so packed that there were not enough chairs, leaving some standing. When I finished, I asked if there were any experiencers in the audience who would like to come up to the microphone and share what had happened to them. Two volunteered. A slender man, maybe in his late twenties, enthralled everyone with his tale of one of the most beautiful, heavenly experiences I had ever heard. There was hardly a dry eye in the place. Then he shocked the audience by saying this was the worst thing that had ever happened to him, that it had fouled up his life and he felt cursed to have had it. Immediately, a woman, probably in her thirties, jumped up and described her experience, a terror-filled scenario of being at the mercy of a raging storm, with high winds, thunder, and lightning. She had to fight to save herself from being sucked into a whirlpool as she swam to shore. What she said next was equally a stunner: "This was the best thing that ever happened to me. It proved to me that we all have a second chance in life and we can succeed no matter what the obstacles are." She was so glowing when she said this that she appeared to be engulfed by a special light.

Before this incident, I labeled unpleasant experiences as negative and pleasant ones as positive. I do not make that mistake anymore.

COMMON COMPONENTS—ELEMENTS

I want to set the record straight. "Tunnels" are not typical. In the first poll done by Gallup in 1982, only around 9 percent of the experiencers surveyed said they saw or passed through anything like a tunnel. In many cultures such things are still unheard of. The idea of tunnels did not become popular as an element of near-death states until after the book *Life After Life* was sensationalized.[17]

Having said that, let's take a look at what really is commonplace, recognizing as we do that faculties are greatly enhanced during almost any near-death state. The experiencer often feels hyperalert, with his or her thoughts hyperlucid and his or her emotions at hyperpitch.

Out-of-body experiences were the most reported element; many experiencers spoke of encountering a special light. Two-thirds claimed to have been met by a greeter of some kind, either at or shortly after crossing over. Forty percent described a life review. Any of these four main elements could comprise a single experience (that's it), or be part of a brief or broader scenario (storyline/narrative) that encompassed multiple components such as walks through meadows, forests, open fields, mountain passes, or alongside a river; passage through the darkness of caves or tunnels; tours of cities, the universe, heaven and hell, history/evolution; discussions with other beings; heavenly assignments, hellish condemnations; attending classes in a special school; learning how to heal; being shown inventions/systems that could help society; suffering from judgment or punishment; torture.

Finding oneself engulfed in an exceptional brightness, with each being or plant lit from within as well, is typical. Darkness is reported too, most often described in loving terms but sometimes considered threatening. Few are open to discuss this, which leads me to believe that hellish cases are not at all rare—just underreported. (In my research, one out of seven experiences was the distressing type.)

I'd like to go a little more in-depth with the four elements I found to be the most frequently reported. What I offer here pales in comparison to the real thing.

Out-of-Body Experiences

Most people, regardless of age or location, experience leaving their body behind as they move up and out in spirit form. Some researchers mistakenly classify the phenomenon of near-death as an out-of-body experience. Not so. Out-of-body, as a unique occurrence of its own, does not have the same intensity, impact, or aftereffects as it does as a component of near-death states. As such an element, wraparound, 360-degree vision is typical, even with people blind since birth. "Trips" can involve things like the dead going home and being there to see who picks up the phone when a nurse calls (accurately describing individuals, apparel worn, words said); those who bob along the ceiling like a balloon (maybe confused about what just happened); or those who journey to far away towns and countries (giving unbelievably detailed "travelogues" of everything encountered). The average skeptic cries foul about lack of verification with out-of-body reports, when, in fact, third-party testimonials validating trip details are so numerous that complaints to the contrary are generally ignored.

A Loving Light That Knows You

Adult experiencers are prone to describe this light as brighter than a million suns and more powerful than a million orgasms. Even the children acknowledge that it is alive, knows everything there is to know (including your name and all about you), and is so loving that being engulfed by it is the purest of bliss. Actually, there is a triune of lights experiencers describe: Primary (luminous)—seen as a pulsating radiance of raw, piercing power, so awesome that prolonged contact makes experiencers feel as if they are about to explode; Dark or Black (can have purple tinges)—velvety and warm, safe haven, usually associated with miraculous healings and sudden genius (seldom ever with evil, although it can be experienced that way); Bright or White (silver tinges) or Yellow (gold tinges)—an almost blinding brilliance that emanates unconditional love and knowingness. Child experiencers sometimes refer to bright light as "Father Light;" dark or black light as "Mother Light;" and primary as "God's Light." Some are adamant that Father Light and Mother Light come from God's Light.

A Greeter of Some Kind

Not everyone is met by a greeter, but most are. Usually it is a deceased relative or pet who appears younger and/or healthier than he or she was in life. Family relationships dominate, for good or ill. Examples: if you couldn't tolerate a particular relative, odds are that that person will be there either as an agitant or as a guide; if unknown or missing, a surprise appearance may unravel old secrets. The importance of grandparents really stands out. Whether recognized at first or not, these "seniors" tend to re-establish deeper bonds of caring. Overriding themes in family scenarios are those of love, acceptance, and forgiveness.

With the kids in my research, 70 percent had angels come to greet them. They described these as humanlike (most said they had wings); either black or white of color (like a black or white color crayon) or colored like real people are (with the variations found in human skin hues). With adults and teenagers, the figure is fifty-fifty. Of those who reported angels, 39 percent saw winged ones; the rest spoke of either special "humans" or human-shaped lightforms/globes/cylinders. Some spoke of angels who were black or dark in color (like the kids did); but, for most, these beings were simply seen as bright or white (often identified as guides or guardians). Religious figures who appeared usually matched the individual's faith tradition, but not always. For those who saw Jesus, the most common response was, "He is so joyful and so loving."

Children experienced stern greeters almost as often as kind ones, and that applied to angels as well. I came to recognize a "critical" or "caring" parent-type of greeter for the young whose job seemed to center around whatever was needed—words of praise/comfort or instructive lectures (as if the child could use a little more attention or "fetching up"). Futuristic events, as well as the child's job or mission in life, were often revealed by this type of greeter.

Among other kinds of greeters were animals (the majority could speak or communicated mind-to-mind). Most were deceased pets, yet some were unknown to the experiencer. Larger animals tended to appear for adults (horses, lions, dogs, eagles), and smaller animals for kids (birds, bunnies, turtles). On occasion, I did run across reports of misshapen, grotesque, or demonic greeters, or those who looked so alien that the experiencer was at a loss to describe them.

LIFE REVIEWS

Not half of experiencers report them, yet life reviews wield an almost unspeakable power. Even in the midst of hellish, frightening, or distressing near-death states, nothing strikes at the core of what it is to be human as bluntly as these. It is your life you must face, from birth to death, in reverse order, or in segments—reviewed or relived as things actually happened, in a moment's flash, or agonizingly slowly. Some of those I studied experienced no buffer between them and any pain that could be experienced. The rest, the majority, were more like objective witnesses during the life review, which gave them a deeply meaningful opportunity to see "the other side" of actions and behaviors.

An example of a life review more radical than most is that of a Mafia hitman whose life review involved him reliving everything he had ever done, good or bad, as well as the consequences. He also had to live through whatever happened to each person he hurt *as if he were them*. He felt all of their pain, lived through their circumstances, and faced their grief. He was incapable of hurting another person after that and devoted the rest of his life to serving the poor through various church programs.

There is no prison term, no punishment that can equal the totality of a radical life review. Some accounts cover the entire impact of a person's existence: everything said, thought, or done since birth, and the effect he or she had on everyone, even passersby, whether met or not, and on the air, soil, plants, water, animals . . . the entire gestalt of one's life—the result of ever having taken a breath. There are those I have had sessions with who could not even step on a bug after such a review, nor swat a fly.

Now that I've scared you, let me ease up some. One of the great puzzles in all of this is why almost mundane incidents tend to be highlighted in the life review over seemingly more important ones. The life review actually highlights the little things in life—how we treat each other, lies we told, what we did about our promises and goals, how willing we were to "walk that extra mile" to get a job done or lend a helping hand. It is as if a life review is actually a teaching mechanism, an opportunity to "peel back the layers" so deeds versus consequences can be weighed and measured.

THE BOOK OF LIFE

Remember those mystical and religious stories you once heard that claim that when you die you will read all about yourself in "The Book of Life" or the "Akashic Records"? Well, about 30 percent of the adults in my research reported having seen the fabled book. (Children, by the way, seldom made such a claim.) Of those who did encounter this, some said it really was an actual book, a large one—found in a library stacked with millions of them or simply lying open on a stand or podium as if waiting to be noticed—that had a record of each moment of a person's life contained in its pages. The majority, however, instead of describing "The Book," told me about what appeared as holograms or television-like theatrical showings of their lives acted out before them. They referred to our histories as recorded upon "the skeins of time" (an information field held at a certain frequency) that were only accessible when we as a spirit "vibrated at a particular energy."

Interestingly, the ancient Sanskrit word for "ether," "radiant space," or "sky" is *Akasha*. It is also said to mean "primary substance." In many of the world's religious and spiritual traditions, "Akashic Records" is used synonymously with the term "The Book of Life," to depict that record of everything that has ever happened said to reside forever upon the rays of light that appear as skeins, threads, or shifts in time.

An extra tidbit: religious and spiritual traditions also refer to a "silver cord," said to be the umbilical that connects our physical body to our spirit body. If it breaks, we die. Rarely do near-death experiencers of any age comment on anything like a silver cord. A few did notice it during their out-of-body episode or when they left this world for another one, waving around in the air like some kind of stretchy string. I only ran across two who said theirs was broken and quickly had to be mended. What does this mean? Research doesn't tell us.

CHAPTER FOUR

ACTUAL STORIES

*"In this uncontainable night, be the mystery at the crossroads
of your senses, the meaning discovered there. And if the
world has ceased to hear you, say to the silent earth: I flow.
To the rushing water, speak: I am."*

—Rainer Maria Rilke

My goal is to wean you from the stereotypical with a variety of stories that reflect the majority. Most experiencers prefer that only their first name be used; a few offer their full name. Some editing has been done to save space.

RICH BORUTTA

Rich was engulfed by a special light during a medical crisis, then successfully resuscitated. His comment: "I came to in my hospital bed later and was angry they pulled me out so fast. I knew that the light held all the answers, and they denied me the chance to explore it." He did go back.

"This time I was challenged, but all I wanted was oblivion and I was defiant. I could not provoke any retaliation and was instead given a choice of how I wanted to take part in the activities of the world from then on. I suddenly became sincere and related that I'd like to straighten out the unfinished business and loose ends of my previous life. To accomplish this, I would need some help from the 'feathery' figures I had seen gathering around the light. I encountered a few of them and was briefly conducted into the light itself. It was teeming with activity, and the experience was exhilarating. I felt very sad that I had to break off the connection with the final 'feather' before it seemed that I had completed the process.

"After I was back in the bed and wondering over the whole experience, I pulled out the IVs in my arms and started to leave the hospital, convinced that everything was all right with the world and I needed to tell everyone. A security guard at the door stopped me, and I was returned to my room. My addiction was gone, and my liver began to function from then on. A biopsy uncovered no evidence of permanent damage even though scans performed before the NDE showed a serious blockage as though cancer or cirrhosis were the cause".[18]

JOSEPH

Joseph's wreck happened twenty-seven years ago. He had just moved to Yakima, Washington, to take part in the apple harvest. He lost control of his tractor on a mountainside, was knocked off by a tree. As he fell, he was hung up on the plow controls and was dragged some distance until slapped against a tree trunk. "I heard a very loud popping sound, just like a twig breaking. It was my pelvic bone and lower spinal area. My boot was ripped off my right leg. I passed out, 'til it started raining some on my face." Joseph somehow managed to crawl and stumble a quarter of a mile to the farmhouse, where an ambulance was called. His breastbone was also broken, although he did not know that at the time.

"The doctor hollered at the staff, 'Hurry, we're going to lose him.'" Joseph never felt a thing. "I woke up in another room with my face covered up with a thin white sheet. I had no idea what was going on. It was dark at the time, so I rose up and went right through that darkness, that sheet, to light, and I was sitting there on the bed thinking how good I felt, not realizing I was dead. I just wanted to get my clothes and shoes on and go home. All of a sudden a spinning circular motion came from the upper left corner of the room. It spun faster, then popped open on me and sucked me into it, feet first. I was being dragged to my left just as I was watching the room slowly disappear. I turned over on my back only to see me floating towards what felt like hell's doorway. I begged for Father's mercy to please don't let me die. Then the pulling sensation started me towards a tunnel, and I went through, and saw all of the clouds beneath me and all of my relatives who had gone on before me. One was a king of sorts and he was looking over British troops and a man on horseback who was going to fight.

"This all disappeared and I ended up in an area that was dark with bushes. I had a sharp pain that was a tearing pain in the lower breastbone area that nearly caused me to stop breathing. The pain was gone as quickly as it happened. I slid through a darkened door that was dropping like a garage door, shutting off the white light in front of me. I came out the other side looking at a fence in a clouded area; trees and sky and ground area with more fence, and a forbidden blacked out area. I landed on the ground feet first. I spoke to a man there who had disappeared, never to be seen again. He told me someone would be with me soon.

"I lifted back up into the air and was talked to by this familiar voice, with a loving sound like that of a father. He told me I had to go back, that he had a mission for me to do in my life before it was my time. I begged him not to send me back to all the pain and misery and headaches. He told me it was not my time to be there. I woke up in the hospital and was told by the doctor himself, officially, that I had been dead for two and a half days." Both Joseph and his doctor were puzzled that he was able to think so clearly after being dead for two and a half days—his brain showed no sign of damage from oxygen deprivation.

MIDGE

Midge was pregnant with her second child. "They started worrying about the baby because I didn't seem to be getting bigger. One day in November I was thrown into the hospital. They had to deliver the baby now. I was in trouble. I was twenty-two and had no clue.

"I was knocked out and woke up very, very cold. I was watching it flurry (heavy). I was freezing. I felt a sharp pain, like someone tearing at my skin, and I lifted my hand to stop it. I grabbed a nurse's hand. I remember telling her, 'It's snowing.' She screamed and ran out. A older woman ran in, and I was wheeled into an elevator. I was on a metal tray bed. No mattress. I was naked. The room was freezing. The woman I scared had a sweater on. White. She was young.

"By this time mother was there. They couldn't find my husband, as he had left the hospital. They said the baby was in bad shape. Mother signed papers so he could be taken to Beth Israel Hospital in Newark. They didn't tell me much, except that the baby's head was gashed open when they were cutting the uterus, and he was two and a half pounds.

"A few days later my mother came to tell me they buried the baby. That's when I was told I was in the morgue for four hours. They had not closed me. I bled out. I remembered the snow and the nurse. My mother told me she was crying. The doctor asked why she was crying. She said, 'My daughter is dead and the baby is dying.' He asked, 'Didn't anyone tell you? She is in surgery and they are putting her back together.'

"My parents lived an hour away from the hospital. So the time fits. From the time they got the call and my sister came over so they could come to the hospital had to be two hours already. My mother and I talked about it afterward. She said she had called the funeral parlor and they said they would go right up and get me. The next day they picked up the baby instead."

Midge's near-death experience actually began when the nurse screamed. "I know I wasn't just out of my body taking a spin outside the hospital. I know it wasn't a dream. I remember walking out the door and into the drive in front of the hospital. I don't remember how I got back inside. I was just there looking back at the nurse who was screaming. At first I didn't feel pain. I felt the pain of the pull at the skin but I didn't feel the surgery that followed. After the nurse fled, I laid there and started to realize something was wrong."

During surgery, her near-death episode started up again as if a continuation of the previous one. "I felt like I was gone for years. Like I was away for a long time. I felt great. I was walking in the flurries but I wasn't cold at all. I felt wonderful. No pain. I was very happy. It was black out except for the flurries. Honestly, I don't remember thinking 'Oh, I have a baby,' or anything. I felt like I could just walk away. No one in the hospital or at the sidewalk talked to me or paid me any mind. No tunnel. No voice or angelic light. I felt free. Nothing was holding me. I was at peace."

Midge added: "Did I change? I realized childbirth is not so natural. I was cocky before that. Hey, it's a baby. No big deal. When I was young I was afraid of dying. Since that day I have never been afraid of death. I have always been religious, but I now have a love affair with God. I know he doesn't punish people. He isn't some tyrant. I just know. I also know angels walk with me, and have since that day. I kind of feel it's my job to show people kindness, that God isn't a stiff-necked Father who punishes you if you're bad. We do that ourselves."

Last year, Midge had another near-death episode. "I was with a man I don't know; I heard his voice behind me. We were just walking the way I walked out of the hospital before. This time I was going with him and we were joking. He asked, 'Won't you miss your kiddies?' I said they were grown and they would be fine. We seemed to be gone a while, like a nice easy walk in the park, when he said, 'I have to show you something first.' He showed me a pine forest. I said, 'Oh look at all the Christmas trees.' He said, 'You're not ready. You cannot love them like you do. You can't care.' He said he would leave me there but when I woke up I would be in terrible pain. I was in snow past my ankles but like before, I wasn't cold. I felt the snow hit my face. I could smell the pine forest, then I started to feel a chill. I opened my eyes and my back between the shoulder blades was in horrid pain. Like someone pulling my heart out from the back. I couldn't breathe. It felt like my ribs were broke. I reached over and hit my husband and he woke up. I was having a heart attack."

MULLIGAN

In February 1970, Mulligan was in the fifth week of Army basic training. He woke up sick and went to the dispensary. His temperature was 106 degrees. He was told to take two aspirin and a cold shower. "The next thing I remember was being in the 'office' area. No one was there. I had a horrendous headache. I stood next to the wall and hit my head against it and moaned. I didn't know it at the time, but I was in an advanced stage of bacterial meningitis. The headache was from the lining of my brain swelling. I did not stop hitting my head against the wall until I went numb and was going into a coma. Someone came and told me to go back to bed. I couldn't move, so they guided me back to bed and covered me."

Mulligan has only a vague memory of being taken to the hospital and of four or five people holding him down so they could do a spinal tap. "I popped out of body—serenity. I didn't feel anything. I looked down. Someone on the medical team said it was really going to hurt. I wondered why it didn't hurt. I sensed my Spiritual Guide. I said (not verbally), 'Who are you?' My Spiritual Guide answered, 'Don't you remember me? I've always been with you. I used to play with you.' I replied, 'Why don't I remember you? Why am I up here?' My Guide replied, 'If you were down there, it would be very painful.' I agreed."

A debate ensued, with the Guide suggesting that they go to the light while Mulligan countered that he wasn't ready to leave. The Spiritual Guide motioned. "We'll go this way first."

"I followed. It got darker, fuzzier, like a fog. Movement became more and more of an effort. It was scary. I was being pushed around and was confused. I indicated this couldn't be the way, but was told, 'This is the way we need to go. Come.' It became darker and worse. Bad beings were taking and getting energy from me. It was painful. I was told to start praying and I did. As soon as I stopped, I was again attacked. So I had to keep praying or 'they' would get me. Finally all were gone. I was depleted. I remember looking up and seeing a small light. My Guide and I started moving up. I went through a long dark tunnel toward a bright light. There were loud noises, popping, cracking, as we proceeded up the tunnel. I saw two beings in the distance whom I knew to be Jesus and Mary. The light became brighter and brighter. When I reached it, there was just light. Welcoming light beings were energy, and not of any form."

Once in the light, Mulligan had a life review and was asked what he had accomplished. It was the small things that were important, like helping people. "I saw my life flashing before my eyes, yet it slowed down at points. I saw how I had treated people and interacted. I felt very guilty and very ashamed about things. I was assured that the overpowering guilt and shame was not mine to take or keep—I was loved. (At that point in my life I didn't remember being abused and that this had caused the guilt and shame, nor did I see it in my review.) I asked who or what caused the guilt and shame. I was told, 'You'll work it out. You'll find out who caused it later.' I asked again and got the same answer, frustrating me." He was then asked if he had any more questions. "No, I don't really have any other questions. My first question wasn't answered." A discussion followed. He said he wanted to go back to his wife.

"We went into a dark velvety light. It was a dark purple light, almost black, but soft and velvety. I felt safe. I felt relieved. I didn't feel guilty. I was very comforted. I remember learning that all spirituality is good. No one belief system was better than the other. I had access to knowledge, but I understood that I would soon forget it. I heard heavenly music. It was like harps. Then I was asked if I wanted to hear real heavenly music, and I said yes. It was like low-pitched chants. I remember meeting but not 'seeing' someone's brother. I was to tell his sister that he was okay. I asked to know more but was told not to worry, that I would meet his sister in due course. I was told that the brother's name would not be on the memorial (it turned out to be the Vietnam Memorial), but that his name would be on the memorial. I was also told his sister was a twin, but not a twin."

Mulligan forgot about this part until, in the mid-eighties, he saw a picture of the Vietnam Memorial on the desk of a woman who had helped to train him. He asked her about it and found out her brother had been killed in Laos. His name was not on the actual Vietnam Memorial but on a scale model done by an Illinois veterans organization. During his next business trip, he told her that her brother was okay. She was very relieved, as she had always wondered. "I told her that I was puzzled about her being a twin, but not a twin. She smiled. 'Oh, of course that's true. As kids, the neighbors always commented about us as twins because of our looks, but we were not actually twins.'"

Mulligan spoke of the tight squeeze to fit back into his body, and of being in a coma for three days. "I could hear, and I knew that I had been given the last rites." After two weeks in intensive care, another week in a regular room, he was given a thirty-day sick leave. "I learned that death is not to be feared, that the spirit is eternal, that there is a higher power, and that the higher power is light and love. Being on earth means being able to see, taste, smell, feel, and hear the higher power through nature and people."

CHRIS RUSSELL

"My name is Chris Russell and I'm a sixty-year-old veteran of the Vietnam War living in North Carolina. My story began in 1999 when I visited a friend of mine in Virginia Beach, Virginia. My friend is a seventy-ish Christian lady who happens to have 'psychic' abilities. To those who would argue that a person cannot be a Christian and a psychic at the same time, I beg to differ. My friend can 'see' and 'intuit' things most ordinary people can't. During my visit, she advised me, 'Chris, you have lung cancer and you're going to die.' Because she has always been accurate in the past, I took her words seriously and checked into the Veteran Affairs Medical Center in Fayetteville." He was given an "Agent Orange" exam and sent to Duke [Medical Center]. Some exploratory testing revealed that he was in "stage 3B" incurable cancer. He was told to go home, get his affairs in order, and prepare to die. Refusing the dire prognosis, Chris went to another center in Houston, Texas. They disagreed with Duke, saying he was in stage 3A. But that center refused further treatment. Thanks to another friend, he managed to fit the criteria for a clinical trial in Greenville, North Carolina.

"Long story short, I had a remarkable reaction to the chemotherapy, as it all but eliminated the 5.2-cm [centimeter] malignant tumor which had been growing in my left lung. While the chemo didn't totally eliminate the cancer, it did eliminate enough that surgeons felt they could operate and remove the lung. All went well. About a month later doctors discovered I had developed a 'fistula' and they would have to go back in and repair it—a fistula is a hole in the bronchial tube." A month after the surgery, Chris developed another fistula. "This time I flatlined on the operating table. The surgical team (which consisted of about five surgeons) grouped together in a football-like huddle on the far side of the operating room. Listening intently, I could hear one of them talking. I realized they were praying for me! Then, all of a sudden, one of my prayerful surgical team members turned and looked directly at me. He noticed that I had my eyes wide open and was looking back at him, then he shouted, 'He's alive!' They all broke the huddle and came rushing back. They were busily checking medical instruments while at the same time telling me how surprised they were to see me alive—because I had died, and they tried everything they could think of to revive me, to no avail. After abandoning their attempts to save me, they decided to gather together across the room and pray for my soul.

"This one physician stayed by my bedside and eventually looked down at me and said, 'You're probably wondering why I'm still standing here.' To which I replied, 'You want to tell me some more about my dying?' 'No,' he said, 'that's not the reason why.' 'Well, what's up, doc?' He replied, 'I've been performing these same surgical procedures for the past twenty-something years, and something happened here today that I've never experienced before. It's had such a profound effect on me that I feel that I have to tell you about it.' I said okay.

"'We had you wide open and were removing some special kind of fat tissue from your heart to use to tie up your fistula when all of a sudden you started talking out loud! Surprised, we all jumped back from the table, as we initially thought that you had perhaps come out from underneath the anesthesia. But when we checked our instruments, we found that, no, you were still under . . . still unconscious . . . so we just stood there and listened while you talked.' 'What did I say?' He replied, 'It's not so much what you said as it was to whom you were talking. You were talking to Jesus Christ!'

"I looked deeply into his eyes, and I could tell he wasn't joking. He was quite serious. Then he added, 'By the way, I'm going to make sure that this gets into your medical records.'"

Ten days later, Chris was well enough to go home. A month later he traveled back to Virginia to visit with his friend. The minute she entered the room, she froze with astonishment. "Chris, you're all lit up . . . you've got lights protruding out from all around and over you . . . you have angels flying all around your head!" Then, with tears streaming down her face, she quietly said, "Chris, you know that you died last month on the operating table and had a face-to-face encounter with Jesus Christ himself!" With little dialogue between them, the woman continued. "When you came to see me last year and I told you that you had cancer and were going to die, that was it—that was your life expectancy. You're not supposed to be here right now. I just wanted you to know that. Now, I'll tell you what happened, what He said, and why you're still here."

"You screamed that you were sorry if you had ever hurt anybody in any way while you were 'visiting' Earth. You screamed it out so loud and with so much emotion and conviction that you startled everybody." Apparently the commotion attracted the attention of Jesus. "Chris, you jumped in front of Jesus Christ and started talking your head off . . . you didn't really know who he was. But you just started telling him that you had just gotten out of prison and were undergoing treatment for cancer and that you were now getting a big government check every month [for exposure to Agent Orange in Vietnam], and that you would never have to go back to work again and that you weren't ready to die. You got them all laughing. It was then that He reached over and touched you and instantaneously cured you of your cancer, and sent you back to your body. You are going to live another twenty-six years, and you are going to spend the rest of your life helping others."

Afterward, his cancer metastasized to his neck—"stage 4 lung cancer." Again, one hospital refused treatment; another did the operation, but they couldn't get it all. Remembering that he had twenty-six more years to live, Chris simply smiled at the doctor and thanked him for doing his best. Several months later, a CT scan revealed that he was cancer-free. That was eight years ago, and he feels fine. In 2005, he returned to school and obtained a Master of Social Work degree and is dedicated to bringing solace and comfort to others. Although Chris remembers very little of his near-death experience, his psychic friend picked up on the whole thing the moment he walked in her house, and, without any cues or word from him, described every minute detail accurately. There is no way she could have known what had happened to him, especially during his surgery, but she did.

CHAPTER FIVE

ACCOMMODATIONS, MULTIPLES, PREVIEWS

*"At the National Institute of Discovery Science, a think tank
for consciousness research, we have learned that near-death
experiences represent the clinical counterpoint to what theoretical physicists are discovering in the laboratory."*

—MELVIN L. MORSE, M.D.

How people die does not determine or influence the near-death experience they might have. Some researchers claim that more women
than men have them—not so in my work. Women by their very nature are
more talkative than men; that doesn't mean they have more episodes—it just
means that it is easier for them to talk about their experience. You do run
into selection and researcher bias in this field of research; this is a caution for
all of us in considering points of view, else we slip into thinking we've found
something significant when we haven't.

We know scientifically that the bulk of each episode occurs when there
is no brain activity: the individual has flatlined. That's why narratives are so
important—and details. The blind I had sessions with, who were blind since
birth, recognized colors and used the right words to depict them. They also
described people who had entered their hospital room—people they had
never touched, heard, or had any knowledge of before. They knew shapes,
sizes, objects, patterns . . . *as if they had once been sighted in a time previous to
their birth.*

Let's admit it: no matter how careful we are, there are still aspects of the near-death phenomenon that defy explanation.

ACCOMMODATIONS

Something very strange can happen with experiencer stories as concerns who or what appears in them, what they look like, and maybe why certain features are there. Embellishments? Well, not exactly. Case in point: the puzzle about "tunnels."

There is no question that, in the early days of near-death experience research, hardly anyone reported such a thing. But after Moody's book became a bestseller, the public fixated on tunnels. People claimed that this explains wormholes; this explains time travel; this explains shamanic visions; this explains the concept of "kundalini" (Sanskrit word referring to that "bundle" of spiritual power said to reside at the base of the spine, which, when aroused, stretches full length up the spine as if a snake, activating endocrine glands and energetic power centers in the body, until bursting through the top of one's head inducing "enlightenment"). Tunnels—the so-called connecting link between life and death, the spiritual and the mundane—have achieved pop-art status. Sorry, folks, but the facts don't match the pop.

It's not only that few people report them. I attended several meetings where experiencers changed their stories right in front of me—changed descriptions of what had seemed dark or strange or confusing into portrayals of a sort of tunnel, as if using that word meant their experience was genuine and they were okay. In defense of the experiencers who did this, I know what it is like to try to describe something that is beyond the range of your language. You want to be understood. When I pushed for these tunnel-experiencing folks to give me specifics on what they saw, I got mumbles instead. Is the cult status of the tunnel element legitimate? Or is it an accommodation of public preference, or the result of psychological modeling?

And what about regionalisms—stories that reflect a certain area's general population base? Yes, I did find them. In my work, people from the American Northwest, Southwest, and Haiti had more animals in their scenarios—mostly as greeters. Those from the Southeast, Midwest, and Central states tended towards themes of good and evil in their stories. I did not find heavy concentrations of hellish scenarios among Bible Belt Christians, as others claim, but I did notice that only Fundamentalists described hell as hot and fiery (the others who experienced this type of scenario spoke of how cold or clammy or void of temperature the place was).

Culturalisms are commonplace. For instance, how an experience is described depends on an individual's language constraints and the societal taboos he or she faces. Within indigenous cultures, for example, the concept of "self" is missing. These people operate from a collective reality, the wisdom of the group. The Lakota Sioux, a people native to the U.S., have no concept or word for "individual self." Their understanding of life is based on relations with all that exists. These people seldom if ever report life reviews as part of their near-death scenarios. If you think about this, it makes sense. If you have no understanding of a "separate self," what good is a review that examines a "self" that to you has little or no validity? Is what we are really witnessing within these "isms" an accommodation for brain development, rather than an outpicturing of regional or cultural traditions and beliefs?

The surprisingly varied nature of the appearance of greeters is an even greater puzzle. Almost always, deceased relatives and friends manifest as somewhat younger—sometimes very much younger, healthy, healed of handicaps, and glowing. Those who died young can still be young, or they can come back at the age they should have been had they lived the length of years the experiencer did. Yet the living can appear too—the child's favorite schoolteacher or the kid down the block, or the adult's treasured friend. What I have noticed with living greeters is that they stick around only long enough for the experiencer to relax into what is occurring; then they disappear and components more typical of near-death states take over. It's as if the only purpose of living greeters is to create a comfort zone wherein deeper and more profound things can follow.

But what about this one? Four-year-old Jimmy John drowned in his parents' backyard swimming pool. He was an only child. Mom was in her late twenties; Dad was in his early thirties. Emergency crews arrived. Fifteen minutes later the boy breathed again. Mom was overcome with relief until Jimmy John blurted out for all to hear: "I met my little brother. He's 'over there,' where I was, and he told me all about Mommy having him pulled out of her tummy when she was thirteen." This was not a grieving mother. Her abortion had long since been forgotten. While her "two" sons became the best of friends, she had a nervous breakdown and her husband left her.[19] Did the much-older brother come as a "younger brother" so as not to frighten Jimmy John? Was this episode an accommodation, a signal of unfinished business that needed attention?

What about those "caring or critical" parent-types? Some of them kind, some not so kind, these greeters tend to be rather specific on certain issues—like the child's behavior, how they have been acting, what is expected of them as they grow, or perhaps the job they will someday perform. Is this an accommodation to instruction needs or needed praise, or, is it a sign of higher orders of participation in the lives we have been given? The soul? Guides? Guardians of some type?

Children typically see God or a God-like figure as a man. Teenagers and adults, for the most part, see The Holiest of the Holy as some form of light, usually a huge sphere. I've yet to hear of a child who challenged what God really looked like, yet they often challenged angels' appearance. Each time they did, the angelic being transformed into light. Is this a social or religious accommodation?

Don't misunderstand me. Near-death scenarios are real and profound, and the otherworldly greeters who attend are just as real—sometimes nothing short of miraculous. Yet, what happens, the experience itself *always occurs in a form the experiencer is capable of receiving, even if otherworldly or bizarre.* With initial greeters, I noticed that they always match the individual's conceptual level of understanding, either to alert or relax, so what is happening can deepen.

Accommodations are "just for us" in how they enable our consciousness to radically shift. This explains, at least to me, the absence or presence of certain near-death components. Although the patterning of the phenomenon is global, components in the pattern can alter, evolve, or change as we do.

MULTIPLES

It is not uncommon for an individual to have several near-death experiences during his or her life. I had three within a three-month period back in 1977. Among the 277 child experiencers I worked with, nearly 20 percent had a second episode during his or her childhood (several had four or more), and 27 percent went on to have additional experiences as adults. Of those I studied, the record-holder was a man who had twenty-three of them over a lifetime of surgeries and pain. He had been born with serious birth defects and was not expected to live past six months. He was in his early forties and wheelchair-bound when I met him. When I asked why so many, he answered: "Each one gives me the strength and courage I need to keep going."

People who die together typically have near-death experiences together. They even see each other in their own separate episodes. This happens with some regularity if parents and their children are involved, or friends, or large groups of people—like passengers in the same vehicle that crashed, or strangers who drowned in close proximity to each other.

Stunning cases of group death/near-death come from the military. Diane Corcoran, a retired Army nurse, was on hand for many of these. She tells of entire platoons blown up; the few survivors talking afterwards about watching their buds rise from their bodies, and, as they did, how they talked to each other, assessed the situation, and learned who would live and who would die. Diane warns that veterans seldom speak of such experiences, primarily because military doctors still consider near-death states a sign of mental incompetency. Diane says, "With blast injuries affecting so many who fought in Iraq and Afghanistan, these soldiers dare not even report NDEs for fear they can't get back into the system for health care."[20]

Arvin S. Gibson, a fellow researcher, told me about one of his cases involving group death. A twenty-person firefighting crew called "Hotshots" all succumbed from lack of oxygen after being trapped by a sudden burst of flames near a mountain top. One by one each of the crew fell to the earth, suffocated, yet each of the twenty saw the others leave their bodies and float upwards (like soldiers in the Army platoons Col. Corcoran spoke of). One Hotshot, Jake, looked down at a fellow crew member who had been born with a defective foot, and exclaimed, "Look, Jose, your foot is straight." Once they were rescued, each Hotshot revived and told the same story: of seeing the others leave their bodies, meet loved ones who had died before them, and engage in a spirit world scenario. Investigators interviewed each Hotshot separately before any man had a chance to talk to the others and compare notes.[21]

The first near-death experiences I ever encountered took place back in the sixties at St. Alphonsus Hospital in Boise, Idaho. Four people died within a short span of time—on the same floor and because of a heart attack. None knew the others previously, nor did they have the same doctor. Yet each one experienced the same hellish scenario and was equally traumatized by it. The four patients were brought together by nurses who were concerned about their strange stories. I was there because I knew one of the patients and she had asked me to come. I could find nothing to explain this strange occurrence. I conjectured that maybe that particular area of the hospital was energetically "imprinted" from other traumas that had occurred there, and that this had affected the four. Today, however, I recognize what happened then as more typical of the kind of patterning found in group events,—where individual scenarios tend to match each other, or nearly so.

Our energy frequency, how we vibrate as living beings, our electromagnetic biofield, is of immense importance when we die, as well as when we almost die. What is drawn together can and often does resonate together.

PREVIEWS

Occasionally dubbed a "flash forward," the experience of being privy to the future occurs in myriad ways during near-death states.

Children often see the effect their death will cause their family and choose to return as a result. Another feature of children's scenarios, especially if the child is from an unindustrialized country, is being told or shown their life's work and how they must prepare and what they must learn. Adults are often shown their funerals. One adult female I had several sessions with accurately saw the man she would marry as well as distinct wedding details.

There are several accounts of previews in the book *The New Children and Near-Death Experiences*.[22] Margaret Evans describes seeing a gigantic mushroom cloud coming toward her in the sky, a cloud that meant instant death to many people, and recalls how busy she and other spirits were, assisting the dead in "crossing over." Years later, she learned what had happened—it was 1945 and atomic bombs had been dropped in several cities in Japan. In another account, Merla Ianello, who had one younger brother, saw a "second" younger brother in a near-death episode, and recognized him instantly as Michael. She said nothing for a while, yet was absolute about the presence of Michael. When she finally told her mother where and when she had seen him, her mother's face went white. Why? Because Michael wasn't conceived until the year after the episode.

There are stories of spectacular near-death cases where experiencers were shown the grand sweep of history, as well as the future. The best-known of these and the most evidential is that of Ricky Bradshaw. In 1975, the torso of his body was literally ground in half when he became trapped between two automobiles backing into each other at a grocery store parking lot. Only his spine and a few cords around it were left intact before the panic-stricken drivers let up on the gas. He was rushed to a hospital and pronounced dead, his body heaped in a corner. A group of medical students noticed the cadaver and requested that they be allowed to experiment with it (the hospital was a teaching facility). After an hour of high jinks, Ricky's heart "reawakened." Two years and twenty-four surgeries later, Ricky's survival made medical history. During that hour when he was little more than a cadaver, he was totally conscious—saw everything that was happening from outside his body, was engulfed in tremendous light, conversed with spiritual guardians at length, chose to come back, and as a reward for his choice, was shown all of history from beginning to end. He will only describe some of what he saw. The rest, he feels, would interfere with human evolution if it were known.[23]

The more famous accounts of people who were given revelations of what is to come are that of Mellen-Thomas Benedict,[24] Dannion Brinkley,[25] Tom Sawyer,[26] and Ned Dougherty.[27] Notice I said "the more famous." Actually, there are millions of cases of futuristic revelations appearing during near-death states—so many, in fact, that hardly an eyebrow is raised anymore if an experiencer makes such a claim. Still, precious few of these have ever been published. One child experiencer, now grown, gave this lament: "Why should I tell what I saw? Who would believe me? I'm just one person. How could I make a difference? When I do say something, I get in trouble. People think I'm crazy."

Of the many cases I've investigated, Cheryl's was by far the most amazing and the most accurate. Never heard of Cheryl? When putting pen to paper to record what was revealed to her, she developed a serious health problem and refused to continue. The world will never know the scope of what she told me, nor do I have permission to pass this information on. Maybe, as with Ricky Bradshaw, this is for the best.

There is a movement afoot to condense into one book the various revelations given to near-death experiencers during their episodes. If this project is finished, I'll post a note about it on my website.[28] The concept of previews, of a future revealed, turns in on itself when we discuss aftereffects (in a later chapter). That's because experiencers typically develop the ability to access futuristic information once their episode is over. This is part of the aftereffects pattern . . . so is the ability to *remember the future before it occurs.*

If this seems strange to you, turn the page.

CHAPTER SIX

MORE STORIES/ DIFFERENT TYPES

"All features of the NDE suggest an urgent need in society to include the extraordinary."

—ALLAN KELLEHEAR, PH.D.

Barney Clark, the man who received the very first artificial heart (a Jarvik-7), had so many vivid and amazingly accurate out-of-body experiences that physicians went scurrying for an explanation. No, it couldn't possibly be the antibiotic and anticoagulant medications Barney took, they decided, nor was it his pain medicine. So they hushed the whole thing up, refusing to talk to the media.

MEDICAL STAFF SEE SPIRITS, TOO

Medical folk—physicians, nurses, emergency crews, medics, chaplains—experience otherworldly episodes themselves in conjunction with their work, and fairly often. Seldom can they admit this without the threat of losing their job or their reputation. Occasionally, though, a few speak up—like Daniel Bishop, Ph.D.

"My experience with NDE was in Vietnam in the city of Huế during the 1967 Tet Offensive, where the resistance was reduced to small pockets and we Americans and our Vietnamese allies were in them. In the days and nights that followed during the biggest battle fought in this war, I saw 100s, and then 1,000s of men and women, and children, fall in battle. As a Second Lieutenant and Intelligence Officer with very little intelligence-gathering to do at the height of this battle, I volunteered to work with my friend and only medical doctor available at an Aid Station and Infirmary that we set up to handle the wounded and dying. It was in this place that I saw many patients die, and have some even return to the living, when they were revived during or after an operation. Having studied yoga in high school, I was aware of [spiritual things] and saw many of our patients go out-of-body and float up to the low ceiling, or to the outside where they disappeared. When I saw this happen, and apparently I was the only one that saw them leave their bodies, I would give a final military salute in deference to their ultimate sacrifice, or wave goodbye to them if they were women or children. One guy, that revived after an operation told me that he had seen me salute him when I thought that he was not coming back. He said I had a bright light around me when this happened. He even asked me if I was really an angel. I answered no, but that I was worried about him and had said a prayer to God to receive him if it was his time to go home. We MediVaced more than 2,500 casualties from Huế in those two weeks of fighting. Most of them survived."

NEAR-DEATH-LIKE EXPERIENCES

I bet you haven't heard the end of the story of Paul's conversion experience in the Bible. Paul was a hard-hearted tax collector who went by the name of Saul, until, on the road to Damascus, a glowing light blinded him and a voice called out, "Saul, Saul, why do you persecute me?" (Acts 9:4). Jesus identified himself as the voice. This so profoundly affected Saul that he changed his name to Paul and began a lifetime of preaching love as a way of life to others. At first people did not accept the change in him and thought him mad. It took a while, but Paul proved himself many times over and went on to "tour" ten heavens and receive innumerable revelatory visions that helped to shape what later became the religion of Christianity.

At first glance, Paul's story dovetails all the patterning of the near-death phenomenon. Papers have been written about this in numerous journals. A glaring omission almost everyone makes, however, seems to undermine the claim: *at no time was Paul near death nor facing death.* He was just traveling along a road when, wide awake and alert, he suddenly faced a light so bright it blinded him—a light that spoke and showed him greater truths. The actual term for what Paul had is a "near-death-like experience." Yup, these are real, and countless people have them: same pattern to the experience, same physiological and psychological aftereffects, same permanency to the changes that occur, before and after photos can differ (a lot, or somewhat). Same phenomenon, sans death. It has been established scientifically that the closer an individual is to physical death, the more apt he or she is to experience the phenomenon. Yet the same thing can happen under other types of conditions, as in the following stories:

> On a Sunday morning, a woman was bent over picking up a large newspaper dropped on her porch. She straightened, looked into the rising sun, and had a full-blown near-death experience followed by a pattern of aftereffects—with lifelong changes.

> A man walking across his living room to peer out the window turned to walk back to his sofa when the room filled with light. He physically and fully consciously walked straight into a lengthy near-death scenario that enabled him to better understand the Bible. Aftereffects were unending, as was his passion to "spread the good news" about biblical text.[29]

> A near-death experiencer who had an incredible episode and revived in a morgue went on to have a near-death-like experience seventeen years later while delivering the eulogy for a friend recently killed. This event was far more powerful than the previous encounter—transforming her in ways beyond her imagining.[30]

These are not typical spiritual or "mountain-top" experiences that awaken an individual to the existence of otherworldly realities. They are breakthrough events that engender total or near-total transformations of an individual on every level of being. Because so many are now reported, a separate category had to be created to include them in near-death studies; hence, the phrase "near-death-like experience."

BACK IN THE GOOD OLD DAYS

Robert Carter III of Nomini Hall Plantation in Virginia freed more slaves than anyone else in American history. He claims to have died, gone to heaven, and talked with God. He set slaves free because of that encounter—what we now call a near-death experience.[31] History is rife with such cases. Don't think for one moment that the phenomenon is only of modern vintage.

The oldest recorded English account of a near-death experience was provided by the Venerable Bede in the eighth century. It concerns a Northumbrian by the name of Drythelm who suddenly arose from his deathbed after a light-filled experience, then proceeded to give away all his earthly possessions so he could join a monastery in service to others.[32]

Thanks to Donald R. Morse, DDS, Ph.D., we also have the story of Dr. A. S. Wiltse, a physician of Skiddy, Kansas, who, in 1889, died of typhoid fever. He was without pulse for four hours, in a state of "apparent death" for half an hour. Said the good doctor when he returned to life: "With all the interest of a physician, I beheld the wonders of my bodily anatomy, intimately interwoven with which, even tissue for tissue, was I, the living soul of that dead body. I learned that the epidermis was the outside boundary of the ultimate tissues, so to speak, of the soul. I realized my condition and reasoned calmly thus. I have died, as men term death, and yet I am as much a man as ever. I am about to get out of the body. I watched the interesting process of the separation of soul and body. By some power, apparently not my own, the Ego was rocked to and fro, laterally, as a cradle is rocked, by which process its connection with the tissues of the body was broken up. After a little time the lateral motion ceased, and long the soles of the feet beginning at the toes, passing rapidly to the heels, I felt and heard, as it seemed, the snapping of innumerable small cords. When this was accomplished, I began slowly to retreat from the feet, toward the head, as a rubber cord shortens. I remember reaching the hips and saying to myself, 'Now, there is no life below the hips.'"

Wiltse appeared to himself something like a jellyfish in color and form. As he emerged from his head, he saw two women sitting at the head of his physical shell and wondered if there was room for him to stand. "As I emerged from the head, I floated up and down and laterally like a soap bubble attached to a bowl of a pipe until I at last broke loose from the body and fell lightly to the floor, where I slowly arose and expanded into the full stature of a man. I seemed to be translucent, of a bluish cast and perfectly naked. With a painful sense of embarrassment, I fled toward the partially opened door to escape the eyes of the two ladies whom I was facing, as well as others who I knew were about me, but reaching the door I found myself clothed, and satisfied upon that point, I turned and faced the company."

Wiltse did not recognize the two women as his wife and sister, as he had no concept of individuality while outside his body. He wandered outdoors and was overwhelmed by the distinctness of everything he saw. "I took note of the redness of the soil and of the washes the rain had made . . . Then I discovered that I had become larger than I was in earth life and congratulated myself thereupon." He looked back through the open door, where he could see his body. "I discovered then a small cord, like a spider's web, running from my shoulders (of the spirit body) back to my body and attaching to it at the base of my neck in front (referred to in the Bible as the silver cord)."

A Presence entered his awareness. "Yet, although the language was English, it was so eminently above my power to reproduce that my rendition of it is far short of the original. The following is as near as I can render it: 'This is the road to the eternal world. Yonder rocks are the boundary between the two worlds and the two lives. Once you pass them, you can no more return into the body. If your work is complete on earth, you may pass beyond the rocks. If, however, upon consideration you conclude that—it is not done, you can return into the body.'" Wiltse was sorely tempted to cross the boundary, when a black cloud appeared in front of him and stopped his advance. He found himself back in his physical body, wondering, "What in the world has happened to me?"[33]

ANOMALIES

Channeling

Did you know that JZ Knight claims that when she is channeling Ramtha, a 35,000–year-old Lemurian warrior, she goes through something like a near-death experience? Let me back up a little here. JZ Knight was once a full-time mother and housewife by the name of Judith Darlene. One day, quite unexpectedly, a tall, radiant man suddenly appeared in front of her and introduced himself. She later agreed to become a channel for him—allow him to use her voice and her body as a physical mechanism for the purpose of communication—to educate, aid, serve, and help others. She has been tested and studied by some of the best scientists in the world. To date, no fraud has been detected. Whoever or whatever Ramtha is, his phenomenal appearances through the vehicle of Knight's body are real. His teachings? Depends on your point of view.

What matters here is JZ Knight's testimonial of what she goes through to allow him physical entry. She emphasizes that neither sleep nor trance are involved. According to JZ: "I didn't like the cosmology of New Age concepts on life at the time I began channeling because that wasn't what I was experiencing... I'm actually having an NDE, and I'm going to the light. I go down a tunnel."[34]

UFOs

Connections to UFOs and extraterrestrials occasionally occur. One of my cases involved an engineer who, when returning from a horse training clinic late at night, lost control of her car on wet pavement and crashed into a forest of trees. The front end impacted a large oak and buckled, shattering the windshield and side windows. As she yelled "Oh, God, help me," her pain subsided and she found herself standing in the brightest light she had ever seen, facing a tribunal of people that were laughing and judging her. A deep voice said, "She's not ready yet," then she heard what sounded like the closing of a very large book before she found herself back in her car. The night was dark and silent. She inventoried her body but didn't feel anything broken. While trying to wiggle free of the front seat, she noticed that her car was now facing the highway! Somehow it had turned 180 degrees away from the point of impact.

"The only way the car could have rotated around was to have been lifted over the treetops, turned, and set back down. Also, the car had been moved away from the oak tree and closer to the road." A trucker stopped after seeing the glare of her fog lights and notified the police. Both police and rescue crews were unable to explain why the extensive damage to the front of her car exactly matched tree markings located to the rear of her car. Her explanation? She was abducted by aliens while driving (it had happened to her before); only this time she could not regain consciousness fast enough when she was returned to her body to prevent the accident. It was the aliens who rotated her car so she could be rescued. She has a clear recollection of the UFO abduction and the near-death experience. According to her, each event was a distinctly separate incident. Whether you believe any of this or not, the impossible anomaly involving the car damage and the trees was recorded in the accident report.[35]

The stats from my research about UFOs and aliens reveal the following:[36]

Adult Near-Death Experiencers (based on 3,000 sessions)

- 20% Identified with being from another planet

- 9% Claimed to have been abducted by a UFO

Child Near-Death Experiencers (based on 277 sessions)

- 39% Identified with being from another dimension

- 14% Claimed to have been abducted by a UFO

- 9% Identified with being from another planet

Child experiencers, whether still young or now grown, have strong ties to the idea of other worlds, other dimensions, other types of beings. Maybe this is because of their unique imaginations. Or perhaps it is associated with limbic development in the brain caused by media exposure; pre-birth memories (from another dimension); or maybe there's more to such narratives than we as a society are prepared to consider. That 20 percent of adults become aware of coming to this planet from another one after their episode—well, this is peculiar. So far, I have been unable to find any patterning that holds up here.

The Void

The void appears in both uplifting and distressing near-death experiences. Not often—sometimes. But it is always described with a type of emotion that is distinct.

If connected with a hellish or frightening near-death state, the fear that is experienced can border on or become utmost terror; all-consuming, almost irrational. Being in a void is like being in a nothing state, either dark or colorless, where you are alone—no sounds, no movement, no objects, no beingness, no top or bottom, no sides—and left with a sense of abandonment. This can be experienced as the ultimate condemnation. There are no demons and dungeons, no punishment, that can compare to this feeling. Individuals who experience this type of frightening void find it difficult to describe, as if it were something they want to forget.

Conversely, voids that appear as components of pleasant and transcendent episodes inspire a certain awe that such a place even exists. This pleasant void is most often described as being the central sourceplace of everything—yet devoid of all, save a sense of thrill or shimmer as if the void were Creation's Womb, pregnant with possibility, ready to "birth" when invited. Experiencers often interpret this "invitation to produce" as somehow connected to our thoughts and attitudes, as if our state of consciousness is important to what issues forth. This type of void is described as a dark space that isn't dark, an emptiness that really isn't empty. Mystics, monks, and spiritual folk speak of the void in this manner, as if it were a special place they feel privileged to visit in deep prayer or meditation.

What makes the difference between a terror-filled experience of the void and one that is uplifting and soul-stirring? As near as I can tell, it has something to do with our egos and how closely we attach to or let go of what we think is real.

Numerous great yogis, shamans, native healers, and religious and spiritual adepts credit their enlightenment with having had a near-death experience as a child. The south Indian sage Ramana Maharshi was one of them. While still attending grade school, he underwent a near-death state and attained union with what his culture terms "Absolute Consciousness." He was transformed in astounding ways. A method of Self Inquiry based on the question "Who am I" unfolded over the course of his life and in the lives of those who came in contact with him. The Divine Presence is said to have revealed itself to him as "Effortless State of Being." He died in 1950 at the foot of Arunachala, a sacred mountain. Maharshi is revered for his down to earth teachings.[37]

Every religious and spiritual tradition has tales like this, powerful stories of youngsters forever transformed by near-death states who went on to affect society in unique ways. In just one week of searching libraries, I was able to find accounts of these people—each one matching the profile of having had a near-death experience as a young person and going on after that crisis to display aftereffects typical of near-death states—Einstein, Abraham Lincoln, Queen Elizabeth I, Edward de Vere (the 17th Earl of Oxford and believed by many to be the real Shakespeare), Mozart, Winston Churchill, Black Elk, Walter Russell, Valerie V. Hunt—plus most of the saints in the Catholic Church.[38]

Is there something about children, especially the very young, that we need to know?

CHAPTER SEVEN

CHILD EXPERIENCERS

"One can't believe impossible things," Alice said. "I daresay you haven't had much practice," said the Queen. "When I was your age, I always did it for half an hour a day. Why, sometimes I've believed as many as six impossible things before breakfast."

—LEWIS CARROLL *(ALICE IN WONDERLAND)*

Near-death episodes linked to pre-birth, birth trauma, after-birth infants and toddlers, are more common than you might think. The very small usually open up about what happened to them once they can speak fairly well or draw or act out their memories. Family and social pressures can weaken those memories; in some cases, they cause the child to block out or tuck away the experience. Repression is far more common with kids than with teenagers and adults. Children's episodes are usually brief and encompass few elements; the closer a child is to puberty, though, the greater the chance for longer, more complex scenarios.

Children of any age undergo the same type of experiences, with the same elements and components in their scenarios, encounter and adjust to the same spread of aftereffects as do adults. Similarities, for the most part, end there.

A DIFFERENT TYPE OF CONSCIOUSNESS

To understand children's cases we need to keep in mind that kids are tuned to different harmonics than adults. Concepts of life and death leave them with puzzled faces. "I don't end or begin anywhere," a youngster once told me. "I just reach out and catch the next wave that goes by and hop a ride. That's how I got here."

Child experiencers, even more so than with average youngsters, speak in the language of "other worlds," one that is less verbal and more akin to synesthesia (multiple sensing—an elaboration or acceleration of the limbic system in the brain). This ability enables them to perceive what we call "reality" as consisting of layered realms, unrestricted by physical boundaries: multi-dimensionality. They can seem multi-sensory, like multi-channelers who live in a multi-verse. Thus, they easily giggle with angels, play with ghosts, talk to sky beings, see colors around people that change with mood, access and sometimes pre-live the future, and hear sounds when nothing and no one visible is present. This can alarm or panic parents.

Such worrisome behavior, however, may well have a logical explanation: near-death states expand faculties normal to us, enabling experiencers to access more of the electromagnetic spectrum. We humans see only a small range of what is available to us. The rest is either infra or ultra to our faculties of perception.

What if something happened to you and you were suddenly able to take in greater bands of that spectrum? What would you see or smell or hear or feel? Who or what might you encounter or touch? Imagine what it might be like to grow up with this "larger view" your dominant or *only* concept of reality.

IMPRINTING AND LOSS OF BONDING

Small children, via expressions, movements, and responses, can show signs that suggest that they may have identified with or been imprinted by the otherworldly imagery and behaviors they were exposed to during their near-death episode. Their earthly family and environs, things typical to culture and place, may seem foreign or of little interest to them. Imprinting, in this regard, means to "fix firmly in the mind," and that is what I am referring to—children who fixed their sense of existing "elsewhere."

The temporal lobes in the brain (above the ear and around the temples) build libraries of shape, size, sound, smell, color, movement, and taste from the input they receive and are exposed to so that we know what things are and how best to respond to them. These libraries change to suit our needs from the day we are born to the day we die. Yet if a child's near-death experience was associated with birth, or occurred during the early days, months, or years of life, it is possible for those budding libraries to accommodate otherworldly models of identification, rather than those of earth. This imprinting can be augmented by sensory responses and intuitive knowing to the extent that the child may seem wise beyond his or her years when, in fact, the youngster is simply responding to what feels natural.

Family and friends are at a loss to understand this, of having a model of life and living different from their own; nor do psychologists and counselors have training in how to interpret why this might be. Hear me when I say this: it is *normal* for the young to lose parent/child bonding. This does *not* mean children cease to be loving and thoughtful, but it does indicate that they can become somewhat silent or distant, independent, or unusually mature and detached. Interests can change from those of the family. For preschool and school-age kids, parent/child bonding is initially quite strong and is the reason they "come back" from the near-death episode. The climate of welcome or threat they are greeted with, as well as how their episode ended, directly impinges on what comes next. Bonding can be re-established for a child of any age through patience and the willingness of both child and parent to share and respect *feelings* as they explore their differing worldviews.

AN ADULT MIND IN A CHILD'S BODY

One of the criticisms I received from publishing house editors when I submitted the manuscript of *The New Children and Near-Death Experiences* was that my accounts of child experiencers portrayed them as much too mature for their ages. No exaggeration, said I. This is how the majority really speak— like they possess an adult's mind in a child's body. This finding broaches topics like reincarnation (the young speak of past lives as casually and confidently as they might inquire about dinner) and physical afflictions ("I knew that I was a powerful, spiritual being that chose to have a short, but marvelous, mortal existence"—a quote from DeLynn, born with cystic fibrosis).[39]

Over half of the child experiencers in my research could remember their birth. Whenever possible I checked out these stories with parents, mostly mothers; I never found an error. One-third had pre-birth memory—most of those beginning at about six to seven months *in utero.* Medically, it has been shown that the fetus at twenty-six weeks or six months gestation experiences many sensations, including pain. This medical discovery of fetal awareness directly applies to the majority of children in my research who reported the beginnings of their memory as *a soul resident in human form* while still inside the womb. Some had recall of earlier than month six *in utero,* even of their conception, and of actively taking part as a spirit in choosing their own DNA. Most of those who spoke of remembering their conception also said they floated in and out of their mother's womb until finally "settling in" when fetal formation was more complete (around the seventh or eighth month).

It's scary what some children remember from their pre-birth experience in the womb. Things like heated debates and arguments, conditions in the home, even how their mother felt about her own life—and her thoughts! Emotionally charged issues are remembered readily, especially if the child's welfare is threatened (like the possibility of an abortion or because of an accident or assault on the mother). And a missing twin—that "extra" who was never born or died at birth or was reabsorbed by the mother because of being damaged or malformed—that being can return in a near-death scenario. On occasion, the one who was aborted reappears.

SOARING INTELLIGENCE AND CREATIVITY

Here are some statistics taken from my studies of 277 child experiencers, aged from around birth to fifteen years at the time of their episode:

- Faculties enhanced, altered, or experienced in multiples   77%

- Mind works differently—highly creative and inventive   84%

- Significant enhancement of intellect   68%

- Mind tested at genius level on standard IQ tests (with little or no genetic markers to account for scores)
  ~ main group, from around birth to fifteen years   48%
  ~ subgroup, between three to five years   81%

~ subgroup, around birth to fifteen months	96%
~ same as previous, but those who had a dark light experience, instead of a bright one	100%
• Drawn to and highly proficient in math/science/history	93%
• Professionally employed in math/science/history careers	25%
• Unusually gifted with languages	35%
• School	
~ easier after experience	34%
~ harder afterward or blocked from memory	66%

I found no difference between males and females with regard to enhanced intelligence and spatial and mathematical abilities. The majority had IQ scores between 150 to 160, past the threshold for genius—and some had IQs up to 174. Those children who had a dark light experience by fifteen months of age scored even higher on IQ tests: into the 200s. Enhancements in music were almost as high as those in math (93 percent). The regions for math and music in the brain are next to each other. It is as if both of these regions were enhanced together as if they were a single unit (another argument for continuing music education in schools—if you want kids who are good in math, you must also provide music instruction).

Another note: the claim that pediatric temporal lobe epilepsy explains near-death states in the very young falls apart if you just look at the facts. Todd Murphy, a well-known researcher in the field, explains: "The temporal lobes do seem to be more labile [changeable/unstable] for kids, but there are 'peak periods,' during which TL epilepsy is more common. For boys, it seems to be from ages 7 to 9, and for girls, from 6 to 8."[40] Most of the child experiencers in my research had their episode before the age of six (when science tells us that the human brain has reached 90 percent of its size). The age of reason begins at about eight. Pediatric temporal lobe epilepsy doesn't even come close to describing what happens to so many of these kids—jumps in their intelligence, in their creative and intuitive abilities, and how philosophical and reflective (and more mature) they become.

LEARNING ABILITY REVERSES

Did you notice what I did? The younger the experiencer, the greater the growth spurt. Tuck these little factoids into that observation: from around birth to fifteen months, the actual wiring of the brain is determined and synapse formation increases twenty-fold; from three to five years, the temporal lobes develop (explore and experiment with possible roles, future patterns, and continuity of environment).

Let's be honest here. Most alien, fairy, and monster sightings, flying dreams, out-of-body episodes, invisible friends, and other paranormal/psychic occurrences experienced by typical, normal children happen between the ages of three and five, along with the bulk of reports of near-death states with the young. This period marks the birth of imagination, and the time when long-term memory begins and storytelling has the greatest influence. Most kids during this time are almost entirely future-oriented—temporal lobe development predominates. But do we really understand this, especially in light of the stats you've just read?

One more thing: near-death kids, almost all of them, come back abstracting. That implies that the normal learning curve has somehow reversed. The average child learns in steps, one at a time, details and facts built upon previously learned material. This is called "concrete" learning. For most of us, this type of education continues through the grades until we are ready for college. What I have observed with near-death kids (the younger, the more pronounced), is that they suddenly start making huge leaps of thought after their episode, clustering ideas and concepts into higher reasoning styles. They pick up answers almost before questions are asked, and they're usually point on; then they probe further, reaching for depths of thought beyond the subject. If you ask them how they do it, they haven't the foggiest. This is "abstracting," where point of focus centers on conceptual levels, sometimes even beyond thought. It's not like "seeing beyond the box." For child abstractors, the box was never there to begin with.

The ability to abstract, educators tell us, typically does not begin until the late teens, twenties, and thirties (if at all). Young experiencers who have the ability to abstract must switch or reverse their learning style to cope with the concrete methods all schools teach. The result is that far too often we lose their genius. (Example: proficient in math/science/history, 93 percent; actually employed in those fields when older, 25percent.)

We need to stop here and ask these questions: Can kids, if near-death states are intense enough, undergo temporal lobe enhancement in advance of temporal lobe development? Would that account for the phenomenal abstractions a child displays afterwards? What if the learning reversals so apparent in child experiencers are the direct result of the brain being "charged" by the intensity of either a "light" or "dark" power surge at critical junctures in its growth?

WITNESS TO MEDICAL MISTAKES

You knew I was going to tackle this one, and you are right. Both adult and child experiencers witness mistakes made by medical staff during the out-of-body component of their near-death experience.

While clinically dead, George Rodonaia, a physician himself, was drawn to the newborn section of the hospital adjacent to the one where his body was. A friend's wife had just given birth to a daughter. The baby cried incessantly. As if possessed of X-ray vision, he scanned the baby's body and noticed that her hip had been broken after birth. Upon reviving, and after his tongue returned to normal size so he could speak (tongues swell up and fill the mouth cavity when a person dies), George told the doctors about the baby's fractured hip, and added, "The hip is broken because the nurse dropped her." Sure enough, X-rays showed the break, exactly as he had described. When the nurse was confronted, she admitted to dropping the child and was fired.[41]

When he was five years old, Robert C. Warth had a tonsillectomy in the doctor's office. Instantly he found himself above the domed operating light looking down at his body. "I could see 360 degrees without moving," he explained. "My mouth was pried open and I was covered up to my neck. There was a frenzy. The nurse yelled, 'Doctor.' He swung around and said, 'Stand back.' The next thing I remember is waking up in the bed." Two weeks later, Robert was taken back to the doctor for a checkup. He described for the doctor everything he had seen and heard. "The doctor winked at my mother and said, 'They tell me stories often. It's the ether. It makes them dream and hallucinate.' What else was the doctor going to say, that the little creep stopped breathing? I saw what he did, and he couldn't get me out of his office fast enough".[42]

During the early to mid-1900s, doctors regularly used too much ether for tonsillectomies. That's why so many of those operations show up in near-death cases during that period (although cases like this are still reported). Apparently, excessive amounts of ether can trigger full-blown near-death states in some children, not just hallucinations.

Medical mistakes are not uncommon, as previously shown with George Rodonaia. The mistakes may be individual incidents, as when the patient while out-of-body witnesses what the doctor or nurse really did; or they may show up as an unusual up-surge of people "dying" from a non-threatening procedure, as what happened with children across the country being overdosed with ether during tonsillectomies. The accuracy of these reports suggests that the range of human faculties is as nonlocal as the mind—something the medical community would be wise to note.

CHAPTER EIGHT

THEIR TURN

"Love's secret is always lifting its head out from under the covers: Here I am!"

—RUMI

"Just call me Chris. I had a near-death experience at a very young age (approximately two years old). I had on cloth diapers which were wet. The floor I was on was marble that had metal dividers in it for decorative purposes. I found a paper clip and put it into an electric socket. What follows is one of the most vivid experiences I have ever had (I am now 50).

"I left my body, and, as I ascended, I remember feeling upset that I had just started my life and did not want to go. I kept thinking that as the walls disintegrated and the horizons looked as though they went on for eternity. There were rings of clouds from the base of the horizon. They became increasingly smaller the higher they went. I started to move up towards a small, beautiful, loving light at the top of this formation. The whole time I felt very natural; however, did not want to keep going because I knew there was work to be done back on earth and did not want to give up. The acceleration towards the light stopped, and then I found myself back in my body. My father found me and was able to revive me.

"This is my earliest memory and, to this day, one of my most vivid. I have ALS (Lou Gehrig's Disease), and I am making a loving transition this year. This video I posted in April of 2008 is meant to be inspirational and loving, and my goodbye."[43]

"My name is Bruna Reyn and I live in Canada. Born in Vienna, Austria, from the age of two to seven I was a ward of the court in the care of The Sisters of Mercy of the Holy Cross. When my mother remarried, my brother and I were returned to her. From a young age I have been drawn to seek information about what happens at death. I had a 'dream' as a child that is as vibrant today as ever. In my 'dream' I was floating in outer space towards a brightly lit figure. The figure was Jesus Christ. He was dressed in robes of brilliant white and blue. Both arms were at His side and were directing 'souls' floating towards Him to pass Him, some to His right and others to His left. This was a brilliant scene in the black space where I was floating towards Him. I now believe this was my NDE when I was three. As a very young child (under 10), although my mother was not religious, when I was sent to bed, I would both pray and try to understand God and eternity. I recall one amazing moment where everything made sense—the fact that there was no beginning and no end, the existence of something beyond my environment—then it was gone.

"In 1994 I received a strange phone call from my mother. My mother said The Sisters of the Holy Cross had contacted her to say that they had been looking for me. The reason: on a hot August day, when I was 3 years old, I had been found drowned in a cistern in a small yard at Laxenburg. The cistern was a very large cement tank for collecting rainwater. They knew I was underwater at least 6 hours. Attempts at resuscitation by the nuns who found me, as well as the doctor in attendance, failed. The doctor pronounced me dead and left. But, following passionate prayers directed towards Sr. Maria Theresia, the founder [of the Order], I opened my eyes. I had a very high fever for 3 days.

"I was told that everyone who was present for this event, including the doctor, was asked to provide a written description of what they had witnessed. Besides having no explanation for this, the doctor also cautioned that they must be prepared as there would be brain and/or organ damage. This did not occur. Once the fever broke, I appeared to be fine. This event was documented, and made its way through various levels until it reached the Vatican. In 1994 the Vatican declared this a miracle. I was invited, together with my husband, to attend the 1995 Beatification Mass for Sr. Maria Theresia Scherer, and receive a medal."

"Kathryn Diamond here. I was 5 years old and swimming in a small backyard pool. My mom was hanging up laundry behind the pool, and my sister and our friend were chatting on a raft. As I swam underwater like a frog, I suddenly realized that I couldn't get up for air because the rafts were jammed together, and I was too weak. I was very scared at first; then I felt a complete calmness and lack of fear. I knew I was going to die. Then I was out of my body and watching it all from above the pool. No one knew I was lying on the bottom.

"Next, I was enveloped in a loving white light. That's when my life review began. I couldn't see the pool anymore but felt like I was in empty white space. My life flashed before my eyes in what seemed seconds. Yet there was a complete understanding that surrounded it—like I knew volumes in those brief moments. I saw every single thing that had ever happened to me, including a birthday party and small details of my life that I had forgotten about. I no longer felt like a child, but like a soul analyzing the experience. I could sense female beings behind me, like stern but loving teachers. They watched, as well, and helped me see how I had not been very kind to others in my five short years—I had a fiery temper to match my red hair. As soon as I came to this realization, the review was over and I was, once again, watching the scene from above the pool.

"I thought again, 'I'm going to die. No one knows I'm down there.' Then my sister stopped talking, perking her head up as if she heard my thoughts. 'Where's Kathy?' she asked frantically. 'Where's Kathy! Oh my God, she's down there!' She must have seen me, because the next thing I remember I was gasping for air. Then I was out of the pool and my mother squatted down to my level. 'I almost died!' I told them. My mother assured me that I 'did not almost die' and that 'I was perfectly fine.' I never stopped insisting that I almost died and never forgot the memory.

"From that moment on, I became totally driven with my writing. I went on to author, among other books, *Rachel's Magic Swing* and *The Day I Almost Drowned: A Child's Near-Death Experience*.[44] My dedication now is to help people. My dad told me recently that I nearly drowned at the age of four, as well, when he found me lying on the bottom of a lake. I wonder if God sometimes plucks children off earth and briefly takes them back to heaven so they will remember their earthly purpose. I believe the most important lesson from my NDE is that we need to treat others with love and kindness. My spirit guide also taught me that it doesn't matter if you help people through books and traveling the world, or if you help save a dying planet—both are equally important. What matters is the act of helping others and to 'walk with love in all you do.'"

"This is about my daughter Maddie. I was on bed rest for five months. She was rather small, but by the time she was delivered she had grown to 'normal' size. Maddie almost never moved during that time. One day after doctors told us she had tested a bit high for spina bifida and that there may be complications, I started to get a wee bit nervous. Well, I was sitting on the couch rubbing Maddie (she was still in me) and talking to her, when I asked would she give me a sign everything was okay. All of a sudden three of the biggest kicks went right into my hand. The kicks were so hard you could see the outline of the foot including toes. It was amazing.

"She had open-heart surgery after she was born and spent the first four months in children's hospital. She had a very difficult time prior to the operation and during recovery. When less than two years old (just speaking two- and three-word phrases), she began to talk in full articulate sentences to my husband and I, and described her near-death experience. We just listened. There is no way she could have ever heard people talk about something like this. She stopped talking after that, and slowly began to speak again over a few months' period.

"When she talked to us about her NDE, she spoke of being in a bright, loud room with lots of people (operating room had a minimum 16–member team and it was very bright and loud). She said she began to rise from her body, and she was looking down at everything from the ceiling, and could see herself on the table. She talked about the beautiful light—'Oh, so beautiful, Mommy'—and how they asked her to go with them, but she didn't want to, she wanted to stay. They asked her more than once. She said she stayed in the dark place until it was over. She mentioned the dark place a few times, and always looked more peaceful when she spoke of it. She was so scared and it hurt so much (operation). She described the dark place as not good or bad. It was just a place to wait and nothing hurt when she was there. It was like a small room. She felt protected. She described seeing beautiful colors and spoke of the tunnel. She didn't want to go into the tunnel. She said she knew it was safe to go back when she saw him. We never asked her who 'him' was, but now wish we had. We were a bit stunned. After she told us this, she was done and never spoke of it again. She doesn't remember it anymore.

"Maddie is now five-plus years old. She was just assessed with autism. She has high-functioning Aspergers and has been tested as gifted. She fits all the categories of near-death aftereffects, but is not gentle with animals, nor is she rough. She has lots of motor-skill challenges and is always dancing on her tippy toes. We have real doubts about the label of autism, and are detoxing her from heavy metals. She is getting closer and closer to recovery. General medicine does not support what we do, but it works. We have an amazing daughter."

"I am Mark Pacana, and I had two near-death experiences. At 6 years I had a hernia operation. While I was being put under and asked to count backwards from 100, I immediately found myself above the operating table looking down at my body. I heard someone say, 'He's out.' I wondered if that meant 'dead.' But I didn't feel dead, so all must be well. Bored of watching surgeons and nurses, I 'flew' out of the operating room through two huge wooden doors to a waiting room where my parents were. I sat next to my mother and held her hand. I don't remember flying back to, or into, my body, but after the operation I recounted the conversation my parents had had. My mom turned white. I repeated almost verbatim what they were talking about.

"I was drowned by a lifeguard in the middle of a motel pool when I was 12. At the bottom of the pool and with a water-filled body, I wondered what would happen next. I accepted that I was going to die. I remember thinking that children die every day; I was just one of them. It was peaceful down there. I sensed beings starting to gather around me. These were good spirits. Angels. I saw them. They were underwater but not wet. Everything slowed down by the split second. I saw my life flash before my eyes. I thought these scenes were all going to be important, and yet I saw mundane events too. I saw birthdays and Christmases, and me wasting time in front of the television. WHOOSH! I felt my 'self' being pulled out of my body. I did not like the separation. I was then 20 or more feet above the pool, watching people dive in to save me. I remember thinking that I was afraid of heights, but, not now. I was not afraid or scared of anything at this moment. I remember not being worried about my family; they would be okay.

"I had seven Angels lifting me up. I knew one of them to be my mother's father, whom I had never known and who passed away when I was a toddler. I saw huge Orbs of God's Pure Love, with the outlined shapes of human souls making up its figure. I looked down to see a brown and dark moving earth. I saw souls. I gained the knowledge that everything you can see, hear, taste, feel, or touch is made up of a soul. God's green earth, every part, is a soul. You can reincarnate into a blade of grass on the side of a mountain, or, you can be an alien from outer space (yes, they exist). I saw, above the heavens, other dimensions of higher and alternate learnings. I know we are here to fulfill God's Great Plan. We have the gift of life. Arriving at a gathering of clouds, a landing, as it were, I saw four more Angels. They had white robes on. I did not see wings. At this landing, knowledge was gained instantly. Communication was by thought. Three of the four Angels stepped in back to discuss how to get me back down to my body. The fourth Angel, a nice, smiling elderly gent, kept me company.

"'I don't want to go back down there. It's painful,' I yelled. 'You must! Your mission is not yet complete,' the Angels shouted back. The Angels were animated and almost mad. Their arms flailed as they talked to each other. The clouds above them lit up and a boom was heard; 'SHOW HIM,' was the response. Immediately I felt shame, for I had not cherished the God-given gift of life. I started saying, 'Don't show me! I want to go back,' but I was too late. I was flown over to the right of pillars where there was another one. On top of it was a book, about three feet thick. It was my Book of Life. The pages flew open, and just like watching myself on television, I saw scenes from what was to be, scenes from my future life. There were things in my Book of Life beyond my control which have since come true. I don't know what my mission is, but I am here for God's sake to fulfill His wishes, peacefully and lovingly.

"After being stuffed back into my body and recovering, I began recounting to my friend what I had seen and what was to be. He, like a lot of others, looked at me without knowing what to say. I don't hate the lifeguard who drowned me. I can't waste time hating. In fact, I feel more loved by Jesus for having had this experience. I was raised Catholic, but now consider myself a Christian. I don't need the Bible nor church. I am the most believing of souls. If I die before we ever get to meet, Trust Me—I will see you on 'The Other Side.'"

"My father, brother, and I were in the woods," said Robin O'Hara, "next to the Monongahela River. My brother and I were doing what we called double-headers on a rope swing. When my brother came back to where I was standing, I would grab his legs, and go out on the rope swing with him. Roughly the fifth instance of doing a double-header, Tim (my brother) did not have a good enough grip on the rope. We were about 20 to 25 feet up in the air when he lost his grip. We fell onto hard ground. Tim, who is three years older than me and heavier (I was 6 then), slammed down on my chest and knocked the life out of me.

"I hurled through The Light and was greeted by a man (which I now believe is my Guardian Angel of sorts). We walked to a Group of People (I did not feel my weight as I was moving). Magnificent, incredible, can't come close to describing the feeling of being with them on The Other Side. I met with this Group and they asked me several questions. They showed me my father (much like with a flat TV screen) who was in a state of panic at the time. They asked if I wanted to go back to my father on earth, and I told the Group, 'No, I want to say here with you.' The Group discussed this, and I believe they judged my father as well. There was a lady in the Group who told me, 'Robin, we have decided that you need to go back to your father.' I pleaded with them to let me stay. I tried to make excuses, but they told me my father was waiting for me. The next thing I knew I had a feeling of falling, and I was yelling, 'No, No, I want to stay here.' When I regained consciousness,

I saw my father looking down on me. Tears were in his eyes. The very first words that came out of my mouth were, 'Dad, why did you wake me up from such a beautiful dream. I want to go back to my dream.' My near-death experience happened during the middle of a bright, sunny day. I was on The Other Side for about four to five minutes. The intensity of time seemed to be longer, as it relates to events on The Other Side when compared to how long I was dead.

"Since my near-death experience, I have met only one other person who had close to the euphoric experience of being with God as I did. Her name is Maria and she owns a restaurant in Berkeley Springs. When I met Maria it was like we were telepathic. It nearly brought me to tears—her feelings of longing and almost anger because she wanted to stay on The Other Side, too. I have had this feeling practically all of my life. I was sent back because of my father's love. He is an extraordinary man. And I know I came back to do good for other people, too. I have spent 10 years in the Army, worked at NSA in Fort Meade, then at Goddard Space Flight Center for NASA. Now I am one of the top web marketing people in the country for search engine optimization and internet marketing. My clients range from a medical company to one who manufactures cemetery headstones."

Jenny stood at the doorway to death when she was eight years old. "I had a mysterious intestinal virus. My symptoms included high fever and vomiting. My symptoms were persistent and severe enough that I became dehydrated and required hospitalization. I entered the hospital and for the next several days was intravenously fed. When my parents stepped out to eat, a nurse brought me a tray of Mexican food, which is my favorite. I ate the entire meal! My body went into shock, which resulted in a coma state for 48 hours. While in coma, I experienced numerous near-death states.

"In one, I hovered over my body and saw people coming to visit me. I watched my next-door neighbor and her mother bring me a Strawberry Shortcake tin can of hard candies. When she placed one in my mouth, the flavor sent me back into my body.

"Another time, I left my body and went down the hall to visit more friends. My boyfriend was visiting his mother and young sister. His entire family was chatting with each other as I hovered over their heads. I left because I realized someone had come to visit me in my room. As I was in the hallway on the pediatric unit, I saw my best friend from school and her sister. They were excited because they had costumes to surprise me with a skit they created. I was hovering above them as they put on their costumes. They had trenchcoats with Groucho Marx glasses and mustache. When they entered my room and saw my body in a coma state, they responded with a gasp. When I experienced their shift from excitement to fear, I went back into my body.

"I decided I was tired of the hospital. I thought to myself, 'I'm leaving.' I began to float up and see the hospital from an aerial view. In the darkness I experienced a set of doors made of energy. They felt like hospital doors with a gate keeper, who was loving and accepting. It seemed like the side of the door I was on was dark, and the other side was light. I wanted to enter, but the gate keeper said, 'It's not your time. You need to go back to your body.' I attempted to bargain my way into the light. Another entity, who felt like God, authoritatively told me, 'YOU MUST GO BACK.' God's message: 'You have a message to bring to earth. It is a message of the existence of a higher power that loves all his children.' I asked, 'What am I supposed to do?' God said, 'You do not have to know now. It will come to you in dreams and insight.' Suddenly I was back in my body. I was told that my parents stayed with me during this time. They were with my body while my soul was with God.

"Over the years I have gone through different stages of denying these experiences and accepting them as well. It is difficult to put into words what happened to me. The paranormal abilities that come with it can be perplexing and confusing. One might say this is a gift with a double edge."

CHAPTER NINE

THE PATTERN OF AFTEREFFECTS

"NDE research threatens the very undergirding of science and our social structures."

—PETER FENWICK, M.D., FRCPSYCH.

Jenny, whose story was told in the last chapter, had this to say about the aftereffects: "Physiologically, I have all the criteria for having had a near-death experience—bright eyes, heightened senses and intelligence, psychic abilities, etc. As an adult, I felt different from others because of my psychic abilities. For example, how do you explain to others how you know the undisclosed details of a murder that happened in a location far from where you live? For many years I kept my psychic abilities to myself. Knowing that I could help others but not knowing how to go about it caused me to feel a great deal of guilt. Psychologically, the near-death experience is a work in progress."

Before we pick apart what happens afterward so we can better understand what Jenny is talking about, let's take a look at the spread of aftereffects—a pattern of physiological and psychological changes that occur—verified not only by the vast majority of both experiencers and their significant others in my research, but by many other investigators in the field of near-death studies. The pattern as presented is based on sessions I had with three thousand adult and 277 child experiencers.

PHYSIOLOGICAL AFTEREFFECTS OF NEAR-DEATH STATES

Most Common (between 80 to 95 percent)—more sensitive to light (especially sunlight) and to sound (tastes in music change); look younger/act younger/more playful (with adults); look older/act more mature/more introspective (with children); substantial change in energy levels (can have energy surges); changes in thought processing (switch from sequential/selective thinking to clustered/abstracting, with an acceptance of ambiguity); insatiable curiosity; lower blood pressure; brighter skin and eyes; reversal of brain hemisphere dominance; heal quicker.

Quite Common (50 to 79 percent)—reversal of body clock; heightened sensitivity; heightened intelligence; metabolic changes (doesn't take that long to process food, bowel movements can increase); assimilate substances into bloodstream quicker (takes less for full effect); loss of tolerance for pharmaceuticals (most turn to alternative/complementary healing measures/holistic medicine); heightened response to taste/touch/texture/smell/pressure; more creative and inventive; synesthesia (multiple sensing); increased allergies; preference for more vegetables, less meat with adults—more meat, less vegetables with children; latent talents surface; sleep patterns change; display indications of brain structure/function changes (also with nervous and digestive systems, skin sensitivity); electrical sensitivity.

PSYCHOLOGICAL AFTEREFFECTS OF NEAR-DEATH STATES

Most Common (between 80 to 99 percent)—loss of the fear of death; become more spiritual/less religious; more generous and charitable; handle stress easier; philosophical; more open and accepting of the new and different; disregard for time and schedules; regard things as new even when they are not (boredom levels decrease); form expansive concepts of love while at the same time challenged to initiate and maintain satisfying relationships; become psychic/intuitive; know things (closer connection to Deity/God, prayerful); deal with bouts of depression; less competitive.

Quite Common (50 to 79 percent)—displays of psychic phenomena; vivid dreams and visions; "inner child" issues exaggerate; convinced of life purpose/mission; rejection of previous limitations/norms; episodes of future knowing/future memory; more detached and objective (dissociation); "merge" easily (absorption); hunger for knowledge; difficulty communicating and with language; can go through deep periods of depression and feelings of alienation from others; synchronicity occurs regularly; more orgasmic; less desire for possessions and money; service oriented; healing ability; attract animals (good with plants); aware of invisible energy fields/auras; preference for open doors and open windows/shades; drawn to crystals; laugh more; become more understanding/wiser.

A further look at how this stacks up with experiencers:

21% claimed no discernible differences afterward (this claim was countered by the experiencer's significant others in every case where I was able to obtain a second opinion).

60% reported significant, noticeable changes.

19% said changes were so radical they felt as if they had become another person (before and after photos often differed, although basic body type and facial structures remained the same).

Those who reported changes of a significant nature after their near-death episode, exhibiting all or most of this pattern, totaled 79 percent. There is no drug (legal or illegal; natural or synthetic), no hallucination, no case of oxygen deprivation, no epileptic seizures, nothing—that can match or mimic this pattern of aftereffects—except a deeply impactful spiritual transformation that also evidenced a kundalini breakthrough (both can and usually do occur at the same time, automatically).

The key in near-death research is to look at the whole phenomenon, not just a few aspects. (A medical corollary: you must use the whole herb, not just the most active ingredient, to obtain the best results . . . because the whole herb has *all of its parts held in balance.* You separate the parts; you lose effectiveness. The near-death phenomenon is just like with herbs: if you separate parts out from the whole, you lose sight of the full effect and larger meaning of the experience.)

SWITCHES IN BRAIN DOMINANCE

After a near-death experience, brain hemisphere dominance tends to shift sides. Those who were once more right-brained (creative, innovative, intuitive, compassionate), often return far more interested in physics, science, experimentation, and history. We mostly hear about the opposite, though, thanks to the many experiencers who were left-brained before their episode. It's curious that the eye's function and the ability to process language are considered more active/male (left-brained), while the ear's architecture and the ability to listen are associated with receptive/female (right-brained). Further, men's eyes have more cone cells in them, which enable a closer focus (perfect for left-brained activities), whereupon women's eyes have more rod cells designed for connecting images into broader pictures (a right-brained trait[45]). If you're into the "Goddess thing," you could reasonably deduce from this that the near-death phenomenon opens us up to realms associated with the feminine. Still, what near-death cases really demonstrate is a melding of art and science (right and left) into a unified whole—the whole brain.

UNCONDITIONAL LOVE

Go back and read again the stats on aftereffects. Yes, experiencers come back more loving. They tend to love others without conditions—none of this "I'll love you if you love me" stuff. Yet they are sorely challenged to initiate and maintain satisfying relationships. Why?

First, we need to be careful how the term is used. The meaning of "love" does not translate as we think it should into other languages and cultures, or even in our own families. What does translate is "empathy" (the ability to understand another's feelings). Words like "peace" and "heart" are universal; surprisingly, "love" is not.

Second, "unconditional love" may not express what we think it does. More aptly known by the Greek term "agape," it is a reference to the highest form of love possible: God's Love, Cosmic Love, Universal Love. Literally, it is love sans object. After a near-death experience, it is as if every woman you see is your mother, sister, aunt, and daughter. Every man, your father, brother, uncle, and son. It's not that you can't tell differences. Rather, everyone takes on "the glow of family"—the human family in oneness with each other—and you want to embrace everyone in a giant hug . . . which isn't cool if some say, "Bug off."

As you might guess, experiencers who feel this outpouring of love must frequently relearn basic cautions. Is everyone truly ready to love each other *unconditionally*—no secrets, nothing held back, no exceptions? I don't think so. The tendency to openly embrace and give without hesitation is generally seen by others as foolish, flirtatious, disrespectful, or unloving. I am continually amazed at how coldly indifferent experiencers can be regarded, when in actuality, they are behaving in an unselfish, friendly, or helpful manner. Maybe this conundrum speaks more to how distant and distrustful society has become, than to how loving and generous most experiencers come to be.

MATTERS OF HEALTH

Notice to all medical and healthcare professionals: have you noticed anything different when treating near-death experiencers? To a rousing chorus of "Yes we have," allow me to "fetch you up."

- Low blood pressure is normal for experiencers. This is not a sign of chronic fatigue syndrome, nor does it require "disease" treatment.

- Less aging. Low blood pressure and looking younger go together, and are signs that cortisol (in the same class as steroids) is less present in the body. Thus, experiencers tend to have slower responses to stress, which creates less cortisol, lowers blood pressure, and slows down the aging factor.

- Light sensitivity. Fresh air is healthy but be careful of excessive sunlight. Especially with the young, limit playtime or sports outside. Adults who work outdoors should consider wearing sunglasses and taking "shade" breaks. Too much bright light could be fatiguing and put the immune system at risk. There are some experiencers who crave light and can't get enough of it. Extremes in reaction to light are commonplace.

- Sound sensitivity. A real challenge for teens and those living in larger cities that are inundated with loud sounds/music. This can be painful. Most experiencers switch to melodic music, the sounds of nature, or silence.

- Less tolerance of pharmaceuticals. Less is more. Please tell your doctor or nurse that you are a near-death experiencer. This alerts them to a possible need to alter treatment. Assimilation is quicker for the vast majority, and it takes less of something for full effect. Seek out the mildest medication possible for your condition. Be careful with child experiencers, as substances for them are administered according to weight and age and often contain unnecessary or excessive sweeteners.

- Sleep cycles can change. The very young tend to nap less and "flow" more (flow states are free of thinking; they help to energize creativity). Many relive their near-death episode or are haunted by it in vivid dream states.

  Sixty percent of adult experiencers wake up between 3 and 4:00 am, and for no apparent reason. Medically, that time is known as "The Hour of the Wolf," and is associated with congestive heart failure and other serious health problems.[46] Creatively, it is called "The Hour of the Muse," when artistic/inventive types receive their greatest ideas and inspiration. That same hour, spiritually, is when angels and heavenly guidance are said to be easier to access; in Islam, the first prayer of the morning begins at 4:00 am.

- Scientifically, it is known that the earth's magnetic fields, pushed by solar winds, peak around 3:00 am each night. This "ambient" or surrounding circulation is considered unstable by scientists, creatively stimulating by artists. Other changes: onset of sleep can be difficult to recognize at first; breathing can stop without cause, even while asleep. Body clock reversals are typical. None of these sleep deviations are outside the norm.

- Switch to alternative/complementary therapies. Those who are able to maintain successful and satisfying states of health are most often those who gravitate toward more natural approaches to health care. This requires re-education as most people are unfamiliar with practices like homeopathy, herbal remedies, osteopathy, psychotronics, and naturopathy, for instance. With acupuncture, practitioners who use gold needles instead of stainless steel note a quicker, better healing response with experiencers—indicative of a biofield shift.

- Overall health. Those who chose to work with and integrate their aftereffects had the best health overall, excelling in self-healing measures and spiritual approaches to life. One out of five became vegetarians. Many came to say grace at mealtimes and meditate on a regular basis.

ALTERATIONS IN THE BIOFIELD

All human beings and other life forms exist in a biofield of electromagnetic energy. Bands closer to the body can be seen, usually in one base color (called an "aura") that shifts in size and shape according to our changing thoughts, attitudes, and desires. This auric biofield has been measured variously as extending twelve feet out in all directions from an average person (thus enabling one to sense or "feel" the environment and whoever is near). Luminous flares or "fountains" of colored light streaking out from the surface of the body have been photographed by Russia's Semyon Kirlian, resulting in what is now termed "Kirlian photography."

There is no question that our biofields are altered to some degree after a near-death experience (hence gold needles work better than stainless steel with acupuncture). Seventy-nine percent of experiencers report having pronounced electrical sensitivity afterward—many experience stopping watches; popping lightbulbs; changing television stations; burning up or short-circuiting tape recorders, small appliances, microphones, computers, electrical systems, phone lines, and car batteries. This is expensive! (What

I learned to do to cut costs, was to enter a meditative state, join with the equipment, introduce myself and state my purpose while assuring no harm, bless the equipment, then return to normal consciousness. Whenever I did this, no problem.) My webmaster, Steff, was able to illustrate on a graph the unusual sound "dropouts" that happen whenever I make a recording. Linda Jacquin, a multiple experiencer, discovered that the battery in her watch was causing problems. She switched to solar batteries, and can once again wear watches.

Cell phones, pagers, Wi-Fi, and microwave radiation, already creating a worldwide epidemic of fatigue and memory loss in the way everyone's bio-fields are affected, constitute a much greater concern for experiencers. Caution is urged.

Near-death experiencers have their faculties expand as well, enhancing sensitivity to taste, touch, texture, smell, pressure, sight, sound, vibrations and shapes of any sort, weather, and subtle movements. Faculty input can also mix or come conjoined in multiples. This is called "synesthesia" and is associated with the limbic system in the brain. An example of synesthesia is when experiencers buy a picture for the sound it makes, not just for its pleasing image. Or smelling color, hearing numbers, seeing shapes, or sensing orbs in the air that correspond to emotional states. The limbic system is the seat of our emotional and survival natures. A lot of what we call "psychic abilities" is really accelerations or expansions of the limbic system—hyperfunctions designed for survival.

THE PSYCHIC/INTUITION

Let's face it. If you weren't psychic before a near-death experience, you become psychic after. If you were psychic before, you become very psychic after. Intuition relates to our faculty of perception, and it is how we piece together information that helps us to live our lives safer and easier.[47] Our brain literally has an "intuition switch" that turns on about every ninety minutes. You can tell that it's on if you suddenly feel spacey, sleepy, or cannot focus (excellent time for a brief meditation or shift into a flow state[48]). The psychic, as I see it, relates to how we use intuition. The word "psychic" derives from the Greek term *psychikos*, which means "of the soul." Traditionally, the ability is identified via mode of usage: clairvoyance (seeing beyond eyes), clairaudience (hearing beyond ears), clairsentience (sensing beyond response), clairgustience (tasting beyond taste buds), and clairolfactory (smelling beyond nose). Psychic functioning is so fast that it cannot be measured via brain waves.

In truth, psychic ability is just another way of listening. Channeling spirits is just another type of self-validation. Intuition is just another avenue to express the spontaneity of a moment and all that it holds.

The paranormal becomes normal after a near-death episode. It is not unusual to hear of experiencers continuing to travel out-of-body; seeing and conversing with angels and spirit beings of various types (as well as ghosts); having startlingly real dreams (66 percent with kids, 79 percent with adults); and experiencing "betwixt and between"—the liminal or threshold states that exist in those areas of the electromagnetic spectrum that are either ultra (the violet area) or infra (the red area) to our faculty of perception. When our intuitive/psychic abilities expand and accelerate, boundaries fade. Considering that plasma is the fourth state of matter, it should come as no surprise to anyone that experiencers often see plasma forms in varied shapes, and that they discover "energy portals" and imprints of spirit worlds at sacred sites around the globe.

FUTURE KNOWING/FUTURE MEMORY

There have been enough rigorous, repeatable experiments to prove that people can foresee the future, at least to a limited degree. This precognition (future knowing) is linked to our emotions, not only in the limbic system of the brain, but also in our "heart brain" (called that because about 65 percent of the heart's cells are neural cells, explaining heart intelligence). Changes in skin sensitivity can also signal this, as skin reflects our emotional state and the same precognitive impulses. The future knowing that emerges from near-death states, however, tends to be more specific and detailed, and not just reflective of feelings.

Experiencers can have episodes of future memory, where they become acutely aware of living the future in advance. Although these episodes can happen in dream states, they most often occur when individuals are wide awake and actively engaged. The general pattern of occurrence: physical sensation at onset (like a "lift" or sweep of energy, perhaps a ringing sound); present time/space relationships freeze in place (this stoppage can be accompanied by sparkles in the air—everything becomes brighter, sense faculties heighten); expansion (as you expand so does space); future temporarily overlays the present (a given scenario manifests in specific detail and is sensorially experienced as if a real event); present time/space relationships resume normal activity (sparkles disappear, rightful proportions return, regular living restarts); aftereffects (sensations of being startled, chilled, or puzzled—event remains vivid as long as it remains in awareness, but, eventually is either forgotten or set aside). These "pre-lived" episodes later manifest. Sometimes experiencers are able to change the timing of what is involved in these memories, but apparently not the event itself.

Timeshifts do not always move forward. Sometimes experiencers are physically propelled back and must relive what they just did. Individuals are shown things during their near-death states, even about people not yet born, that later happen—always on cue. Timeshifts are like tales from the *Twilight Zone*. An amusing curiosity is that the majority come to think outside of time, as if the perception of time is merely a reflection of where one is in consciousness.[49]

THE IMPORTANCE OF MUSIC

Why researchers don't focus more on this I do not know. There is certainly no shortage of examples. During many near-death scenarios a distinct kind of music is heard unlike that on earth; dubbed "music of the spheres" for lack of a better term. Afterward, sound enhancements skyrocket with most, creating relationships to music that are sudden, passionate, fully dimensional. Yes, there are stories about experiencers who, without thought or intent, suddenly began to sing grand opera or play a musical instrument or compose incredible scores like pros. More numerous are the stories of experiencers who work to bring special music into hospice and healing environments (like Gilles Bedard, who became a specialist in contemplative music and now works in collaboration with a neuroscientist to explore the spiritual aspects of the brain[50]).

Back in 1988, Dr. Susumu Ohno of the Beckman Research Institute in California converted the chemical formulas of healthy living cells of various parts of the body into musical notes. It was found that DNA molecules of different bodily areas had their own musical melody; some had an uncanny resemblance to the works of the great composers.[51] What should interest all of us is that Ohno's work has since been duplicated and expanded upon by the French anthropologist Jeremy Narby.[52] Narby found that DNA emits and receives both phonons and photons—electromagnetic waves of sound and light. He writes that according to shamans, it is impossible to enter the world of spirits and remain silent, for everywhere there is *visual* music and endless sound. Today DNA is considered a text, a keyboard, a musical score that follows the rules of grammar and language. Pythagoras believed that "all things are numbers," that every structural form is "frozen music." Goethe declared that "architecture is crystallized music." These discoveries interconnect—whether universe, multiverse, or innerverse, there is sound and there is light. Even within the mathematics of structure, shape, and form, melody or dissonance prevails. With child experiencers, I found that enhancements in music (85 percent) were almost as high as those in math (93 percent). Since the regions for math and music in the brain are located next to each other, it is obvious, at least to me, that they accelerate as a single unit.

There's a clue here—a big one. Background sound and melody (similar to "hoomi" singing/bell-like overtone harmonics) are present in the majority of near-death experiences; some experiencers return with full-blown musical talent; most come back either craving certain types of music or dedicated to using music as a healing tool. Math and music tend to merge for many (just like science and art do); our bodies are made of light and sound at the most primal level, and so are the worlds of spirit and the structures of matter.

Life and death are coded in the language of light and sound. We stumble upon this coding in near-death states, not knowing what we've found until we come to realize that the essence of otherworlds, of origin, is implanted in our very genes.

CHAPTER TEN

A MYRIAD OF EXAMPLES

"If the doors of perception were cleansed, everything would be seen as it is, infinite."

—WILLIAM BLAKE

Dian Curran was a senior systems engineer when she had a performance review in 2005. Her supervisor gave her this note: "Dian has progressed significantly during 2005 by working on interpersonal relationships and by not being defensive when code errors were found or changes were required." Her overall rating was: "Meets requirements." That was a nice way of saying she was difficult to get along with, argumentative, and seemed to have a chip on her shoulder.

She "died" not long after and had a near-death experience. What makes her case unique is that the 2006 performance review was done by her old boss. The year following she had another review conducted by both old and new bosses. Her 2008 review involved only the new boss. The comment for 2008 was: "Her excellent work was noted by the instructor to her functional management." In 2008, her review stated how well she worked with little or no supervision, had excellent leadership skills, rating, "Exceeds Requirements." (I have a copy of all three reviews on file.)

At issue here is the 2007 report. Content is missing as a result of a dispute between her two bosses. Her former boss squabbled with the new one, claiming he "must be blind" to see anything praiseworthy about Dian, whereupon the present boss countered by saying she was an excellent employee and easy to be around. Neither one could recognize the other's description of Dian. She had changed that much—even her before-and-after security pictures (one was a work ID taken November 2006 and the other a passport photo taken March 2007) differed enough that you had to do a double take to make sure it was the same person.

I asked Dian to make a list of the aftereffects following her near-death experience. Here's what she gave me:

Physical: "Waking up in the middle of the night for no apparent reason. I have little or no trouble falling back to sleep afterwards. Extreme sensitivity to light and loud noises. Increasing adverse reactions to certain scents and smells. Needing less sleep that before, and seem to sleep deeper than I used to in spite of waking in the night. Sensitivity to cold, more tolerance to heat. Drastic changes in appetite and diet. I eat less red meat and am drawn to fish. I hated fish before, now I prefer it to all other meat. Drawn to eat more vegetables and fruit." Blood pressure used to be high, took medication. Diastolic went from around 100 to low 70s, meds no longer needed.

Psychological: "Much higher ability to handle stress. I used to be prone to outbursts of anger; that has disappeared. Much increase in empathy and charisma to the point that people seek me out in random places like the grocery store. Several unrelated people have said to me, 'It's not that you've changed, it's that you are an entirely different person.' Apparently there are aspects of my personality that have changed, but that has more of an outward manifestation than what I notice from inside myself. What I do notice from the inside is that I am a happier person, and I feel there is meaning in my life. I have no idea why I was sent back, but my life has more value to me now. Spirituality is an inseparable part of me, thus my life. I do not have to do rituals or meditations to be spiritual—I live it. I often do these things but they are usually when I am trying to focus on something particular. Before, I was somehow separate [from things spiritual] and struggled to get in touch. That struggle has ceased."

Additions/Subtractions: "I feel that the NDE kind of re-wired my brain. Channels were opened up that weren't open before, which started a process that continues. Telepathic abilities increased immediately. I had some abilities before, [but not like this]. I have learned to control a kind of on/off switch.

Ability to reach other people's emotions and give them a feeling of safety and trust. This allows people to open up to me. Ability to diagnose a physical/psychological ailment. I can look at someone and get a kind of knowing of what is wrong with them. I have been suggesting to people 'get this checked' or 'that checked' when I do the diagnosis. I was able to clear up some clogged arteries in someone, but that took regular treatments over several months. I used a visualization technique to make the buildup dissolve into the blood, go through the kidneys and out through the urine. Within a day or so their urine got cloudy and continued to be cloudy until the end of the treatments. Then it was normal again. When they had a calcium recheck, the buildup was gone. Others I have worked on expect whatever they have to go away after one or two treatments—it doesn't work that way. Ability to interact with beings from other planes—meaning spirits, whatever. I think people call this mediumship. I feel their presence and have no trouble interacting with them. They do not interfere with my daily stuff or 'command' me or anything else that would indicate I'm out of my mind, although I wondered at first. I thought maybe I hadn't fully come back. Not sure how to categorize this: I think that my 'silver cord' has never been the same since. I accidently almost harmed myself when I 'went as far away as I could' in an experiment not long after I came back. I had been taught that one would always come back to one's body if there was any strain—that there were automatic controls on this. Well, I seemed to have lost those automatic controls and nearly died again. It either got damaged or is not in place. I often have to kind of force myself to stay present in my body. Over time, this has become easier. From this I am able to recognize someone else who has had an NDE. I look at this cord and if it has a 'kink,' they have had one. Some 'kinks' are more noticeable than others, but all seem to have them. I have not been able to read my own cord. I have vivid, sometimes prophetic dreams. And am able to read someone's deeper layers of mind. I just seem to get a 'knowing,' and am then able to navigate with the real facts. It is quite effective in dealing with people without making myself appear threatening. The difficulty I have had integrating back into this world is that I live a different reality now, and have these abilities, but it doesn't pad my ego. I feel that I am somehow in a separate reality than those around me, and am no longer part of this world."

THREE EXAMPLES OF HEALTH ISSUES THAT BECAME LIFE-OR-DEATH CHALLENGES TO NEAR-DEATH EXPERIENCERS BECAUSE OF HOW THEY HAD CHANGED

Linda was feeling poorly—a cold/flu thing—so she went to her doctor and was given antibiotics. The same night she went out for dinner with friends and became quite weak and had difficulty forming words. She was rushed to the hospital where all manner of tests were administered. The doctors told her that the antibiotics were shutting down her system. "I knew better than to take them," Linda admitted. "I always use homeopathic remedies now but, well, I just thought I'd be okay this time."

Tonecia's lupus was affecting her heart. She had to be taken to the hospital. According to the doctor there was no basis for her failing heart. She told him about her near-death experience as a child, how she nearly drowned. He had an "aha" moment in recognizing that her heart had the pattern of someone who had suffered trauma (the drowning). Apparently the doctor had some knowledge of near-death aftereffects, because he changed her medicine to the mildest available, and then reduced its potency even further. She was out of the hospital the next morning, feeling fine.

"I have experienced unusual reactions to various pharmaceuticals prescribed for me at different times in my life," said Joe Ann Van Gelder, who experienced multiple near-death episodes when she was a child. "In fact, I believe that my last NDE (after back surgery as an adult) resulted from an 'overdose' of anesthetic—a dose used for 'normal' people. I had marvelous results with a two-year homeopathic treatment for the post-polio problem I've had. Regrettably, that homeopath has died and I haven't located another."

A timeshift—"My husband and I were driving in the car toward the bridge," said Jennifer. "Just before we got to the bridge I took out my usual dollar to pay the bridge toll. Next thing we knew, we were about 10 miles back, on the same road, passing a stone building we had just passed 10 minutes before. I looked at my husband and said, 'Didn't we just pass here?'—then we both noticed the dollar bill in my hand, which I always took out seconds before crossing the bridge. We realized that we had been 'set back' . . . in time and space."

Slow brain waves—"My EEGs show this slow brain wave," reported Lucia. "I am an accountant. I can't stop learning since my NDEs. I love science. I have the theta waves, the voices, the visions. Theta waves are rare in the awake individual, unless they are in deep meditation. I am 'high-functioning,' as the doctors and psychiatrists have told me. Now that research is showing things in this area, of theta waves and the area of stimulation triggering memories, maybe I can help somehow. I can be of assistance in proving that consciousness never dies. That it goes on. That we go on. That we 'tape' absolutely everything into our minds. Everything we notice and even that which we do not."

Strange sleep pattern, future knowing, different view of lifetimes—Lee speaks of many changes. "I have the taste of metal come up in my mouth when I have been 'zapped.' I'll be wandering around, minding my own biz, walking in the mall, standing at the sink, and suddenly have a sharp pain in the arm or someplace—like a small needle has just stabbed me. It is so shocking to the system that one needs to be caught before one falls to the floor. Looking at the spot one never sees any wound, but the taste of anesthesia wells up in the mouth and within 15 minutes sleep is just about uncontrollable. One sleeps for about five hours and wakes with the same taste in one's mouth, as if just waking up from an operation. The metallic taste is there for about five hours more. These sleeps are extremely exhausting. We call them 'working sleeps'—like dreams where we are set to a task or forced to learn something.

"I have been a stickler for avoiding making things happen that I saw in my NDE preview. If they are intended for my life, and if I am following The Light in each moment, then these events will happen of their own accord. I seem to have some sort of gut feeling about things—that has interfered with my academic career. I'll hear something and just know it's wrong. I can't even make myself learn it sometimes. I tried Sociology in college, but the ideas they were making us learn were so idiotic that I just couldn't make myself remember it long enough to take a test. I went back to college in this last decade and took anthropology and economics. The stuff was marginally better, yet still very moronic and self-aggrandizing in parts. I often felt I was learning more about the authors and their little egos than anything important about humanity or the world in general.

"Since the early 80s I've had what can only be described as 'auto-particle physics.' I'll be sitting there and suddenly an image of some math formulas will come streaming into my head, and I'll have to write it down before it will stop. I'll go and find some of the formulas in college textbooks or reference books at libraries—but only parts of them. It's as if I get the initial formula, and then the rest of the function is detailed but corrected from what's in the textbook. The formulas seem to be about fluid dynamics and gravity—yet they're all partial.

"My Dad had an NDE seven years before he died. During the experience he found that after he had gone through the 'tunnel' and out into the area where souls were congregating around the Central Light, he could 'Go anywhere in Space-Time just by thinking about it. Go to any moment in my life or yours, even times where I was dead and gone. I could decide to join a new place, or universe, or time, and that would be where my new life would take hold.'

"I feel that our lives are sequential only in our experience of them. I've a set of lifetimes; some are here, some are in other universes, in time frames that wouldn't even correspond to anything here. Some are not only in this universe, but on this world. Some are overlapping with this life as I am living it right now. I may even meet myself as I pass through this life-path. Some are a flicker away in the next-over possibility line, or more than a flicker over. I may have a lifetime in the deep past of this world and the next in the far future. And, as I meet myself in another life-path, I may be the one further along the journey of our 'sequences of lives,' or they may be. Perhaps this is the True Meaning of the idea from the Oriental religions when they speak of the Divine living every life . . . as a dream. It may be the Core Truth of the Commandment, 'Love One Another AS IF YOU ARE THE VERY SAME PERSON—because you are, or may be. As we cross paths with others in our 'lifetimes,' we need to remember that the person we hurt may just be ourselves . . . or a person we deeply love . . . in another body, another context. I am my brother's keeper because: I LITERALLY AM MY BROTHER."

A list of some of my own changes afterward:

Hair and nails now grow faster, blood pressure lower.

Muscle strength decreased while energy levels increased.

Sun tolerance decreased. Would turn bright orange the first seven years and become nauseous and dizzy if exposed to direct sunlight for over 15 minutes. Orange coloration finally ceased, but some sensitivity remains.

Both temporal lobe areas of head thicker, more spongy than before, and so sensitive even finger pressure cannot be tolerated.

Body clock reversed to mornings (was a night person). No awareness of tiring at first. Would suddenly collapse when sleep came. Took several years before adequate sleep control returned and could withstand longer hours.

Food flushes out of digestive system within 15 to 20 minutes if tainted or not in agreement with body. Jaws and teeth hurt if say an untruth or falsehood.

Hearing range increased and have become more tonal. Now hear pain (not just feel it), hear paintings (not just see them), and follow tones in travel.

Taste and smell more acute, can also taste words and feelings. Allergies developed to pharmaceuticals necessitating a switch to natural remedies.

Had difficulty handling the great sweeps of joy which would overwhelm me. Meditation and prayer helped to redirect this ecstatic energy into modes of healing and help for others. Still challenged by and delight in joy.

Memory seemed disconnected and hard to access at first, as if it belonged to someone else or somewhere else. Energy flows were fragmented. Exercises and intention corrected this (plus a lot of effort).

Could "hop" among the clouds and "split" into other dimensions with ease. Still can.

Much more sensitive to electric and magnetic fields. Can no longer wear a watch. Look younger, feel younger. Eyes, skin, and hair brighter.

Cognitive abilities reversed. Where once analytical, now intuitive. Where once intuitive, now analytical. Ask more questions, probe, verify.

Intelligence increased, developed an insatiable hunger for knowledge. Once memory disconnection and energy fragmentation were corrected, ability to concentrate skyrocketed. Mind now like a laser-beam. Fully exist wherever my attention is, as if physical body has been vacated.

Quit going to funerals. Could see the "dearly departed" enjoying his or her own funeral and couldn't stop laughing.

CHAPTER ELEVEN

INTEGRATION

"We shall be changed, in a moment, in the twinkling of an eye."

—CORINTHIANS 15:51–52

The majority of near-death experiencers come back as positive "can-do-ers," ready to transform themselves, their families, their careers, their religion, their politics, and their pocketbook. Almost immediately worlds collide. The world they glimpsed during their episode is another reality and a grander truth that does not match the one that they left. A sense of loss can follow—it's usually subtle—until boundaries, benchmarks, and the "dream of self" (who you thought you were and what you thought you would do with your life) take on different dimensions. Incredible joy for what you gained mixes with incredible sadness for what you lost. A great love blends with deep grief. You leave "the circle of the familiar" for "realms of the miraculous"—life as always, little more than memory.

This needs to be said up front so no one misunderstands: the phenomenon *reorders* (not disorders); you *adjust* (not recover); it is *a new reality* (not pathology). Mental health professionals miss this. Their expertise centers around how to work with what breaks down or afflicts—not with what uplifts, heals, and makes new. Give experiencers a supportive environment, a good listener, plenty of info, and time to "feel" their way through the many conflicts that invariably pop up, and they will amaze everyone with how readily they can take what they learned from their experience and integrate it into daily life—to their benefit and that of others.

There's the catch: how many experiencers actually receive any degree of support or validation? Not veterans—military experiencers are virtually ignored; those who dare to talk about near-death states are usually diagnosed as mentally ill or hallucinating. Not fundamentalists of any religion—still today these folk consider the phenomenon the work of the devil; experiencers are either ignored, ridiculed, or punished; families curse children who have them. In Muslim countries even today, experiencers are targeted for murder to "protect the family's honor."

Integration is like walking through a door that can no longer close.

DIVORCE, MONEY, AND SUICIDE

You've had a chance to look at the pattern of aftereffects in the previous chapter. We'll focus on more of what is the typical here. But since the integration process has many sides, let's begin with some important "glitches."

Divorce

Between 75 and 78 percent of the experiencers in my research divorced, most within six to twelve years after their episode. This figure is much higher than the national average. Of interest: both spouses usually voiced the same complaint: "I don't know that person anymore." The non-experiencer wants what he or she once had. The experiencer no longer relates to others the same way, and the past holds little real interest. Misunderstandings between spouses and lovers could be cut substantially if enough information about the phenomenon were readily available.

Money

The desire for and interest in money often fades after the near-death experience. A commitment to service and helping others—working because one enjoys the work—replaces prior fixations on the corporate model of "profit first." This can free the individual to live a simple life more in tune with spiritual values, or it can open the door to extremes of poverty, sacrifice, and perplexing behaviors. Even the rudiments of logic and caution can be cast aside, as happened to Steve. He went on a spending spree, traveled with his wife and children, bought expensive things no one needed, planned to buy a bigger house—all of this to help out his family. When he "hit the wall," with family finances seemingly beyond repair, he sought the aid of a financial advisor. She found a way he could turn the mess around, but before she could show him how, Steve committed suicide. The shame of what he had done overwhelmed him. Steve's last request was that near-death experiencers receive guidance about the real value of money and what it's *really* for. The magic of compound interest completely eluded him.

Suicide

No one wants to talk about this, but we must. What happened to Steve happens to others. For the most part, near-death episodes are a suicide deterrent, especially if that episode sprang from a suicide attempt. But not always. In my research of child experiencers, 21 percent attempted suicide within about fifteen years of their experience. Some in five years. We don't recognize what goes on with children because we have forgotten how a child thinks. Their logic says: "I was in a bright-filled world with loving people when I wasn't breathing. Now that I'm breathing again, the bright ones are gone. The way to get them back is to stop my breathing." A child does not see this logic as harmful or hurtful to parents and family. To a child, it makes sense. An easy way to counterbalance this thinking is to teach the child how to get "back there" through guided visualizations: calming the heart and mind in a brief meditation, seeing once again that wonderful world (in detail and with great feeling), being there for a while, and then returning to full consciousness, wide-awake, and refreshed. The child should be encouraged to do this simple exercise occasionally, but not too often, as this life, where we are now in consciousness, is where we need to remain. The exercise should never be used to escape; only enrich. With adult experiencers, my figures for suicide were between 4 and 5 percent, and linked entirely to conflicts in handling the aftereffects. Whether challenged by relationships, situations at work, or by money (as with Steve), the aftereffects of a near-death episode can be daunting. Most integrate successfully. Those who don't need a little help.

VISIBLE/INVISIBLE ENERGY FIELDS

Near-death episodes often broaden one's perception of what exists. Experiencers come to realize that they are a soul living in a physical body that operates through various levels of energy fields:

- Physical—temperature, odor, electromagnetics, density factors; all of which are measurable scientifically.

- Emotional—feelings, sensations, attachments, expressions; all of which are automatically sensed or felt organically.

- Mental—thoughts, ideas, perceptions, memories; all of which are analyzed and processed intellectually.

- Spiritual—insight, wisdom, knowing, creativity; all of which transcend definition.

These energy fields interpenetrate and enable us to function as we do. They are seen by most as layered sheaths or coverings that circle our visible body in much the same fashion as onion skins layer around an onion's core. Each layer is finer and more subtle than the previous. They extend out from the body about a foot or so, perhaps a number of yards—depending on a person's mood or health.

This is ours, the supportive "energy package" we wear, that formerly we could neither see nor admit to knowing. Is it any wonder, then, that we could be adversely affected by electromagnetic fields from power lines, home wiring, airport and military radar, substations, transformers, watches, computers, electric blankets, and the like? In my case, I took up the art of dowsing, simply because dowsers know a thing or two about sensitivity to energy fields and how to turn negatives into positives.[53] So do a myriad of "energy workers" in the health field and in shamanism.

OUR PSYCHIC GIFTS

Society tends to toss anything that exceeds acceptable definitions of reality into the "dustbin of the dubious," alias—the occult. "Occult" means "secret."

If you've gone to a newsstand or watched television recently, you've been flooded with stories about extrasensory perception (ESP), psychic abilities, and psychic phenomena. Forget "secret." Occultisms no longer apply.

Hear this: psychic abilities are enhancements and extensions of faculties normal to us. They are *varied expressions of one mechanism that helps us to survive and thrive.* Such an awakening of gifts and talents enriches our lives immeasurably.

In my research, I noticed a consistent pattern to how a person's faculties spread out, and then enlarged afterwards. This is how I would describe what I observed:

Faculty Extensions

Physical Faculty	Psychic Extension	Collective and/or Spiritual Extension
See/Sight	See without the use of eyes; research term—"clairvoyance."	VISION
Hear/Sound	Hear without the presence of sound; research term—"clairaudience."	MUSIC
Feel/Touch	Feel, or have an effect on an object, without touching; research term—"psychokinesis."	ART
Taste/Flavor	Flavor without use of taste buds; research term—"clairgustation."	DISCERNMENT
Smell/Scent	Odor without use of nose; research term—"clairolfaction."	INTEGRITY
Sense/Intuition	Aware without or in advance of recognition; research term—"clairsentience."	GRACE
Perceive/Perception	Apprehend without or in advance of physical stimuli; research term—"precognition."	KNOWING

This amazed me—how our faculties really jumped or spread out twice in the extension process. That initial step always encompassed things psychic, what might be called the paranormal, but appeared related more to personality-self and communication/listening issues than anything else. The largest number seemed to stay at that level. Those who not only integrated their aftereffects into daily life but went far deeper than that in a quest of understanding the fullness of life experienced a decided shift to what I would call "spiritual maturity." It's like they began stretching farther into the collective—humankind as a family of one, life and death as complements in a journey without end, spirituality as our daily breath and each beat of the greater heart. When I recognized this pattern to be universal—not only with experiencers but also with anyone who had gone through an impactful spiritual transformation of any type—I began to realize that the spiritual aspects of near-death states might actually be the real driver of the transformational process.

As a brief aside, I discovered that individual learning styles directly relate to how and what experiencers or people like them access from the invisible worlds. Example: auditory learners tend to hear voices or pick up on specific sounds or music. Visual learners respond more readily to shape and color, such as symbols, visions, images, and light. Kinesthetic learners can be very touch-oriented and speak of feelings as if sensation itself was their primary language.

Phases of Integration

Phase One: First three years. Impersonal, detached from ego identity/personality traits. Caught up in desire to express unconditional love and oneness with all life. Fearless, knowing, vivid psychic displays, substantially more or less energy, more or less sexual, spontaneous surges of energy, a hunger to learn more and do more. Childlike mannerisms with adults/adultlike behaviors with children, a heightened sense of curiosity and wonder, IQ enhancements, much confusion, challenged with communication. **REBIRTHING.**

Phase Two: Next four years.* Rediscovery of and concerned with relationships, family, and community. Service and healing oriented. Interested in projects development and work environment. Tend to realign or alter life roles; seek to reconnect with one's fellows, especially in a moral or spiritual way. Unusually more or less active/contemplative. Can resume former lifestyle, but more desirous of carrying out "mission." **RETRAINING.**

Phase Three: After the seventh year. More practical and discerning, often back-to-work but with a broader worldview and a confident attitude. Aware of self-worth and of "real" identity (soul). Tend toward self-governance and self-responsibility. Spiritual development an ongoing priority, along with sharing one's story and its meaning. Dedicated. Strong sense of spiritual values. **REBORN.**

Phase Four: The fifteenth to twentieth year.** Immense fluctuations in mood and hormonal levels. Often discouraged or depressed while going through a period of "grieving"—reassessing gains and losses from the experience, while fearful that effects are fading. Many problems with relationships, money, and debts. A crisis of "self." If can negotiate "the darkness light can bring," a depth of spiritual maturity and confidence emerges that is unique to the long-term effects of a transformation of consciousness. **BORN AGAIN.**

---

* Child experiencers in my study who turned to alcohol for solace (1/3), began drinking during this phase.
** Child experiencers who attempted suicide to get back to "the other side," did so in this phase.

OPPOSITE REACTIONS

Child experiencers do not integrate near-death experiences in the same manner as older teen and adult experiencers. A child's job is to survive, grow, learn. Anything that obstructs this instinct is either ignored, repressed, set aside, forgotten, or jumbled. Thus, they seldom evidence the same distinctive shifts that adults do until Phase Four. Why? Take a look.

Adults deal with changes afterward, and the necessity of finding new reference points. They are challenged to redefine themselves and the life they live from another perspective. Before-and-after comparisons can be made, and the results are oftentimes quite striking. For many, it is as if they go through a process similar to rebirthing and rediscovery.

Children deal with the strangeness that what they encounter in the world around them does not match what they know and can identify with. They are challenged to recognize the source of their uniqueness and accept the validity of what they have gained from their experience. Seldom can comparisons be made, because what happened to them is the basis of what they know. With the very young, there is no "before-and-after," only what applies in the now moment and is usable. *Adults integrate. Children compensate/adjust so they can "fit in."*

Children are perfectly capable of balancing two differing worldviews in a healthy manner if they have supportive parents or relatives who are good listeners. This is done by being open and encouraging while still maintaining basic discipline. Where psychologists and counselors slip up is in not realizing that the young tend to bond with spirit beings and imprint to "other worlds." This is *not* imagination gone wild.

WHAT CAN MAKE A DIFFERENCE

There is a movement afoot in the mental health community to update the DSM (*Diagnostic and Statistical Manual of Mental Disorders*) with a special v-code (section). According to Rev. Karen E. Herrick, Ph.D., LCSW, LMSW, CADC: "This v-code was created to help differentiate between spiritual experiences and mental disorders, and to aid in the integration of the growing numbers of different cultures entering the U.S. population with their different beliefs and practices. Spirituality is used to describe 'the transcendent relationship between the person and a Higher Being, a quality that goes beyond a special religious affiliation.'"[54]

Currently, psychiatrists are turning more and more to psychotrophic drugs to treat anything that seems odd in the way of child or adult behavior. Be armed, should you need it, with this wondrous news: in 2004, Oxford University Press and the American Psychological Association published *Character Strengths and Virtues: A Handbook and Classification*. This book is the DSM-1 of "Positive Psychology," focusing on that which uplifts in life instead of disorders.[55]

In 2008, a bill was introduced in Canada that would have outlawed 60 percent of natural health products. I mention this because a goal of the United Nations is to have every country institute a "Codex Alimentarius" (a standardization of vitamins, minerals, herbs, and other natural health products). This seems like a necessary step to protect world health, but the codex is written in such a way that in many cases, it would recommend pharmaceutical treatments rather than natural ones and supplant individual choice. This would be detrimental to near-death experiencers and others like them.[56]

OTHER SUGGESTIONS

A near-death experiencer by the name of Yolaine Stout had a great idea. Why not create an organization for experiencers, by experiencers? With this in mind, she organized the American Center for the Integration of Spiritually Transformative Experiences (ACISTE) for the purpose of creating safe, healing, therapeutic, and supportive programs for experiencers of all types of transformative episodes that were life changing. Although the goals of ACISTE are ambitious, the organization should be operational by 2011. Inquiries are welcome.[57]

In most of my books and on my website are in-depth resource sections on ways to integrate experiences like the near-death phenomenon into everyday life. Of what I have done, the best for children is in *The New Children and Near-Death Experiences;* and for adults, *Beyond the Light.*[58]

Day-to-day living, though, requires quick, useful, and dependable strategies. Programs are great. Taking part in them does make a significant difference, but there's still nothing quite like old-fashioned common sense. If you need help, use your M.A.P. It's always available and it always works:

M = Meditation

A = Affirmations

P = Prayer

Use your M.A.P. I do.

CHAPTER TWELVE

SPEAKING OF THE SPIRITUAL

"Can we not understand that exclusivity is a condition that
we, not God, invented? That the same energy enfolds the
Buddhist's prayer wheel as it does the fondly-held rosary? We
are here to share God's light, not claim ownership of it."

—REV. MARGARET STORTZ

Linda Jacquin, a two-time experiencer (once as a child, once as an adult), gets very excited about the spiritual aspects of the phenomenon. "This IS the overriding issue," she claims. Linda's voice echoes thousands, maybe millions around the world—except for those in Germany.

A German survey conducted in 2001 surprised many. It revealed, among other things, that the majority of West German experiencers felt positive about their episode; among East Germans, the reverse held true. As an after-effect, both groups claimed that their lives had improved afterward. But, in their words, "religiosity" was rare. Perhaps that's because they confused the spiritual with the religious. Many do. To better understand why the confusion, let's take a historical approach.[59]

RELIGIOSITY?

You never hear a word like "religiosity" associated with near-death states. Should it be? Take a look at the work of William James in his seminal book, *The Varieties of Religious Experience*.[60] Acknowledging that religious conversion experiences could be gradual or immediate, he states: "It is natural that those who personally have traversed such an experience should carry away a feeling of its being a miracle rather than a natural process." Elements he associates with conversions:[61]

- Voices are often heard, lights seen, visions witnessed.

- Automatic motor (movement) phenomena occur.

- After surrender of personal will, a higher power floods in and takes over.

- Radically new nature, sense of renovation, safety, cleanness, rightness, jubilation.

- No words can describe the experience.

- Bodily accompaniments, loss of sleep and appetite.

- Period of unconsciousness, convulsions, visions, involuntary vocal utterances, sense of suffocation, nervous instability.

- Hallucinatory or pseudo-hallucinatory luminous phenomena.

- Ecstasy of happiness, field of consciousness opens up, magnetic fields.

- New levels of spiritual vitality, the impossible becomes possible, new energy.

- Loss of worry, sense that all is well, peace, harmony, the willingness to be even though outer conditions remain the same.

- Perceiving truths not known before, a sense of assurance about objective change, an appearance of newness beautifies every object.[62]

James admits that this type of conversion experience can happen numerous ways. "However it comes," he cautions, "it brings a characteristic sort of relief, and never such extreme relief as when it is cast into the religious mould."[63]

Did you notice how similar his elements of religious conversion are to the characteristics of near-death states? As per aftereffects, are you aware that there are more records (not just myths) of paranormal and enhanced abilities and psychic phenomena *within the religious venue* (you name the religion) than any other place—including mystical, esoteric, spiritual, and metaphysical traditions?

For instance, St. Joseph of Cupertino (1603–1663) was often seen levitating across considerable distances. He was observed flying over the heads of bystanders by an ambassador to the Papal Court. Even Pope Urban VIII witnessed St. Joseph rising high into the air during a Vatican visit. He could read people's thoughts, had gifts of healing, and produced rain in a drought. So did countless others—Zoroaster, Jesus, the Prophet Mohammed, Buddha, Moses, Bahá'u'lláh.

We wouldn't know about any of this, nor could a mind like William James's have been so inspired, if religion had not existed. Huston Smith, a well-known scholar on world religions, reminds us: "Religion has preserved history's greatest wisdom teachings. If the Buddha had not founded the *sangha*, the community of monks, the four noble truths and the bodhisattva vow would have evaporated in a generation. If Jesus had not been followed by Saint Paul, who founded the Christian church, the Sermon on the Mount would have been forgotten in a generation or two."[64]

WHAT WAS PRESERVED

Sage Bennet, Ph.D., gives us a taste of what the various religions of the world have gifted humankind in her book *Wisdom Walk*.[65] That "taste" covers practices such as (from Hinduism) home altars that personalize worship; (from Buddhism) meditation's peace and clarity; (from Islam) surrender to the power of prayer; (from Judaism) weekly Sabbath for rest and renewal; (from Christianity) the act of forgiveness; (from Native American Wisdoms) the interconnectedness of all life; (from Taoism) release and trust in the universal flow; (from New Thought traditions) the art of visioning for higher guidance.

What has been saved from the dusts of time are literally treasure troves of sacred history, inspiration, and guidance. Still, we need to admit the obvious: religion is organized spirituality. The core truth or root of all religions and all sacred traditions is virtually the same throughout the world and always has been. It is the spiritual. It is that personal experience of Source/Deity/Allah/God. The majority of near-death experiencers glimpse that core truth in a moment of self-surrender they neither understood nor were prepared for, and they are forever changed.

THE PERENNIAL PHILOSOPHY

What is the core truth at the root of everything spiritual or religious? What is the basic core essence of near-death states, as claimed by the very people who underwent the experience? Traditionally, it is known as "The Perennial Philosophy."

One God

One People

One Family

One Existence

One Law—Love

One Commandment—Service

One Solution—Forgiveness

From this ageless and ever-present core truth emerged the recognition of universal laws, those laws that govern human existence and the universe itself.

I mention this only because experiencers, either as part of their episode or shortly after, discover that there really are universal laws that operate unerringly; and that they had better wake up to this, pay attention, and change a few things in their lives.

THE UNIVERSAL LAWS OF EXISTENCE

These laws were codified via oral historians from each age and around the world. A written version that survived antiquity is known as "Hermetic Law." It was set to papyrus by the Egyptian god-king Hermes Trismegistus (thrice greatest). Early scholars and scientists considered these laws the foundation of alchemy—not just the transmutation of lead to gold, but the greater formula for the transmutation of the baser self to the Higher Self (from dross to spirit). Additions have been added over the years, until today, nearly a hundred universal laws are claimed to exist. Those I learned about after surviving my own bouts with death/near-death are:

Law of Polarity (opposites)

Law of Correspondence (as above, so below)

Law of Relativity (all things exist in relation to each other)

Law of Vibration (energy permeates and enlivens matter)

Law of Rhythm (regular movement, flow, pulse beat)

Law of Karma (cause and effect)

Law of Repulsion (reject, turn away, resist)

Law of Gender (all things possess positive or negative charge)

Law of Attraction (energy follows thought plus emotion)

Law of Balance (harmony, peace, rest)

Law of Abundance (the ability to manifest)

Law of Grace (gratitude, protection)

Law of One (virtually the same as the Perennial Philosophy)

A uniquely accomplished individual who had near-death experiences as a child was the late Walter Russell. He had his first episode at the age of seven, followed every seven years thereafter by another near-death state or a near-death-like one, culminating when he was forty-nine in the full illumination of cosmic consciousness. This illumination lasted thirty-nine days and nights without abating. Once he regained use of his faculties (which took a while), he penned *The Divine Iliad* (about his experience), and then spent the next six years writing *The Universal One*, a text containing drawings and revelations given to him about the universe and how it worked—covering such topics as chemistry, physics, and electromagnetics. He later corresponded with Albert Einstein about his own theory that ours is a "thought-wave" universe created for the transmission of thought.[66] I have these two books plus

The Secret of Light, and marvel still at the stunning depth and detail of what he received while enveloped in light.

Like an early 20th-century Hermes Trismegistus, Russell considered Mind to be the One substance in the universe. "This is a universe of appearances," he wrote, "all of which are relative, and not one of which would have even the appearance of existence without the relation of others. Without the illusion of separability, space could not be. Without events, time could not be. Without motion-in-opposition neither heat, cold, color, sex, mass or any of the effects of thinking could be or appear to be. Without the variability of motion-in-opposition there could be no appearance of variability in the chemistry of the One substance."[67]

In the summer of 2009, students of Russell admitted that he was deeply into alchemy, not as per Hermetic Law; rather in accord with revelations given to him and what he himself knew was possible. He had an invention of his tested at Westinghouse Labs back in 1927. I saw the lab report, which showed that with this invention, transmutations of elements into other elements did in fact occur. Lab officials didn't quite know what to make of this then. Recently, a physicist, not knowing what Russell had done, virtually duplicated that invention and obtained the same results. The man's name is Nassim Haramein. He too had a light experience, and is in the process of further testing.[68]

Transfiguration and transmutation—whether of people, conditions, or the very elements that make up the universe—are common themes of near-death experiences.

PERSONAL EXPERIENCE OF CORE TRUTH

Speaking of the spiritual, it is that personal experience of revelation—that peek at a greater truth and a grander reality—that spins one around. Rarely do experiencers meet or witness what they previously believed or were once taught. Invariably, an experience of this impact really stretches them.

One way to appreciate what this means is to learn something about the legacy of Tibetan storytellers called Gesar Artists. These storytellers, although usually illiterate, are able to recount numerous lines of extraordinary sophistication—tales of their most venerated hero Gesar, a knight from the

Kingdom of Heaven sent to earth to save and protect Tibetans. Gesar's story has been passed from generation to generation, but not by memorizing it. To be a true Gesar "Artist" (not just a storyteller), one must be "god-instructed." One must go through something like a near-death experience or what shamans call "dying unto the self" (an ego death) in order to achieve the personal experience of what Gesar came to earth to teach.

God-instructed . . . that's what the Gesar Artists call it. For those near-death experiencers who had longer or more complex episodes, that's exactly what it felt like, as if they were instructed by God . . . about living, the afterlife, heaven and hell, borderlands and shadow areas, spirit beings, angels, the soul, creation, God. Yet even brief encounters with life on the other side of death leave a mark. Many try to forget it, brush it away, or find some excuse to dismiss the whole thing. The "gotcha point" is the question: what if it was real? Can you imagine what it might be like to believe God spoke to you? To have toured heaven and hell? To have been touched by an angel or a being of pure light? To smell a flower not of earth?

Linda Jacquin was inspired to initiate spiritual retreats for those who have had near-death experiences. IANDS sponsored the first one at the Mercy Center in St. Louis, Missouri. Dave Bennett and Bill Taylor (fellow experiencers) joined her, and now the trio produces popular annual retreats.[69] Their concern is with the personal. All of their programs, including art, poetry, and photography, are geared towards being completely open and honest. One attendee remarked: "I found my family. I can talk about anything and it's alright." Linda believes that sharing what you learned from your near-death episode is the real mission of all experiencers.

Personal: a woman whose case was discussed in Raymond Moody's *Life After Life* went through years of depression after she was featured in the book.[70] Why? She felt shame that she couldn't match Moody's portrayal of the kind of "perfection" experiencers exhibited afterward. She was afraid to admit this.

Personal: a mother and wife of a fundamentalist preacher said to me, "He's wrong. I know now deep in my heart he's wrong. What he's preaching, that's not the way it is. I feel like he's telling everyone a lie and I don't know what to do about it. I love my husband and I love our children. I don't want to upset him or anyone else. I don't want a divorce or anything like that. But I can't listen anymore. I try to pretend I'm too busy to come."

Personal: "Me/Barbara, watched my sister pass over, twice, at Fairfax Hospital. I was ALIVE, standing there at her feet as her own deceased father, our deceased great-grandmother, and (to me unknown) her deceased grandmother helped her pass both times. They actually infused her with golden/white light energy under her shoulders, which crackled and changed the energy around her as she lifted full-body up from her dying body. And, well, the scene goes on in great detail, complete with telepathy, an open beautiful space-filled door surrounded by golden/white flame-like energy. She died twice that day, and did leave us. I can never be convinced that this and other experiences are JUST the brain dying. I've seen deceased attend their own funeral. One lady came back much younger, and in her old-fashioned wedding dress. One guy sat on his casket and snapped his fingers to the rhythm of the music, and got a kick out of the fact that the preacher struggled to find something uplifting to say about his somewhat irresponsible lacking-in-religion lifestyle."

Personal: Retired near-death researcher Kenneth Ring wrote a moving eulogy to Tom Sawyer (yes, that's his real name) when he passed away from pulmonary fibrosis.[71] Sawyer was well-known as a near-death experiencer who gave back to others to an almost unbelievable degree. Several books were written about him by Sidney Saylor Farr.[72] Lynda, a paramedic, who only briefly spoke to him before he passed, suddenly (and without any interest or desire in doing so) began to channel Tom. That is to say, Sawyer (even though dead) was communicating through the paramedic as clearly and in character as the experiencer known to thousands. This confused Lynda at first, but she has since managed to parlay the strange occurrence into classroom studies about spirituality. And, at Tom's direction, she has delivered messages to his family, inspired his friends, and caused a group he once led to become active again in contributing to the spiritual welfare of humankind. Kenneth Ring was deeply moved by Tom's continued "life after death."

Personal experiences of this nature are too big to keep to ourselves.

A LITTLE MORE ABOUT RELIGION AND THE SPIRITUAL

In my research of adult experiencers of near-death states, two-thirds either left organized religion after their episode or never had a religious commitment to begin with. One-third stayed with the religion they always knew. Those who stayed became more active and seemed devoted to making improvements in their church. Those who left either went on to explore other religious venues, including Native American spiritualities, or adopted meditative, mystical, or contemplative lifestyles. What interests me is that most of those who left, after about fifteen to twenty years, came back to a church of some kind (often a more metaphysical type like Unity, Religious Science, or Center of Spiritual Living) in an effort to rejoin the fellowship of spiritual community in service to others.

Of interest is this tidbit: A more accurate translation of the biblical passage "Be ye therefore perfect, even as your Father which is in heaven is perfect," is *Every one of you, therefore, be inclusive even as your Father in heaven is all inclusive.*[73]

CHAPTER THIRTEEN

SHIFTS IN PERCEPTION

*"Their life and their identity don't end when the body dies.
They simply have the feeling they're taking off their coats."*

—PIM VAN LOMMEL, M.D.

Decades ago a linguist by the name of Benjamin Lee Whorf asked an important question: "Does the language we speak shape the way we think?" This set off a flurry of research that is still ongoing. The upshot so far is that yes, language shapes our thought—language even shapes what we see—and it may even affect how we construct our ideas of causality.

I caught on to this, the importance of shifts in perception and languaging during the early days of my work. There are near-death scenarios that appear to follow religious precepts. Yet when you study these accounts, you begin to recognize that the interpretation of what was seen or heard or sensed, the *languaging* used, has more to do with what the episode *seemed* to be than with what it actually was. Even trying to validate experiencer claims is risky business if you aren't careful. One way to validate an experiencer's "real" scenario is to have them draw it or act it out. Invariably, truths universally present will pop up in unique ways. We tend to name and claim in accordance with previous teachings and taboos.

The simple chart on the following page shows what I came to recognize when experiencers used certain words to express their points of view.

Basic Element	Religious Conversion	Spiritual Awakening
The experience	Baptism of Holy Spirit	Light of God
What it represented	A new covenant, being born again	Enlightenment or illumination, an awakening
What it was	Heaven	Home
A life force	Angel	Light being
Words spoken	Message from God	Conversations held
Words felt	Gift from God	Telepathy
Opinion of self	Chosen of God	Child of God or a light worker
The return	Appointed mission to be God's chosen messanger	Unfinished business to complete or a job yet to be done

PERCEPTUAL PREJUDICE/PREFERENCE

A team of scientists experimenting with babies found that the only time babies startled was when something happened to them that defied common sense. This discovery suggests that we all have a certain level of perception and a genetic predisposition (basic prejudice) that is reinforced by the way our faculties and our brain work. We depend on life being what we think it is, and we accept the bias of that perception. In our day-to-day existence, *we recognize only what we are prepared in advance to see.*

Alternate realities and other dimensions of vibration are missed or bypassed simply because we are not aware that we are missing or bypassing anything. We accept what we perceive, and it seems illogical, if not impossible, to do otherwise.

But this tightly knit package of natural perceptual prejudice (often referred to as "environmental integrity") is actually based more on assumptions from individual belief systems than on genetic predisposition. Often, it is more a *preference* than a prejudice.

This is so because of the way we mix together acquired tendencies with natural perceptive skills through the thoughts and languaging we use. We allow our loved ones, our schools, our jobs, our fellows, our society, and our governments—not to mention our own notions of what we think we perceive—to define and interpret our lives. We allow this because it is fundamentally easier, more practical, and less risky, to accept rather than challenge the bias of mutually accepted belief. (Society owes its existence to this tendency among people to accept majority opinion as personal truth. Messiahs owe their deaths to the same principle.)

TRICKS OF PERCEPTUAL PREFERENCE

To help us understand the impact that can occur when an experiencer's perception is suddenly shifted, a little or substantially, here are some everyday tricks of perception that fool us every time. As you read them, imagine what it would be like if tricks like these lost their "cover."

With movies, you go to a theater to see a good show. But what do you really see? A continuous projection of still frames separated by periods of darkness. Your perception creates the movement of a solid picture. Movies are nothing more than optical illusions.

With television (before digital), you sit down to enjoy a good program. But what is it that you really watch? A television tube ("gun") fires electrons at a screen as raster bars roll from top to bottom separating incoming electrons (dots) from outgoing ones. Your mind connects the electron dots into picture images while ignoring everything else. Television is a mental illusion (digital, as well).

With music, you love to listen to a good song. But what is it that you really hear? A series of notes separated from each other by intervals of silence. All any voice or instrument can produce is a single sound, one at a time. It is your perception that supplies melodic sweep or dissonance, what is termed music or noise. Music is an auditory illusion.

Our subconscious mind regularly absorbs over a billion pieces of information per second. The bombardment is so great that less than one percent of what comes in ever reaches the conscious mind. Within a fraction of a second, 99 percent is filtered out. The area within the brain/mind assembly that does the filtering is the reticular activating system, a small bundle of densely packed nerve cells located in the central core of the brain stem below the limbic system. What directs the filtering, though, is *perceptual preference* . . . not necessarily anything inborn. What is automatic, even from infancy, can be altered, expanded, enhanced, or changed.

Meditation and other similar practices help us to retrain our perception so the sequences of both activity and rest (described in each of the perceptual tricks just given) can be viewed or heard simultaneously and separately at the same time. A near-death experience or a spiritual awakening shifts the capacity of our brain further still. Such a brain shift cleans out our filters, blocks, beliefs, and unfinished business and enables us to "slip between the cracks" of perception into alternate realities, parallel realities, and coexistent realities. This convergence of information (the chaos of "all-at-once") is disorienting at first, but eventually we are led to that wellspring of clarity and insight formerly masked by what is inborn, what is acquired, what is culturally accepted.

This brain shift can be subtle enough that others recognize what is happening before the experiencer does. But, for the majority, the chaos that can result is more than just disorienting—it is downright confusing.

Example: shortly after my near-death episodes in 1977, I began to experience sensory input unlike anything before. At that time, phlebitis and the damage done by blood clots and other physical traumas required that I relearn how to crawl, stand, walk, climb stairs, and run. Therapeutic exercises were ongoing. A letter I wrote then describes a particular sunny day in downtown Boise, Idaho, when I could at last run an entire city block without falling and without pain. Note the sensory alterations that accompanied this feat:

> "Each minute sensation from my legs was received in my brain like
> an afterclap from a sonic boom. That loud, and I could both hear and
> feel simultaneously. If I couldn't hear a sensation then I couldn't feel it
> either, because, for some reason unbeknownst to me, both faculties had
> merged. They were now equal halves of the same sensory mechanism,
> reverberating in shouts of feeling/sound throughout my body.

As I cried out for the joy of being able to run again, I noticed rays of energy protruding from me and spiraling out into the air. They looked like pulsating flares glinting in the sunlight. A car honked when I wobbled off the curb into the street, feeling somewhat dazed and giddy. I jumped back and when I did, those energy flares flipped into fireworks, setting off a cascade of what appeared to be miniature rockets shooting off in all directions.

I could taste it, the sun, and I could taste the satisfaction of being there standing on the sidewalk. Whatever I saw or thought about deeply had flavor, a taste. My faculties for sight, thought, and taste had also merged. Feeling/sound. Flavored sight and thought. Who in their right mind would believe any of this? Me? Anyone?[74]

My tears of joy at being able to run rolled into wracking sobs that day, for I was overwhelmed by the strange sensing multiples that assaulted my brain. This wasn't the first time since my near-death episodes that the sensory stimuli I received did not match the perceptual conditioning I was used to. Still, this incident was a turning point for me because it forced me to realize that more than my body needed retraining.

I have come to believe that the extremes in sensory distortions I had to deal with immediately following my near-death episodes were the result of losing much of my inborn perceptual prejudice. I now recognize that the strange sounds I heard and the energy flares I saw were, in all probability, a magnification of biological processes normally not discernible to conscious awareness. This magnification made my world seem oddly different, when it was really my perception of my world that had shifted the most. It could well be that my reticular activating system had been damaged; certainly my limbic system was stimulated or altered in some manner. Regardless of cause, these novelties of perception eventually worked to my advantage—they greatly enhanced my awareness. After I learned how to control them, my life greatly improved.

Once your consciousness transforms, whether biological processes magnify, as I believe they did for me, or whatever else begins to shift, the very first thing you lose is a sense of time. The second is a sense of space. The world reorders itself; the paradox of perceptual tricks and illusions begins to fade.

British scientist Peter Russell once said: "A change in consciousness is a change in perception—a change in how we see things. The real secret—and it's only a secret because we keep forgetting it—is that we always have a choice in how we see, experience, and interpret reality."[75]

"I GOT WHAT I NEEDED"

Almost every experiencer I worked with said it at some point—"I got what I needed." I suspect the sentence continues to roll off the lips of experiencers worldwide. Whether talking about their actual near-death state or what happened afterward, experiencers point out that a cause-and-effect connection exists and that this connection directly impinges upon the perceptions they once had versus what they know now. They come to question whatever appears to be "accidental."

Nancy Evans Bush, M.A., President Emeritus of the International Association for Near-Death Studies and retired pastoral counselor, who had a frightening near-death state when in her twenties, advanced a rebuttal to my discovery of four main types of the phenomenon.[76] "The global Atwater assessment," she cautioned, "does not recognize that *everyone*, even those who report dazzlingly transcendent experiences, has 'deeply suppressed or repressed guilt, fear, and angers,' nor does it acknowledge that people self-described as guilt-ridden, fearful, and angry have reported glorious accounts. It is not enough."

She is right on one hand. My initial charting (in chapter 3) was by necessity brief so it could appear on a single page. Perhaps Nancy missed my insistence that *every near-death experience is valuable*, regardless of type, even if it consists of only one element and nothing more. In that same chapter, I tell a story about two people who volunteered to share their episode at the talk I gave. The man felt cursed to have had a heavenly experience, and the woman, although terrorized by hers, felt blessed and grateful for the whole thing.

You cannot judge good or bad with near-death experiences! Nancy makes this point with her criticism. So do I. Nonetheless, I feel it necessary to repeat what I said at the close of chapter 2. (Take a deep breath, everyone.): There was one pattern, and only one pattern, that I found present in every single case I saw, and that was that during the near-death scenario, experiencers had the opportunity to come face to face with whatever existed and was fully integrated within their deepest self. If you are honest about near-death episodes and examine them in context with the life of each experiencer, you will discover what I did: scenarios complement on some level the inner reality of those who experience them.

A PATTERN TO AWAKENINGS

Yes, we all have guilt. Yes, we all have joys. Neither defines us—we are deeper than that. And on that deepest of levels, that's where I saw what I claimed. What do I mean by this? Certainly, I keep my work objective and stick to protocol, so what I do can be duplicated by other researchers. But for further insight and to cross-check what seems obvious, I allow enhanced subjective sensory input to function as another "tool" in my researcher's toolbox. Yes, I admit it . . . I can see energy. This extra source is what enabled me, at least in a general way, to recognize the growth potential freed within the experiencer. I offer the following to you as a synopsis of what I really saw when I looked deeper:

Initial experience: An introduction to other ways of perceiving reality; stimulus.

Unpleasant or hellish experience: A confrontation with distortions in one's own attitudes and beliefs; healing.

Pleasant or heavenly experience: A realization of how important life is and how every effort that one makes counts; validation.

Transcendent experience: An encounter with Oneness and the collective whole of humankind; enlightenment.

If you are objective about this synopsis, what emerges is a fascinating panorama suggestive of what could be the natural movement of consciousness as it evolves through the human condition via stages of awakening. These stages of awakening extend from the first stirring of something greater—an initial awareness—to confrontations with the bias of perception, followed by opportunities to cleanse and start anew. This leads to the bliss and ecstasy of self-validation and the discovery of life's worth, until at last the moment comes when unlimited realms of truth and wisdom are unveiled.

This panorama of awakening consciousness indicates to me that the near-death phenomenon is more than just a singular anomaly. More importantly, it seems to be part of an ongoing process of transformative adaptation within the human family as a species, a growth process that appears to shift individual souls from one stage of vibratory awareness to another and from one state of embodiment to another, a process that parallels and duplicates what happens during a spiritual transformation. We get what we need because we're all on the same journey. We enter into invisible realms, ones we can scarcely imagine, to discover who we are, why we're here, and where we are going.

Let's look at this issue yet another way:

Distressing experiences—encountering one's shadow and whatever aspect of self has been repressed or denied.

Radiant experiences—a reunion with one's authenticity and worthiness, *equally repressed and or denied.*

The world around us exists as perceived because of how perceived.

We are real. Our world is real. What happens to us is real. Slip in between the varied aspects of this realness . . . and everything changes.

CHAPTER FOURTEEN

CROSSOVER

"There is something mysterious and whole which existed before heaven and earth, silent, formless, complete, and never changing. Living eternally everywhere in perfection, it is the mother of all things."

—LAO TSE

Dateline: May 27, 2009. *Whitehorse Leader Newspaper*, Australia. In an article entitled "A Feared Call, 'Save' Result," by James Dowling.

It is the call all fireys dread and on February 15 at 3 am Nunawading fire station's B shift of Gary Easte, Steve Tanner, and Scott Hardy got that call. A 47-year-old woman was 'non-breathing and non-alert,' which Mr. Easte, the Nunawading station officer, knows usually means one thing. 'We don't look forward to getting those calls; we usually know it will be a negative outcome,' Mr. Easte said. But this time, after 47 minutes of intense CPR, five electric shocks, and two adrenalin shots, Nunawading resident Carmel Bell, who suffered a cardiac arrest, survived. Mrs. Bell, who had no history of cardiac arrest, was also lucky her husband, a former paramedic, was able to start CPR straight away. Despite the lifesaving effort, her brain had lacked constant oxygen for more than 45 minutes, usually leading to brain damage. Amazingly, and Mrs. Bell would argue 'miraculously,' the mother of two made a full recovery.[77]

Carmel Bell had a near-death experience during her cardiac arrest. Today she deals with the mystery of forty-seven minutes without oxygen, brain function improved, life on the other side of death a sudden reality, and the unstoppable spread of aftereffects. All this was a puzzle until she learned more about near-death states.

Please remember, even though the primary material in this book came from people who died, there is no question on whether or not to resuscitate a dying person: the near-death experience "flowers" because the individual survived. Whether brief or lengthy, the narrations that result stop us short. So do other factors associated with the crossover from life to death.

WHY LEFT?

On October 25, 2006, at the IANDS near-death conference at the M. D. Anderson Cancer Center in Houston, Texas, a nursing supervisor reported that 85 percent of the patients she saw who were near death looked up and to the left, smiled, and sometimes talked to "people" there right before they died. The appearance of "visitors" coming in from the left has become a gauge for the nurses at that hospital to anticipate the timing of crossover.

Claims from medical staff in my research reporting the same thing have varied from 80 to 88 percent. Certainly there are nurses who are skeptical: "We are trained to approach patients from the right. Whatever else is present has to be to the left." Dianne Arcangel, M.S., a medical researcher of near-death states, found no preponderance of anything left with the eighty-five respondents to her "Afterlife Encounters Placement Survey."[78] Still, neither of these sources addresses the broad scope of what I keep finding.

Historically, shamans are taught that magical or mysterious acts must be carried out with the left hand. Gypsies and palmists believe that our destiny, our heritage, and things unknown to us, rest in the palm of our left hand. Energy workers and massage therapists focus to the left to better see their client's energy field, and say that energy beings who help out enter from the left. One professional pointed out that because so few people focus to the left, uncommon perceptions have a chance at evading being "filtered out" by coming in that way. Brain imaging has shown that meditators have increased activity in the left prefrontal cortex, a part of the brain that produces positive feelings and lower levels of the stress hormone cortisol. In dreamwork, the left side represents the subconscious mind; the right, the conscious aspect of mind. There is a teaching in esoteric studies that says the left eye emits one's soul essence, while the right eye, one's personality essence.

From Dolores J. Nurss, a dreamworker and journalist: "My father wrote deathbed messages to each of his children. Mine told me to listen for his voice after he died, 'to your *left*.' (underscore is his). I often wondered about that. He was politically conservative, and identified with the right wing. But he was also a Raven Medicine Man [Native American Shaman]."

From Vicki Jones, a university extension program officer: "When my father was close to death last year, he reached up as if to take the hand of someone with his left hand. My sister and I watched him smile (as he did this). She asked him about it, but he wasn't able to tell her anything. He died within days. On his left was the wall. He was clearly looking up and reaching up at a 45-degree angle. There was nothing physically there for him to see. My father hardly ever smiled, but his face lit up as if he was seeing someone that he hadn't seen in a long time."

Does this mean that everyone leaves their body at death through their left side? Not necessarily. But the left clearly has some significance. Is this because our heart is on the left, or because the left side of our body is controlled by the right hemisphere of the brain, that realm of subconscious abstractions? Or, might it have something to do with the fact that on earth the amino acids in all living things twist to the left, and that out in space most spinal galaxies rotate to the left? Believe it or not, left really is the preferred direction our universe leans and all of nature prefers.[78a] No one knows for sure, but F. Gordon Greene, a well-known near-death researcher, has some ideas—not about left, but about why the dying move upward as they leave their bodies, and why near-death experiencers once out of body seem to hover in ceiling corners before moving on.[79] Greene, who has a background in hyperspatial geometry, explains: "We are trying to interpret near-death experiences according to our limited view of reality. We are forcing a three-dimensional understanding on hyperspatial experiences. Leaving the body distorts what you see looking back. Corner ceiling positions are so commonly 'occupied' by OBErs, then, because these positions serve as the *natural* point of contact between space and hyperspace."

The puzzle of why left may not be a puzzle at all. We automatically turn in the direction that offers open portals to deeper reaches of mind when we shift in consciousness. We are made that way. For most of us, that turn will be to the left in accordance with nature's basics and because of what already occupies that space within our very bodies. Regardless of the exit direction taken, though, we move up and out of our bodies at the moment of death. Once we do, experiencers tell us we can still see, hear, taste, feel, move, smell, and tell jokes if we want to. Our physical body remains where we left it as a pasty shell, looking somewhat plastic. The biggest surprise in looking back down is the realization that we are not our body. We are a soul, and our real body is spirit.

THE SOUL

George W. Meek, in his book *After We Die, What Then?*, describes several attempts to measure any weight loss at the moment of death to see if an unidentified mass exists within human beings that could account for the presence of a soul.[80] Meek describes the work of a Dr. McDougall, who was able to measure the loss of between one half and three quarters of an ounce of body mass in tests done in the early 1900s. Later, a team of five physicians at a Massachusetts hospital replicated McDougall's work, showing in their tests over a six-year period an average loss of one ounce at the moment of death. Why so small? Meek wondered about this until he stopped to realize how much information a microchip can carry. A whole ounce could contain unlimited amounts.

Did you know that Thomas Edison believed in life after death? He was convinced that the soul was made of "life units"—indestructible, microscopic particles that could rearrange into any form while retaining full memory and personality. He died before he could finish building a machine that could detect them. Along a similar vein, ghost hunters of today are using electromagnetic field (EMF) detectors to find certain electrical elements at sites of active reports. They claim that when ghosts are present EMF readings are higher than what the device can produce by itself. Life units? Electrical interference patterns?

Near-death experiencers say yes to the soul. We all have one, they claim. It is the real us. Some call it the Higher Self; others the Greater Self. It is described variously as filmy, vaporous, fog-like, plasma, similar to smoke, ethereal, brilliant, or like a spark of holy fire. Experiencers are pretty much in agreement that souls have no gender and are immortal extensions of the Divine. Even though we identify the soul as who we are, have always been, and return to once we cast aside our physical bodies at death, there is still an understanding that the soul has a will of its own and an agenda apart from what we as personalities have. It's as if we move from "the little" to "the larger" once we cross over.

Memory of our true identity is not necessarily automatic. What we went through in our lives, what we believed, our passions, joys, and grief—all of this takes time to assess. Emotions can overwhelm. We awaken in stages according to what we can handle.

HEAVEN, HELL, AND BORDERLANDS

The scenarios of near-death states show that once you—the real you—leave your body in death, you eventually find yourself moving to or present within a vibratory energy frequency you resonate with. What you find there corresponds for the most part to what you are capable of responding to (i.e., beings, shapes, forms, activities). These frequency realms resemble a "layer cake" of many levels, each separated from the other by degrees of lighter/finer or heavier/denser vibrations.

To understand what this array is said to consist of, hang out with experiencers as I have. Snuggle up with them and absorb their words, feelings, their sense of awe tinged with the fear of too much, too simple, too perfect. It's as if the symbols of their culture, their religion, and their dreams fail utterly in comparison with the real thing—the afterlife of heaven, hell, and borderlands. The sharing I offer here is a summary from over three thousand of these voices. I could listen as I did because I was one of them.

Hell

The heavier, more dense vibrations hold what most people call "hell" in that they consist of negative or lower forms of thought that reside in close proximity to the earthplane. It is where we go to work out whatever blocks us from the power of our own light: hang-ups, addictions, fears, guilts, angers, rage, regrets, self-pity, arrogance, resentments. We stay in hell (and there are many divisions of this vibratory level) for however long best serves our development. We do not leave until we have changed our attitudes, thoughts, and feelings, and are ready for another opportunity to improve and advance.

Heaven

The faster, higher, more subtle vibrations are what most people term as "heaven," and they also are fairly close to the earthplane. We go there to recognize or enjoy whatever reveals the power of our own light: talents, abilities, joys, courage, generosity, caring, empathy, virtue, diligence, patience, thoughtfulness, loving kindness. There is a sense of benefit here, as if one has found one's true home. We stay in heaven (and there are many levels here, too) for however long it takes to experience the glory of love and the power of forgiveness. We leave whatever level of this positive, supportive domain we are in once we have further advanced as an awakened soul and are more unified in spirit.

I have counted what appear to be twelve heavens and twelve hells from experiencer descriptions. Yet, this "layer cake" of energy frequencies (realms we can inhabit) appears to be open at both ends. I have found nothing to indicate otherwise. Claims of souls forever and eternally trapped or condemned in the heavier levels, or basking in the glory of ascension in the finer, lighter ones, do not hold up. When you study what people encounter on the other side of death, you come to recognize the power that can be unleashed out of awakenings. To whatever degree an individual awakens, the soul responds and consciousness expands—personally and collectively.

Borderlands

Yes, "detours" do occur—to places like borderlands or shadow areas where individuals in spirit form may tarry. In some cases the ego personality refuses to merge with its soul, and that spirit can remain "apart." This situation can be temporary or long-lasting; the cause most generally is the intensity of an individual's desire not to leave, or perhaps from disorientation or confusion, feeling lost, or maybe because of a vow or a promise the individual is determined to fulfill. Spirits in these areas can be seen as "ghosts" to those who are still embodied. The idea of "way stations," places where spirits reside until helped in some fashion, perhaps by other souls, angels, or beings of light, is upheld. These catchall places appear to be necessary diversions so that one can shake free of that which initially hinders. Many religious and spiritual traditions make allowance for such death distress by encouraging the living to pray for the departed, so any who are lost might be found.

What matters the most throughout this entire arrangement of heaven/hell/borderlands is the resonance factor: like attracts like, and you go where you fit in accordance with your attitudes, beliefs, and feelings. Our religions insist that it is deeds done or not done that are the final determiners of where we wind up once dead, yet nothing from experiencer cases fully validates this. Their testimony indicates something else is primary—that self-acceptance or self-rejection is what actually creates our energetic "signal." You may be a doer of great deeds, pay out millions to help the needy, but inside be an empty mess. Or you may be nothing more than a petty thief with a string of failures, yet you really tried and you keep on trying to pull yourself up. You cannot fool your soul about who or what you are.

THE SOUL'S AGENDA

You get a very real sense from some experiencer testimonies that souls have their own will but that, whatever their agenda is, it straddles the spread between fate and destiny (our choices as an individual ego versus what is more in keeping with the completion of our life's purpose). We get "soul nudges" when we need them, what some of us call "course corrections" or "intuitive prompts" to keep on track. We can ignore these nudges or pay attention. For most of us, life is easier or at least more fruitful if we do the latter.

The soul itself appears to go through learning cycles of its own—big ones—that can arc over many time frames and varied types of lives. Souls can and often do "move" in groups to accomplish specific goals and tasks on a grand scale. The soul level of our being is said to possess perfect memory and an almost unbelievable grasp of Creation's Story and our place in the overall scheme of things. On this level, which experiencers consider a higher level of existence, the goal of continued incarnations in human or other forms contributes to the furtherance of our true goal, our highest purpose: to become Co-Creators with the Creator. Winding our way through the peaks and valleys of humanness appears to aid in this process. You get a sense from this that life and death and the forms we take on fulfill an even Greater Will for an even Grander Purpose.

Four words . . . the vast majority of near-death experiencers say the same four words after their episode: "Always there is life." Look at those words. If you take them literally, and there is no reason why you shouldn't, they show us that there is no afterlife, no before life—only the now of life itself, forever in motion.

It is not my intent here to be sappy or feed into some kind of "religion of the resuscitated," but it is my desire to give voice to the millions who have something to say. And those four words are certainly worth hearing.

CHAPTER FIFTEEN

COMPARE IT TO LIGHTNING

"Thunder is good; thunder is impressive . . . but it's lightning that gets the job done."

—Mark Twain

Near-death states might be unique in critical ways, but they fit the pattern of what happens when our consciousness broadens, deepens, and transforms. These commonalities, (referred to in mystical/spiritual/religious lore as "The Inner Journey"), signal that a person is undergoing or has undergone the early stages of this shift. A pattern common to those in the initial throes comes next, followed by the "gold standard" used for over a century in how to recognize people who have attained the goal of awakening . . . *enlightenment.*

INITIAL STAGES

Initial stages of an awakening mind, according to Tricia Nickel, M.F.T., include: alteration in thinking (difficult to concentrate, thinking blurs); disturbed sense of time (timelessness, slowing of time); loss of control (losing grip on reality); change in emotional expression (emotional extremes, depression); body image change (boundaries dissolve); perceptual distortions (increased visuals, visions); and change in the meaning of one's life ("eureka" moments of profound insight). Nickel reminds us that, "In the intuitive, psychic openings, we are still experiencing duality. In the transformative mystical state, we are one with all that is; there is no sense of separation."[81]

ADVANCED STAGES

What follows is a partial list of traits indicative of having attained a higher, spiritual level of mind, from discoveries made by Richard Maurice Bucke, a Canadian psychiatrist, after launching an in-depth study of people he felt had reached "cosmic consciousness."

- *Subjective light.* A brilliant light is seen, unearthly colors, everything expands.

- *Moral elevation.* Becomes moral and upright, has a greater duty and service to God and the human family.

- *Intellectual illumination.* All knowledge is given, overwhelmed by total and complete love, a sense of being "reborn."

- *Sense of immortality.* Thinking replaced by knowing, realizes Divine identity.

- *Loss of the fear of death.* Knows death does not end anything.

- *Loss of the sense of sin.* Knows that evil is good misused, all is good in God's eyes.

- *Sudden instantaneousness of the awakening.* Actual moment of illumination is unexpected; can last minutes, hours, or even days.

- *Previous character of the person.* Latent abilities surface including genius, strong desire to learn and excel.

- *Age of illumination.* Usually happens to adults in middle years.

- *Added charm of the personality.* Attract people/animals, Divine protection.

- *Transfiguration.* Marked change in appearance, behaves like a new person.

The precedent established by the work of Dr. Bucke was originally published in 1901; it survives today as an invaluable guide for recognizing the kind of aftereffects that indicate that something far greater and transforming than just a change in attitude or a renewed appreciation of life has taken place in the lives of those who have experienced a transformation of consciousness.[82] Bucke cautioned that there are no guarantees during or after the episode. A person can backslide if ego or greed is allowed to overshadow the illumination. In some ways, his research reflects the prejudices of his day (for instance, he was puzzled as to why women and blacks never attained cosmic consciousness); yet overall, his work stands as the best test we have for identifying traits that can lead to spiritual enlightenment.

ANOTHER TYPE OF PATTERN TO NEAR-DEATH STATES

There are other patterns that link near-death states to the larger genre of "transformations of consciousness" and to the various traditions of an enlightened mind. Some are surprisingly powerful in what they imply.

When I wrote *Coming Back to Life* in the eighties, I introduced a particular patterning that spanned every case I had observed (up to that point and since). It was part of the underpinnings for "Brain Shift/Spirit Shift: A Theoretical Model Using Research on Near-Death States to Explore the Transformation of Consciousness." The model grew as my research expanded. Phases I and II were published. Phase III, which completes the model, is this book.

I never had any idea of creating a theoretical model when I began my research. I didn't even know what one was. I just knew that near-death states were both personal and collective, and that all of the imagery, revelations, and symbols could be interpreted on multiple levels. My experiences in Idaho during the sixties after several awakenings turned my life around, led me to work with, observe, and study nearly every bit as many people then as I later did researching near-death states. What I learned from that earlier effort gave me an eye quick to notice the slightest of clues and an ability to "merge with" that allowed me to look *inside* what people were describing. I didn't just observe near-death experiencers. Whenever possible, *I joined them in consciousness* (especially the kids). This methodology was my multi-angled approach to examining near-death scenarios and what followed. The result was this version of how things looked, sounded, smelled, and felt.

Disconnection from the physical body. We are somehow jiggled, hit, shaken, or broken loose from connections inside our physical body.

Conscious mind ceases to function. There is momentary silence, darkness. Nothing moves. Survival systems are on extreme alert, waiting.

Preparations for crossover. All disconnections are not made, allowing additional chemicals to further activate and empower the upper brainstem and the limbic system. To ensure survival, a brain shift takes place, diverting mind from a separate but parallel condition to full death. Possible futures switch. There is a jerk, sound, sudden movement, snap, or perhaps something like a wind. Lights can flood by or flash. Our field of vision can be light or dark. There is a feeling of great activity and a whiff of newness.

Scenario journey—possibility number one (external experience). Speed accelerates. There is a sense of forward and out, of changing places and moving rapidly. We are now out of our body but still within our familiar world of conscious reality. We have no weight and no restrictions: we can float, hover, or fly anywhere. The body and the death scene are viewed dispassionately. Exploration begins with the desire to contact others present. Contact attempts cease when we realize we are invisible. Otherworldly ones can visit, but these visits are usually brief. Feelings of peace, of being free and unhampered, abound. At this point, the individual usually returns to his or her body, reconnects, and is revived. The physicality of external experiences and what was seen/heard/ smelled/felt is often verified as accurate later on.

Scenario journey—possibility number two (internal experience). Speed accelerates. There is a sense of forward and up or down, changing places, and moving rapidly. Dark or light fields of vision still prevail. Movement is very much akin to moving up the brain stem and the limbic system and spreading out through various parts of brain, or moving down the spine and spreading out through the "gut brain" (solar plexus area). We traverse a tunnel, or enter through a doorway or corridor, or pass through an emptiness or darkness by flying, floating, or somehow rushing along. This in-between space, this scenario journey, functions very much like a pressure chamber or preparatory compartment where one can readjust and get ready for another environment. While we are in this preparatory space there is a marked change in our structure or mass and frequency of vibration. This space is quite literally a safety zone. Beings and/or animals can appear, lights can flash, and telepathic communication can take place. A brilliant flood of yellow, yellow-gold, yellow-white, or white light appears, or a darkening of light that intensifies as we near the end of this zone. There is often a veil or curtain, like a force field, we must pass through to reach our destination.

Scenario destination. Often there is a greeter, guardian, or keeper at an entryway or gate to assess passage. Or we can instantly be where we are meant to be, in an "other" world similar to but beyond that of dreamscapes, more like spiritual/religious visionary experiences—either heavenly or hellish, radiant or distressing. Radiant realms are unusually bright, clear, and often musical, with colors not of earth. Distressing realms usually have subdued colors, threatening beings or storms, desolation, or evoke a sense of being trapped or having to fight. Faculties are heightened in either version. Suddenly we know things. There is a sense that we have found our true home in the radiant realms, or that we are lost, maybe waylaid, in the distressing realms. Love, peace, and joy are intensely felt as euphoria builds, or growing alarm and a sense of hopelessness takes over. Either way, there is initially no thought of loved ones "back on earth."

Involvement on the other side. Not everyone who enters gets involved, but for those who do activity is more intensely experienced than ever before. This intensity seems to shift the world we have reached into yet another, more advanced or reduced octave of sight and sound—a world almost beyond our ability to comprehend. People previously dead can be met and conversed with (they usually appear "youthful" but not necessarily younger than when last seen, or hauntingly despairing or threatening). Interactions can occur with inhabitants—transactions involving instructions, explanations, messages, or judgments. Any religious leaders or religious symbols encountered will match the deep beliefs of the experiencer, yet the experience itself reflects all beliefs. We discover the truth of our Divine identity in the radiant realms; we are filled with regrets, sadness, or anger at disappointments revealed in the distressing realms. Interactions either shatter or confirm previous knowledge, as the experience becomes like a giant "washing machine" in how it cleans out our concept of inner self and all that we repress or deny. A life review can occur followed by evaluation or judgment (done by self or others). It seems that before we lose all ties with our past, we must first understand who we are and the consequences of the choices we once made.

Leaving the other side. There is a feeling of restriction or a line of demarcation separating or preventing us from further passage or longer stay. We have experienced the depths of our own being and glimpsed the universal, but further entry is not allowed. We must return. We are told or have a feeling of mission, a job yet to do, more to learn. Movement begins—usually back and downward, maybe upward—to retrace our journey here. There can be a jerk, snap, or pop as we return like an overstretched rubber band back into our body.

Reconnection with the physical body. For those who can remember, there is a feeling of returning larger and bigger than the body size, thus necessitating a need to shrink or diminish somewhat in order to fit back in. There is a marked contrast between our lack of weight and the body's heavy weight. Dizziness and disorientation are usually experienced when consciousness is regained, perhaps because of the speed of leaving and reentry and the various chemicals we were "bathed" in. Speech might or might not be possible right away. Inner systems switch again as the brain begins to shift back to a more normal state. Revival is seldom pleasant. Reactions vary.

Only seconds or minutes may have lapsed, but for the experiencer it seems more like hours or days. Once begun, the near-death experience is no longer dependent on the condition of the physical body nor its close proximity, and will play out until conclusion. Episodes can be interrupted, however, if significant others forcefully intervene. Scenarios experienced are personal in the sense that we face our own beliefs, attitudes, and life choices; they are collective in the sense that all human beings are very much alike and are desirous by nature to improve and make better the world around them. The near-death experience is, to my way of thinking, both a movement through brain (head/gut) and a movement through mind (limitless potential). It is both literal and symbolic. Phenomena thought unique to it by researchers are by no means unique.

EASTERN AND WESTERN

Without a doubt, many near-death experiences are awakenings of one sort or another, usually leading to things spiritual. I can caution that reaching enlightenment is not the same thing as attainment. It takes time and much discipline and dedication to refine skills and insights gained out of a near-death experience, and to truly understand what was revealed.

Bucke's list of traits indicative of having attained a higher, more spiritual level of mind does indeed apply to near-death experiencers, as well as to others who have also undergone an impactful transformation of consciousness. But it also applies to history's steady procession of revelators and avatars (great teachers or messiahs) who claimed Divine authority to reveal Higher Truth. These great ones exhibited unusual powers. They healed, taught, preached, and performed miracles for the benefit of those in need. They assured the multitudes that anyone can do as they did and offered to teach how. What they taught was invariably a course in self-development that involved discipline, sacrifice, virtue, and a lifetime commitment in service to humankind—not unlike challenges given to near-death experiencers. Because the processes of awakening and enlightenment are central to the genre of transformational events, near-death states share in this greater journey—complete with accompanying phenomena and aftereffects.

Even though history's best were products of their prevailing cultures, their teachings about spiritual development have key elements in common. They can be condensed into two basic patterns of how thought, emotion, and energy can form a system of practice that works. These basic patterns link back to that part of the globe where their practice evolved and are loosely referred to as "Eastern" and "Western."

Each pattern is like the other, but mostly opposite in application, representing mirror reflections of the same goal. If you follow the predominate energetics of that tradition, amazingly simple pathways stand out—that may well be the missing links in understanding the purpose and power of the enlightenment process. Let's take a look at the basic essence of each pattern and then follow the energetics of the patterns and their core philosophies.

Western pattern: Predominate energy flow from outside the self, considered "top down." The Western version emphasizes descending force originating from outside a person's body, passing down through the top of the head or through the chest area, then spreading throughout the body. It is an outward directed process that seeks outside guidance and looks for God On High. It receives outside energy in. The most familiar teaching of this version is Christos (Descent of the Logos).

Eastern pattern: Predominate energy flow from inside the self, considered "bottom up." The Eastern version emphasizes ascending force, originating from within a person's body, usually from the base of the spine, rising up until it bursts through the top of a person's head. It is an inner process that seeks inner guidance and looks for God Within. It projects energy from inside out. The most familiar teaching of this version is Kundalini or Ku (Ascension into the Godhead).

Note: Both versions also feature practices that involve the opposite flow of energy.

What is shown here is the predominate or main thrust of that particular tradition's energetic (which underlies their basic philosophy).

Western teachings (basic philosophy)—Christos (Descent of the Logos)

"Christos" (Kristos) is the Greek word from which "Christ" was derived, and comes as close as possible to translating "messiah" from the ancient phrase that meant "The Anointed One." As near as anyone can tell, Jesus rarely if ever accepted the label *messiah* as applicable to him, preferring instead the title "Son of Man."[83] Long after his crucifixion, it was the Western mind that named Jesus "The Christ" and established his identity as the Son of God. Since then, *Christ* has also come to symbolize "Christ Consciousness" or "Christ Mind," which, it is said, anyone can possess. Jesus himself is said to have stated, "All these things I have done, you can do, and more also" (John 14:12), thus indicating a state of consciousness others can attain.

The entrance/activation of Christ Consciousness is sometimes called "Baptism of the Holy Spirit," and is characterized by descriptions such as: being struck, as if by lightning or a blinding flash; being consumed as if by fire or great heat; being torn as if by an explosion or great wind; being immersed as if by heavy rain or flood swells. The spiritual force seems to enter the individual's body from outside the self, from heaven, God On High, or through some saintly emissary or angel.

The sudden descent or passage of the illuminating force is said to come only when the recipient is ready and worthy. It usually enters through the top of the head or through the heart center and fills the entire body. This activation of Divine spirit energizes and illumines, thus transforming the individual's concerns from mundane to spiritual. This tradition also indicates that the event is *not* the culminating union with God/Deity, but rather a beginning or a step toward that goal. Various stages or initiations are necessary after illumination before true divinity can be attained.

Eastern teachings—(basic philosophy) Kundalini (Ascension into the Godhead).

"Kundalini" is a Sanskrit word that means "coiled serpent." The term may actually be derived from the much older word "Ku," meaning "The spirit force of God awaits within each person." (Taken from Mesoamerican traditions that predate the Maya, *Ku* comes from *Hunab-Ku*, "the sacred name of God," and is symbolized by Quetzalcoatl, the Feathered Serpent.) Both Kundalini and Ku refer to the "serpent power" that is said to be coiled in a ball at the base of a person's spine. When stimulated, it is said to uncoil and rise up the spine and brain stem, like a serpent stretching full length, until it bursts through the top of the person's head. While rising, it supposedly ignites or expands seven whirling vortices of energy that are located in or near certain areas of the body trunk, neck, and head. These whirling vortices, called "Chakras" in Sanskrit (meaning "Wheels") or termed "Flowers" in the Mesoamerican tradition, are like spinning energy generators. They relate to each of the seven major glandular centers (endocrine glands). Thus, people are said to have a channel within for spiritual energy to travel through (the spine) and power generators to speed it along its way (the endocrine glands). Details of how all this works and which *Chakra* or *Flower* is an extension of which gland depends entirely on what interpretation of which traditional teaching you study. The various versions agree only in principle.

It is claimed that once Kundalini/Ku rises full length, after stimulating, activating, expanding, and enhancing each of the seven major *Chakras/Flowers* and bursting out through the head, enlightenment occurs and reunion with God/Deity is possible. In actuality, however, this bursting forth is a signal of a shift from one mode of awareness to another—a shift, if you will, to the spiritual path. Just as mundane life goes through various phases of development in order to spiritualize, the spiritualized life goes through numerous phases of development before *attainment* is reached. A Kundalini/Ku breakthrough does not guarantee complete or lasting enlightenment.

THE MODEL LIGHTNING GIVES US

Stop for a moment. Be as objective as you possibly can. Doesn't what you have just read remind you of a formula for exposure to strong doses of highpowered energy? It could well be that the path to God/Deity revolves around the challenge of how one handles intense power—how one deals with "The Force."

The only real difference between Eastern and Western versions of spiritual development is the directional path of energy currents. That's it. When we are talking about spirituality or religious conversions, I believe what we are really talking about is the force of energy itself, differing by degree and type of voltage, and how this force can be accessed and utilized.

During the sessions I had with near-death experiencers, rarely was I able to isolate what would show me that a singular path of energy was responsible for either the experience or its impact. Indicators of Kundalini/Ku or Christos directional currents were present, but they seemed more auxiliary to me than causal.

What caught my eye were indicators of both power flows converging together and causing what I would call an implosion. In a way, the condition reminded me of lightning.

Science tells us that the lightning stroke is a huge spark. It equalizes the potential difference between clouds in a thunderstorm and the polarity of soil in the ground. It is, in effect, the culminating result of ascending and descending forces, which in meeting release pressure through a visible charge. Lightning, then, is not some "heaven-borne" bolt of electricity hurled to the ground. Along with releasing pressure, lightning also releases nitrogen compounds already present in a form more readily usable for healthy plant growth.

Compare what happens with lightning and what I suspect may be happening in major transformational events such as the near-death experience.

In the evolution of the natural world, to equalize pressure differences between clouds in a thunderstorm and polarity of soil in the ground, descending bolts of electricity (from the clouds) and ascending bolts of electricity (from the earth) meet to create a huge light flash (external explosion/lightning) that stabilizes environmental integrity while stimulating plant growth through the release of nitrogen compounds in a form essential for fertilizer.

In the evolution of human consciousness, to equalize pressure differences between latent spiritual potentiality and mundane personality development, descending currents of force (possibly from the soul level, Higher Self, God) and ascending currents of force (perhaps from ego states, lower self, personality level) meet to create a powerful light flash (internal implosion/illumination) that stabilizes and balances individual body/mind integrity while releasing human growth potential through the expansion and enhancement of consciousness.

Think about what this might mean: whether external or internal, explosion or implosion, a light flash seems to occur whenever opposing forces of energy current converge to release pressure and potentiality.

A light flash!

Enlightenment by its very definition means an experience of light whereby knowledge and information are imparted for the growth and expansion of human consciousness. What makes us think that this experience is only symbolic? Or just an exercise? Or merely an attitudinal shift in consciousness? Or the product of wishful thinking?

What if it's literal?

CHAPTER SIXTEEN

THE KEY IS INTENSITY

*"All matter originates and exists only by virtue of a force...
We must assume behind this force the existence of a conscious
and intelligent Mind. This Mind is the matrix of all matter."*

—MAX PLANCK

Back in chapter 9, I said: "There is no drug (legal or illegal; natural or synthetic), no hallucination, no case of oxygen deprivation, no epileptic seizures, nothing—that can match or mimic this pattern of aftereffects—except a deeply impactful spiritual transformation that also evidenced a kundalini breakthrough (both can and usually do occur at the same time, automatically)." The model I just gave of converging power flows and lightning serves to explain this statement. It also serves to invite us to consider this whole subject from another angle—that of stress and what else can occur at the moment of implosion/explosion.

As the aftereffects are a dead giveaway (pardon the pun) to specific aspects found within the near-death phenomenon itself, so are the "before-effects."

BEFORE THE EVENT

Yes, there is a "before." There are stressors, conditions in the experiencer's life, that point to either unrest or inattention. These are present to some degree in nearly every case. What caught my eye were episodes that occurred under these circumstances:

- during major life junctures;

- when a decision needed to be made and at times of deep dissatisfaction, disappointment, frustration;

- when feeling hurried all the time or excessively strained;

- while "running a tight ship," insisting on personal control;

- as lifestyle maintenance toppled one's ability to keep it going;

- alongside pushing limits—at work, at play, in everything;

- when demanding and strict rules limit one's beliefs and activities;

- without existence of meaningful goals, or when in strong denial;

- during "happy" times that were really a façade;

- when overly satisfied or complacent.

Any common threads here? You're right. One. Lots of stress, excessive stress—whether acknowledged or denied, short-term or long-term—the common thread is still stress. Even with babies and the unborn. Mother's stress, even that of the father, can readily become the child's stress. Sometimes it's as if the child has the experience for the parents or doctors or significant others . . . to relieve or heighten their stress.

And the type of stress I recognized was the kind that pushes a person beyond his or her limits, beyond that which is "safe" (a threshold experience).

On February 29, 2000, the *Daily Progress* in Charlottesville, Virginia, reported that Bruce Greyson, M.D., a professor of psychiatry and near-death researcher at the University of Virginia, was able to show a link between the phenomenon of near-death experiences and a natural physical response to trauma.[84] He found that experiencers have more dissociative episodes—the normal kind, not the pathological kind—than those who were close to dying but did not have a near-death experience. "It's basically narrowing your focus so much that you block out things that are going on around you," Greyson was quoted as saying.

Did you catch that? What he is describing is what shamans, spiritual and mystical folk have for aeons of time referred to as the goal of "high stress" . . . what it takes to push one past the threshold of what is known.

HIGH STRESS

Narrowing one's focus to such an extreme that everything else is blocked out—why would anyone do such a thing? What creates this goal? Being driven into and through what overwhelms (the stress threshold)?

Through the ages sacred initiations of the greatest order demanded a "death"—seldom physical. They required the death of the ego. One had to "die unto the self," leaving behind previous desires and wants, to take on the trusted role of healer-guide who then dedicated the rest of his or her life in service to others. The core of shamanic vision quests ("calling for a vision" or asking the spirits for guidance) still today consists of ceremonial rituals that mimic or come close to actual physical death. Probationers are prepared for this; still, there is no real preparation for that overwhelming, "over the top" fear that pushes one's panic button. Once that threshold is breached, the individual either passes into madness or breaks through the threshold into otherworlds of spirit that accompany a transformation of consciousness.

Consider the mythological traditions of the "hero's journey" or the making of "wise ones." High stress was always the deciding factor: how the individual faced "the watcher at the gate" (the stress threshold), overcame fear (passed through/ascended), or entered the otherworlds of spirit (that null space where everything is said to converge/suspend/expand—into the collective whole), and is imprinted from the aftereffects (bears the "mark" of ascension) . . . *which establishes the extent to which the individual is changed/ transformed.*

The formula then for a transformation of consciousness (the basic energetics in brief): intense trauma, high stress that narrows one's focus, feeling driven or accelerated beyond states of fear/panic, encountering a threshold (maybe a greeter), passing into a null space of energy convergence, infused with knowing, imprinted or changed by null space exposure, returning as one who has been expanded or enhanced by the experience as if "marked" by the pattern of aftereffects. Sounds like I'm repeating myself, doesn't it? Actually I am.

POWER PUNCH

I've seen them thousands of times—experiencers who behave as if they have been punched, jerked, hit, pushed, or somehow spun around. Something physical happened to them, something separate from any mind play or otherworldly visitation or event that put them at death's door. And that "something" shifted their futures, pushed them into a unique arena of experience. The "something" that set them apart I call a "power punch." It is a force. It is an energy. It is intense.

This intensity, what narrows the focus in high stress, is the key, the hinge, to understanding near-death experiences and their aftereffects.

The 21 percent of near-death experiencers in my research who claimed they did not have aftereffects worth mentioning, or at all, were the same ones whose episode was so seemingly superficial to them that they described it as a simple, fleeting dream.

The 60 percent of those I had sessions with who reported significant, noticeable changes after their experience were openly expressive about how intense their episode was and how it had impacted their lives in dramatic ways. They exhibited most or the entire pattern of aftereffects. Many seemed stunned at how much they had changed once they compared "before" with "after."

The 19 percent who were so radically affected it seemed as if they had become a different person or at least an altered version of who they had once been, bore the full brunt of the "power punch"—and showed it. Before and after photographs illustrated the depths of what they had been through and how it had changed them. Almost to a person they displayed the full pattern of aftereffects.

And, with the 73 percent in my research who had electrical sensitivity afterwards, I was able to establish that it was the intensity of their near-death episode that had been the determining factor in causing this aftereffect—not how long or short their episode, or how much light they had been exposed to during their scenario.[85] No matter how I approached this, cross-comparing brief and longer near-death states, complicated and simple—regardless even of imagery or how it was described—I still reached the same conclusion: what mattered most was the intensity of the episode, not the episode itself. The intensity is what shifts us.

COLLOIDAL CONDITION

Just as there is a corollary in nature between lightning and enlightenment, so exists one between the energetics that produce the power punch (brain shift) and those that cause a colloidal state. I've given you the formula for the actualities of the transformative shift; here's the rest.

A colloidal condition is a peculiar in-between state that occurs when forces suddenly collapse and then converge. This in-between state creates antiforce, which is antigravity. Particles caught in this unique state between implosion and explosion transmute and remain forever changed by that transmutation. On a molecular level, these particles show evidence of enlargement and of having taken on different and enhanced characteristics.

Recognize this? No? Well, maybe this illustration will help.

Let's take a look at what happens when water is stirred. There are several ways you can stir water. For the sake of this discussion, we'll rotate it. Spin the water. Round and round. Faster and faster. Really spin it. Then stop it suddenly, and reverse directions.

Did you see what happened? When you stopped the spin, the water collapsed into itself, creating an implosion. But just before you initiated the reverse spin, where the water could explode back out again, conditions mysteriously changed. Both the water and everything contained within it were briefly held in suspension. This is called a colloidal condition; the particles caught therein are referred to as colloids.

The same thing can happen to the human brain if suddenly hit, jarred, or severely jiggled, especially during an automobile accident or as a result of a fall. Typically a colloid-like suspension of consciousness will follow such trauma, whereby the environment appears to expand out as time slows to a standstill. The individual feels somehow caught *in between* realities when this occurs, as if he or she has slipped through a crack in time and space and suddenly become resident of a world neither here nor there. This peculiar feeling of being suspended in between realities affects a person so deeply that it can permanently alter the way the individual regards the world at large and his or her place in it.

Of interest is that consciousness, even if simply released from the bias of thought as in a flow state or during meditation, will behave somewhat the same way.

Also of interest is another state, termed the "acute dying experience," that produces "peritraumatic dissociation." Described medically as depersonalization in the face of life-threatening danger, the acute dying experience occurs when one's sense of time ceases at the same time that profound feelings of unreality and hyperarousal occur—as well as out-of-body experiences, decreased pain perception, disconnection from body, disorientation, tunnel vision, dissociation, numbness, and dreamlike states.[86] This state, although tossed around in near-death circles as a possible corollary, doesn't fit research, mine or anyone else's.

Of every possible explanation for what might happen to consciousness as it undergoes an impactful transformation, no other theory compares, step by step, with the actual energetics involved—except the colloidal condition. Here's why.

A colloidal condition occurs when:

1. forces suddenly collapse, then converge;

2. a momentary state of suspension results;

3. everything caught in that suspension expands and enlarges as anti-gravity is created;

4. inherent or unlimited potential is released;

5. whatever is present is imprinted (becomes permanently altered by what happened);

6. whatever is present then transmutes (takes on different characteristics);

7. as reversal of motion is completed, forces are restored, suspension ends, but the imprinting (transmutation) remains.

COLLOIDS

Remember, a colloid is any particle caught in a colloidal condition. Once suspended in this manner, the particle will automatically enlarge, expand, and remain permanently and forever altered by the experience.[87]

The process that creates a colloid correlates almost exactly with what happens to those who undergo spiritual transformations and near-death episodes. The majority who go through such processes experience an enlargement and expansion of consciousness, exhibit the sudden surfacing of latent abilities, face a confusing array of psychological and physiological aftereffects, and are never quite the same again.

It is my belief that the reason this process of convergence and transmutation (transfiguration) is universal is because all of us, now and through the ages, are and have always been imprinted by the same creative impulse that originated us. The mark of our creation is what we display whenever our consciousness is set free to rediscover itself and the source of its being. After such transformative/threshold experiences, we feel as if we have found "home" because the home we think we've found already exists within us—and always has.

We recognize the place because we never left it to begin with.

Separation, what makes us think we have left our source, is really but a slip of memory, a case of mistaken identity. We make this mistake by identifying with the "projection" we have become, rather than with the source of who we are.

The true purpose of a transformative experience, in my opinion, is to help us remember what we forgot.

THAT WHICH EXPANDS

The idea that consciousness might have the capacity to grow/change/evolve—individually and en masse—brings me to mention this fascinating tidbit: the word "heaven" comes from the Greek. In the language of the Bible, which is Aramaic, the same word was often referred to as "leaven." Jesus is quoted in the 33rd verse of Matthew 13 as saying: "The kingdom of heaven is like unto leaven." Leaven causes dough to rise, like yeast. Leaven expands, yet the Greeks understood that heaven was *that which is already expanded.*

With that clue from the Greek version of what heaven might be, allow me to conjecture: The near-death phenomenon may well function as leaven does, expanding the consciousness of its experiencers into the next phase of their growth and learning.

Their consciousness, once expanded, could enlarge to such an extent that it would be capable of accessing other dimensions of reality and greater levels of consciousness—perhaps mass mind or even the One Mind. Once an individual's consciousness has expanded in this manner, regardless of cause, that individual could become *more than before* . . . perhaps permanently, if intense enough.

My research shows me that the common denominator linking consciousness with creation itself—*the single linchpin that governs the alteration and evolution of consciousness—is a colloidal state* not just within a single individual's mind as that person matures and changes, but collectively through the combined effect of human consciousness as a whole.

CHAPTER SEVENTEEN

BRAIN SHIFT: SENSITIVITY AND SYNCHRONICITY

"A new view of nature is emerging, which encompasses both galaxies and neurons, gravitation and life, molecules and emotions. As a culmination of centuries of studying nature, mankind has been approaching the thorniest subject of all: ourselves."

—Piero Scaruff

Whenever consciousness expands, we retain the imprint of that expansion. The hinge to the process is the intensity from high stress. The linchpin in that hinge that enables it to bend, shift, alter, expand, and enlarge is a colloidal condition. The imprint of what we retain is the pattern of colloids that results—the characteristics and traits of the aftereffects. The most noticeable one? Hypersensitivity.

Some of us are born that way. Arthur Rubinstein, the Polish-born American pianist widely considered one of the greatest piano virtuosos of the 20th century, said: "When I was a small boy, about 8 or 10, I was sitting at the piano while taking a lesson from my teacher. As I was sitting there ready to play, and had my hands on the piano, I felt ghostlike hands slowly coming across my shoulders and merging into my own hands. Then 'my' hands began playing a piece of music which I had never heard, nor played, before. Actually it seemed it was not me but my hands that were playing! After the piece was finished, the teacher was aghast, and said that what I just played was a very famous classical piece of music, and that it was played perfectly, in fact, better than he, the teacher, had ever heard the greatest of piano players play the piece." Rubinstein paused, then told the interviewer, "Makes you wonder, doesn't it?"[88]

French Islamic scholar Henry Corbin coined the term "imaginal" to refer to incidents like that of Arthur Rubinstein to distinguish sensitivity to secret and hidden powers from negative, belittling labels like "imaginary." Science counters, however, that such hypersensitivity "reflects a deep dualism in the human psyche" that, when in doubt, defaults to a belief that everything is alive. Sharon Begley, in her article "Why We Believe," says: "During intense prayer or meditation, brain-imaging studies show, the structure is also especially quiet. Unable to find the dividing line between self and world, the brain adapts by experiencing a sense of holism and connectedness."[89] Is imaginal hypersensitivity, then, just a trick of the brain? Hardly.

BRAIN WAVE CHANGES AND ENTANGLEMENTS

Mario Beauregard of the University of Montreal discovered that the brains of near-death experiencers showed marked changes in patterning when they were asked to mentally visualize and emotionally connect with "the being of light" from their episode. His finding evidences a shift in brain function.[90]

Although unrelated, an experiment I was privy to back in the late seventies and early eighties is relevant here and extends the scope of how brain function can shift. At that time a number of dowsers were using the Mind Mirror (spectrum analyzer) during field trials to measure the "dowsing mode," that state of mind they attained when searching for water, missing items, or people with their tool of choice, be it a forked stick, dowsing rod, or bent clothes hanger. With headbands and electrodes in place, the participants achieved (through intention) a "search state" in their mind that "felt right." The researchers began tracking. The device measured electrical voltage in participants' brains, separating brain-wave frequencies into bands which printed on readout charts.[91]

Differences in brain function showed up immediately and in every chart I saw. Voltages for high frequency beta waves or gamma (super wide awake, focused) and low frequency delta waves (deep sleep, unresponsive) *were both so high that they were beyond the capacity of the instrument's measurements.* Alpha (natural rest state, creativity, intuition) registered fairly strong; theta (dreams, hypnotic states, deep meditation) registered weaker. The charts shocked everyone. Alpha was expected to be the dominant frequency, yet the opposite occurred. Each chart contradicted the hard science that suggested that "only advanced and highly trained meditators and yogis can be fully conscious while in delta." The "dowsing mode" turned out to be *the synchronization of the highest and lowest electrical outputs in the brain.* Of interest is that many dowsers have trouble meditating. They find it too confining for how their mind spreads. (Contrary to popular notions that state centering one's mind at the delta frequency is the best way to develop an evolved mind, research shows that gamma waves—extremely high frequencies of beta—can also take you to oneness and bliss.[92])

What does any of this have to do with near-death states? I "saw" this same pattern of brain-wave function in about 42 percent of the adult experiencers I had sessions with and close to 65 percent of the children. Each was fully conscious while in this mode, yet behaved as if he or she were downloading information or plugging into other levels of existence. No switcheroo between left and right hemispheres of the brain with this (although that does happen); rather, what appeared with brain waves was the emergence of a new or at least different electrical field array.

This type of shift creates a kind of "active rest." The subject is hyperfocused, hyper-aware, and hyper-sensitive, while at the same time exquisitely at peace and comfortable. Near-death experiencers and those like them sometimes speak, as dowsers do, of being in that mode, that "feel" of mind, that locks onto "spots of knowing." This pattern of brainwaves is very stimulating. One feels linked to everyone, everywhere, as though there is only one mind—with "knowing" universal.

Physicists are moving closer to the idea that, at the quantum level, all minds are part of each other, entangled in a giant web of interconnections streaming from a common source.[93] The idea that anything can be separate, that distance can ensure separation, is untrue. Once paths cross, even slightly, what affects the one will affect the other. There is a corollary for this in the

Huna traditions of the Hawaiian Islands and throughout Polynesia. It is called "Aka threads." (Huna is a philosophical knowingness that applies to all aspects of existence.) "Aka" means "life"; hence, Aka threads are life threads. The understanding is that once you touch something or someone, part of your life essence remains there—a tiny filament, a thread. No bother, really. Still, the more you touch, the thicker the thread becomes. Touch enough and that thread can become a cord binding the two parties together. Life after life doesn't break these cords; Huna offers that only love can break them—the unconditional love that streams from a forgiving heart.

Life threads, webs of interconnectedness, linkages that defy reason . . . are now as much a part of the language of science, as mysticism.

THINGS FUTURE

Look for it—a signature feature of transformations of consciousness, no matter how they occur, is the comfortableness of things future. The individual is able to access the future, see the future, know the future, or live the future before it occurs. Things future: a marker of brain shift.

Children up to about the age of five or so spend more time in the future than they do in the present. Acting out their "fantasies" is the major way they have to establish continuity (recognize and trust the existence and continuance of what fills their world), and prepare in advance for demands soon to be made of them. Those fantasies are really rehearsals, a necessary step toward becoming acclimated to earth life, wearing a body, performing tasks, handling disappointments and expectations, and branching out to attract more possibilities as they gain in confidence.

Until children become social, their time sense is in the now. In maturity they move past the larger-than-life archetypes of childhood, then the stereotypical demands of adulthood, until at last they truly begin to individuate—they become their own person living a life they consciously chose.

Invariably, those who have undergone a near-death experience and/or a transformation of consciousness flip back to a behavior similar to the early years of childhood. Aware again of the power of *now* and cognizant of broader archetypes as universal themes common to us all, experiencers begin to spend more time in the future, acting out, preparing for what could occur, literally rehearsing the new and the different. I view "things future" (that intrude into or blend within present moments) as an absolutely healthy and necessary component for integrating breakthrough experiences. Without an awareness of and comfort with future, we cannot connect where we were with where we are, or how we prefer to be. We too easily lose ourselves in the drama of what happened to us and the mythology that describes it (archetypes). Futuristic episodes help us to re-examine and reassess. Even Freud observed that pathology occurs with the loss of future orientation.

While considering the value of futuristic knowing, be aware of these notes:

- Future memory is not déjà vu. It is the ability to live the future in advance in detail, sensorially and fully, without knowing you are doing so; then, at a later date, facing the same episode—living through it again, while recognizing that the prior incident was just practice, getting you ready for "the real thing."[94]

- In dowsing for a target, it has been demonstrated that the dowser's hand responds *before* the target is reached, as if its location is already known.[95]

- Scientists at the Max Planck Institute for Human Cognitive and Brain Sciences in Leipzig have discovered that several seconds before we consciously make a decision, its outcome can be predicted from unconscious activity in the brain. Knowing, then, actually happens in advance of decision making.[96]

- Presentiments or "pre-sponses" are quite common. Even though it has long been established that a person cannot respond to a stimulus before it occurs, modern experiments are proving the opposite—we know in advance.[97]

- Large numbers of people knew hours, even days in advance about the disaster that hit New York City on September 11. Some described airplanes striking towers. This type of occurrence implies that "mass mind" exists, a central vibratory matrix we interact with.

Get this . . . from *Science Digest*, October 1982 . . . "The flow of time is a psychological, not a natural event. No physical experiment has ever detected the flow of time."

Another tidbit . . . the languages of most indigenous people contain no words for "time." None of the hundreds of words in the language of Australian Aborigines refer to time, nor is space perceived as distance. For them there is only the perceptible and tangible conscious mind, and the invisible subconscious involved in the continuum of dreaming.

One more . . . in experiments with clairvoyants conducted by Harold E. Puthoff, a Stanford University physicist, each participant was able to describe the destination of target subjects a half-hour to five days before any of the targets knew where they were to go, much less arrive there. Other experiments are currently in progress that suggest that time can work backwards as well as forwards. Already known is that in the energy field, there is no difference between a memory and a new experience. *The brain retrieves "old" and "new" information the same way! Past, present, future can become—and often are—merely options.*

WAVE PATTERNS AND THE FIFTH DIMENSION

I have consistently observed a sensitivity I would not define as "simply psychic" in both adult and child experiencers. What I have recognized are signs of alterations in the brain/mind assembly that enable experiencers to encompass a broader range of frequencies in the electromagnetic spectrum while wide awake and keenly aware. When most experiencers speak of other dimensions, realities, matrixes, or levels, they are *not* losing touch with the world around them, the world they have known since birth. They are instead referring to a larger panorama of what already exists and always has. Nothing magic or mysterious here . . . only awakenings.

James E. Beichler, Ph.D. "woke up" one day and in so doing came to understand the fifth dimension. He said during one of his recent talks:[98]

> The expanding role of "mind" within its environmental envelope
> evolves "consciousness," an awareness of its own being, self, and the
> conditions in which the body functions within its more complete

surrounding four-dimensional environment. "Consciousness" is the result of an evolutionary process toward a still higher or third level "resonance" pattern between memories, knowledge patterns, "mind," and the living body. Consciousness exists completely in the fifth dimension as an extension of the living body. It is a resonance pattern, a harmony in the fifth dimension. Through the fifth dimension, all particles in existence link to all other particles. We can detect the fifth dimension through emotions, intuitions, intangibles. It is a single field—wave function is actually a volume in the fifth dimension.

The more Dr. Beichler described the fifth dimension (that it consists of resonance patterns), the more I realized that what he was detailing is in essence the colloidal condition. Could the two be the same? I suspect they are.

SYNCHRONICITY

The Swiss psychologist Carl Gustav Jung coined the term "synchronicity" to describe the phenomenon of seemingly unrelated events occurring in unexpected relation to each other, not connected by cause and effect but by simultaneity and meaning. Defined as "meaningful coincidence," this phenomenon is unpredictable and seemingly random in occurrence, yet Jung posited that there was so much order to the randomness that the implication was—there is no such thing as a true coincidence.

Crazy? Look again at how I found most of the near-death experiencers in my research base—60 percent through synchronicity! During the initial years of my work I never introduced myself, said I was a researcher, or exhibited any particular behavior other than being open to listen to whatever people had to say. Seldom was I ever given references, even within the families I visited. They came—sometimes ten or more a day—year after year. I'd turn around (that's all it took) and there would be another one, almost as if waiting his or her turn. If you are a near-death experiencer, you know what I am saying. Those I had sessions with (between 50 and 79 percent) reported "meaningful coincidences" every day; the rest reported having them once in a while. There were phone calls, repeating numbers, coincidental meetings between people who had been trying to get in touch but couldn't, or turning on a radio and hearing the exact thing you needed to hear at the exact moment you needed to hear it. Could this be random? Not when it occurs every day.

Synchronicity, although surprising and unlooked for, can presage some very dramatic or important turns of fate. Take what happened to Einstein. He was attending a class taught by Albert von St Gallen Heim (a professor of geology in Zurich) when Heim's paper was published. Heim had fallen when climbing in the Alps and had what we now call a near-death experience. He was so changed by his experience that he sought out others who had had similar experiences with falling. He wanted to see if people who fell from a great height reported that time seemed to slow down or stop completely. He discussed his findings in class, and very probably focused on the idea from his research that time and space were relative to each other. There is every reason to believe that Einstein had a near-death experience when a child and that any such discussion would have fascinated him.[99]

Einstein developed his theory of relativity after he saw a man fall from a Berlin rooftop. The man survived with little injury and told Einstein that he had not felt any of the effects of gravity. What the man told him duplicated what he had heard previously in Heim's class. A new view of the universe resulted.[100]

Synchronicity is so commonplace with near-death experiencers and those like them that it becomes almost routine. When the phenomenon occurs, you feel as if you are caught in a flow state: things connect, somehow everything just flows together on cue . . . without any decision or effort on your part.

We know a lot about flow states. Unlike concentration, which increases brain action, flow states decrease it. Distortions disappear and we just flow. Nothing happens, yet everything happens. You emerge from such a flow state refreshed, inspired, and invigorated—as if you had been asleep—yet you know more than you did before and you have no idea why or where the information came from.[101] I compared mental (internal) flow states in my book, *Future Memory*, with that external sense of flow that can happen when synchronicity becomes almost routine.[102] A chart in that book that shows this is worth repeating here:

Aspects of Flow

Internal to Self	External to Self
Subjective environment	Objective environment
Without a focus	More in focus
Release of thoughts	Release of goals or vested interests
Stimuli fade away	Stimuli increase in clarity
Blank out to nothing	Perk up to new possibilities
Consciousness expands	Experience expands
The mind flows	The life flows
You know more	You do more
Connect with a source of wisdom	Connect with a source of guidance beyond self
Gain information	Gain harmony and an orderly rhythm to life experiences
Unify in consciousness	Unify with the world at large
A state of mind	A state of being

Based on the thousands of cases I have studied (including what I did back in Idaho during the sixties and seventies), synchronicity's only purpose is to catch our attention. It signals that an external flow has been activated, for however long. Get that? Synchronicity is a signal of movement "switching gears."

Study fluid dynamics—how birds in flight maintain organized formations even when individual birds make mistakes, how rotating colonies of bacteria stay together regardless of challenge, how a herd of buffalo maintains order even in full gallop, how people in crowds pour out from an event as if "directed." Flows occur whenever we shift into a wave pattern—a natural rhythm of movement that results when we function as if one mind. To put this another way, synchronicity is the fluid dynamics of mind on the move.

Colloidal states lead to new order; flow states continuously reorder (whether internal or external). Walter Russell says we live in a thought-wave universe.[103] There are twenty-two basic wave patterns that have been identified. All the early alphabets represented these patterns in how characters were shaped. Think fluid dynamics if you want to understand how consciousness works, what happens to us when we change (like after a near-death experience). Think fifth dimension and waveforms and resonance patterns. Then, know this:

Science tells us that "excited" or highly charged fluids can reach a state called "superfluidity." When that happens, the least expected thing occurs—the fluid can no longer be contained. It will pass through glass, walls, even floors as if nothing is there, as if once it moves past the containment threshold it changes dimensional function.

What I have observed with experiencers who have passed through an intensely transformative episode is that their consciousness tends to behave as if highly charged "superfluid" that now operates "beyond containment."

CHAPTER EIGHTEEN

BRAIN SHIFT: LIMBIC SYSTEM

"Knowledge has three degrees—opinion, science, illumination. The means or instrument of the first is senses; of the second, dialectic; of the third, intuition."

—PLOTINUS

You knew the limbic system was next. How could it be otherwise? When you think survival, think limbic. The limbic system consists of various parts and components that wrap around (like a vine) the top of our brain stem. It translates our basic instincts for sex, hunger, sleep, fear, and survival into more flexible, social forms of behavior. Often referred to as our emotional or feeling center ("gut" brain), the limbic is also the seat of our immune system and the body's ability to heal itself, and operates like an "executive office" in deciding what information is stored in memory, what is forgotten, and what will be further elaborated upon and refined in the two brain hemispheres and throughout the brain/mind assembly. It has a direct neural connection with the heart. Emotion is necessary to accelerate and prolong limbic involvement (which jumpstarts learning). Odors access the limbic instantaneously. All other stimuli take longer to register; therefore smell is primary, especially as a memory cue.[104] Although reptilian by design, this ancient and complicated structure is what makes us *specifically human*.

CORRELATIONS IN THE BRAIN/MIND ASSEMBLY

Stimulating the limbic activates the imagination and "imagery patterns" found in the temporal lobes. Note the linkup in the limbic system between heart, emotions, smell, immune system, temporal lobes, and survival. Overlay symbols to each of these and you get love, ecstasy, integrity of memory, upliftment, otherworldly realities, awareness that life continues . . . a symbolic spread that *exactly matches and identifies the universal elements of a near-death experience or any impactful transformation of consciousness!*

Hold on, folks, we're going to play with this.

Many professionals now believe that if the limbic does not originate "mind," it certainly is the gateway within the brain to higher realms of mind; certainly to more powerfully diverse and collective types of consciousness. Yes, I know about all the research that indicates that the Sylvian Fissure in the right temporal lobe is the seat of things spiritual (we'll talk about that in the next chapter); still, nowhere in the brain but the limbic qualifies as the actual *staging arena* where the organ called the brain accesses and filters what is referred to as mind. How I spread this:

Left-brain hemisphere (conscious, objective mode of awareness): Mainly analyzes, clarifies, categorizes, and separates data. Intellect and reason are its regions of expertise; science and education its preferences.

Right-brain hemisphere (subconscious, subjective mode of awareness): Mainly collects, absorbs, enhances, abstracts, and connects data. Imagination and intuition are its regions of expertise; religion and symbology, its preferences.

Limbic system (superconscious, synergistic mode of awareness): Mainly senses, embraces, and knows that it knows (gut response). The collective whole and memory are its regions of expertise; mystical knowing (gnosis) and convergence with realms beyond self (unification with a Greater Source), its preference.

Using the same type of spread, we can change the headings to read:

Modes of Awareness

Conscious	Normal ego awareness
Subconscious	Altered state of awareness
Superconscious	Expanded state of awareness

States of Existence

Objective/Physical	Wide awake, alert: externalized, outer world
Subjective/Symbolic	Dreamy, subliminal: internalized, inner world
Convergence/Synergy	Mystical knowing: unified, collective whole

How our mind responds is a reflection of how easily our degree of consciousness operates in and through the various brain support structures. This alters with each challenge and new opportunity we process and/or integrate. Nothing is static in brain/mind functioning. We either grow or diminish. Today's researchers consider feeling the basis of consciousness. "There was an emotional brain long before there was a rational one."[105] Put this in context with the immediate feedback loop between the limbic and heart and you will understand why near-death states are most often accompanied by "floods of love."

Looking back at the pattern of physiological and psychological aftereffects, we see that *almost every one of them can be traced to enhanced, accelerated limbic system involvement as a point of origination.*

When the limbic is stimulated, it leaves "prints." With a little bit of stimulation, we get excited, perk up, emotions flow, and receptivity is enhanced (music, rituals, and celebrations are geared for this). Passion/compassion turns on with more stimulation; along with displays of psychic/intuitive abilities and the inspiration to take action (charismatic speakers or shocking headlines can lead to this response). Overwhelming surges of love and light, faculty changes, panoramic visions, and the emergence of wisdom and knowing most often occur when the limbic is deeply impacted by the intensity of a sudden shift in function. "Prints" can include: multiple/conjoined senses (synesthesia); clustered thinking (a marker for creative genius); parallel processing/simultaneous brain-wave function ("awakened" mind or mind in the state of "active rest").

When the limbic system is spun around or receives a blow, it's as if the temporal lobes, nervous system, and heart are signaled to do one of two things: shut down or speed up. Shutting down means damage or death. Speeding up means healing or enhancement. What we refer to as the aftereffects of near-death and similar states I consider to be *the cascade effect* or *imprinting* that various bodily systems exhibit as they react to and correspond with the specifics of limbic system enhancement, enlargement, or acceleration. The extent of the cascade effect indicates the degree to which the limbic was impacted.

DEATH FLASH/CHEMICAL YELLOW

Attending physicians claim, and verify, that brain waves are most often zero during near-death states. No breath. No heartbeat. No brain. Oh? What if the brain, specifically the limbic, *is* in operation—just not in ways we are trained to recognize? What if the limbic can redirect its ending to a new beginning?

An October 6, 2009, *Discovery News* article by Irene Klotz reported about a study of seven terminally ill patients that "found identical surges in brain activity moments before death, providing what may be physiological evidence of 'out-of-body' experiences reported by people who survive near-death ordeals. . . . Moments before death, the patients experienced a burst in brain-wave activity, with the spikes occurring at the same time before death and at comparable intensity and duration."[106]

A similar study came to my attention around 1987 and I wrote about it in *Coming Back to Life*.[107] "A Polish physicist named Janusz Slawinski, a member of the faculty at the Agricultural University at Wojska Polskiego in Poznan, is convinced that a 'deathflash' takes place whenever any organism dies, humans included. He explains that this flash is an emission of radiation ten to one thousand times stronger than normal, and contains within it information about the organism that just released it."

A parallel study of George W. Meek in his report about a team of doctors who weighed dying patients at the actual moment of death, and discovered an overall, unexplainable loss of about an ounce.[108]

This relates to research on the Italian Holy Shroud of Turin, which is believed to be the burial cloth that covered Jesus after his crucifixion. The cloth exhibits an exact imprint of a man's body in both positive and negative formats and contains detailed information that matches the Bible Gospels; the imprint is said to have been caused by flash photolysis (the breakdown of materials under the influence of an intense burst of light[109]).

Surges of brain-wave activity, of energy, of yellow light. Yellow?

Although yellow is neutral to the spectrum and is not a color in the energy world, it does pop up in some very peculiar ways. The retina of the eye has color cones for red, green, and blue, but not for yellow. Yellow is created by a chemical reaction in the brain. Color photography is no different, with yellow hues the result of chemical reactions during film development. It is surmised by medical researchers that the ability to see yellow signaled a crossover in the evolution of eyesight from purple rods on the retina (which enable us to see in dark or shadowy places) to color cones, with "white" probably next. There is no arguing that yellow has always been associated with change, good cheer, brightness, and spirit. Most of us get a lift just from seeing the color. Yellow, gold, and white hues are associated with holiness, halos, spiritual illumination, rebirth, and transfiguration.

Some doctors claim they use a penlight when checking the pupils of patients thought to be dead, to determine if the soul is still there. If the back of the eye is yellow, the soul is gone.

Here's the stunner. During the many years I trained people in how to have out-of-body experiences, they would invariably pass through a yellow haze before their sight switched to normal color hues or bright, enhanced colors. During the three decades I have been researching near-death states, adults and children would consistently comment on being bathed in yellow, white, or gold light. (Same color range when shifting from embodiment to spirit.)

We're not talking symbols here—or tradition or mysticism or religious belief. This is physical, the way our bodies are constructed, and the brain is far more capable and surprising than science has established. The limbic system can indeed switch its own future around through a sudden, intense burst of energy and light . . . to guarantee life *or* death.

Should life return, that switch-over can disrupt breathing and sleeping afterwards. Many experiencers report periods of breath stoppage while wide-awake activity continues. Although appearing as if a type of sleep apnea (falling asleep suddenly, even if standing), breathing oddities correct themselves in a year or two. There is a tendency for experiencers to begin to flow with the rhythm of the earth's pulse beat, which peaks between 2 and 4 AM.[110] What is natural re-establishes itself, thanks to our emotional feeling center, the limbic.

HOLOGRAMS, COHERENCE

You don't need a brain to access mind. A college graduate with an IQ of 126 discovered, much to his and everyone else's utter amazement, that he had only one-eighth of an inch of actual brain matter. That's all. The rest of his head was filled with fluid. So what about the brain in conjunction with the mind?

Physicians researching the near-death phenomenon are beginning to think that memories are really stored outside the human brain. According to Pim Van Lommel, M.D., near-death experiences can only be explained if you assume that consciousness, along with all our experiences and memories, occupies energetic frequencies apart from the brain. Where might that be? Van Lommel can only speculate. "I suspect there is a dimension where this information is stored—a kind of collective consciousness we tune into to gain access to our identity and our memories."[111] Neurophysiologist Karl H. Pribram believes the answer lies in how memories are encoded—not in neurons, but in patterns of nerve impulses that crisscross around the brain in the same way patterns of laser light interference crisscross the entire area of a piece of film containing a holographic image.[112]

What is Pribram suggesting? That the brain itself is a hologram. (Holograms possess an astounding capacity for information storage, which might explain how the human brain can store over ten billion bits of information during an average lifetime.) The brain operates like a hologram enfolded in a holographic universe. With around seven billion brains pulsing away on any given day, each one generating between ten and twenty-three watts of power (enough to power a lightbulb), what would happen if even a simple majority of us, our brain power, came together (cohered)? That question sparked the idea that a Global Brain, created from the collective field of consciousness, must exist. The Global Consciousness Project is an international project that sought to explore whether interconnected consciousness could be scientifically validated.[113] They succeeded, in essence constituting step one in a string of experiments by other groups that are still on ongoing. The goal is to measure the effect human emotion has on the earth's magnetic field.

In chapter 3, I spoke of the Akashic Field, the name coming from the Sanskrit word for "ether" or "radiant space." The Book of Life or the Akashic Records—same thing—contains the memory of all we have ever done, thought, or said, held forever upon rays of light that appear as "skeins" or "threads" or "wave shifts." We reconnect at this vibrational level with the all-ness of us, while being drawn into coherence with the universal field. The chaos theory applies: during a near-death or near-death-like experience, systems become disordered and break down, so an underlying order (previously thought random or non-existent) can emerge and reorder—at the next highest level possible.

DRUGS

Okay, time to face the subject of drugs. Those most often associated with near-death states are ayahuasca (a favorite of shamans), DMT (the most potent hallucinogen on earth), oxytocin (a hormone), ketamine (an anesthetic/psychedelic), ibogaine (hallucinogen hailed as a possible cure for addiction), psilocybin (feel-good magic mushrooms), LSD (a psychedelic associated with Woodstock and the birth of the hippie generation), and peyote (part of Native American spiritual rituals).

Admit it, four needs drive our instincts, not three. You can name food, sleep, and sex without hesitation. But the fourth? Intoxication. This universal drive for mind-altering substances is common not only in human beings, but in animals and even insects.[114] Sometimes that mind-altering urge can lead to positive changes with individuals afterward, like with ibogaine as a possible cure for the addiction response. And, believe it or not, ecstasy can have positive effects on humans. While in Hannover, Germany to deliver a paper on near-death research, I learned that Dr. John H. Halpern of Harvard Medical School was conducting trials using the drug ecstasy in treating end-of-life patients who were struggling with grief and fear. I saw film of Halpern's trials and was impressed with the results—patients were lively; interested; and had more self-acceptance, grace, and a better sense of their place in the greater reality—none appeared drugged.[115]

Did you know that Nobel Laureate Francis Crick, who is credited with codiscovering the double helix structure of DNA, said the image of the structure came to him after taking LSD? There are many stories like this. Native peoples and shamans are vocal in their belief that to reach the true teachers of humankind, one must prepare for sacred ritual where a special potion is taken to ensure contact with otherworldly beings. Elders are always present to help the seeker. There is no comparison between these sacred ceremonies and the so-called pleasure trips today's addicted pay dearly for.[116]

I offer these comments to let you know that I have seen great good come from the taking of drugs under the right circumstances. Still, if you want to compare those I have mentioned with genuine near-death experiences, you wind up with counterfeits that either do not match the depth and scope of the real thing or cannot produce the pattern of physiological and psychological aftereffects. Claims about ketamine do not match, either. You simply cannot compare "trips." Near-death states are so much richer and multi-textured—consistent, coherent, verifiable—with aftereffects that, in most cases, engender positive changes that increase with time.

I was about to toss DMT too, for I did not find Dr. Rick Strassman's book about the drug as interesting as a lot of other folks did (his description of near-death states was incomplete[117]). Then a close friend whose life was transformed by a near-death-like experience surprised me by saying that his episode was the result of his taking DMT as part of obtaining his degree in psychotherapy. My apologies to Dr. Strassman. DMT is actually "manufactured" by the pineal gland in our brain. It facilitates the soul's movement in and out of the body and is an integral part of birth, death, and higher levels of the meditative experience. This means that DMT, the most powerful hallucinogen on earth, is natural to us—a part of our life, our growth, and our journey into spirit, available free of charge through meditative and contemplative states and spiritual awakenings. You can take it as a drug, which my friend did (under supervision in a clinical setting), or benefit from the natural processes it is designed to initiate and support.

In the mid-sixties, on a day I was scurrying to catch up with my family for a picnic, I stopped short, fascinated by a man dressed in white, sitting on the stage of the bandshell at Julia Davis Park in Boise, Idaho. He was describing to a small crowd the states of ecstasy he had reached while taking LSD. His name was Ram Dass. As I listened, a little old lady ran over to the stage, craned her neck to see him, and yelled, "I have those same experiences every time I crochet." He laughed. I joined in because I too had experienced the same thing sitting on the roots of great trees.

Can drugs be dependable or even valuable for inducing near-death states? I vote no. But, I will admit, the jury's still out on this one.

PSYCHOLOGICAL LABELS

In their book *The Spiritual Anatomy of Emotion*, Michael A. Jawer and Marc S. Micozzi discuss the various traits of "unusual" personalities as defined by professional psychologists.[118] Categories that bear some semblance to how near-death experiencers and those like them change afterward are high sensitivity, sensory defensiveness, over excitability, absorption, fantasy-proneness, transliminality, metachoric, shared perceptions, blind sight, extreme perceptions, and, what Jawer believes is the best of labels—thin boundary. It's no wonder experiencers worry about being labeled crazy. Our psychological community really doesn't have a clue as to what is normal after a typical near-death state (for adults or children).

Complaining about this accomplishes nothing. Instead, I'm listing the most common traits the *healthiest* experiencers exhibit afterward, irrespective of age.

- Unusually empathetic, rich inner lives, some healing ability

- Complex, vivid dreams; good recall

- Highly perceptive, creative, intuitive, strong feelings (especially of love)
- Faculties enhanced, synesthesia (conjoined senses), psychic ability
- Susceptible to environmental changes, more allergies than before
- Sense of being able to merge with others and with nature
- Surplus energy for many; restless, curious
- Strong reactions to positive/negative sensory stimuli
- Much in the way of visuals, aesthetic awareness, knowing
- Intense focus, love to question, hunger for knowledge
- Feel things deeply, can have past-life/anomalous memories
- Identity more with soul than self, mystical awareness
- Comfortable with things future and otherworldly states/beings
- Can at times influence physical objects, electrical sensitivity
- Out-of-body experiences can sometimes continue
- Tend toward self-deception, need to relearn basic cautions
- Tend to identify life as a waking dream

Millions of people. All ages. Wake up, psychologists. This profile is normal.

CHAPTER NINETEEN

BRAIN SHIFT: TEMPORAL LOBES

"You're only given one spark of madness. Don't lose it."

—ROBIN WILLIAMS

I wonder sometimes about assumptions. I don't know a scientist or researcher who hasn't made a few (me included); that's why we do so much cross-checking. Example: did you know that all the older Venus figures, relics from Cro-Magnon days, are almost dead-ringers (there's that phrase again) for the shape of animal brains and that of the human limbic system?[119] Why? Did our ancestors know something about the brain and the limbic system that we moderns have forgotten? Have we misunderstood the meaning of their relics, assuming that what appeared to be heavy-breasted women as examples of a goddess culture were, possibly, symbolic renderings of other things as well?

This possibility is in line with older shamanic teachings that placed great emphasis on the limbic system of both animals and humans in regards to rituals that invoked the sacred. Today we know that if the limbic system is excited or stimulated enough to activate areas other than its normal "house-keeping" and maintenance chores, one can slip through the "zero-point" gateway it offers into the in-between realities commonly referred to as otherworld journeys and, I believe, under the aegis of the temporal lobes. Those Paleolithic goddess figures were powerful in what they could have and probably did represent—the fertile energetics of the subconscious (symbolized by the feminine) that unlock the deeper reaches of brain (the limbic plus the great libraries of the temporal lobes).

TEMPORAL LOBE LIBRARIES

We have two of them, located on either side of the brain in the temple area. They have numerous functions, but they are most important as the "libraries" of shape, form, size, dimension, sound, taste, and smell. I regard them as containers of our original template for existing on the earthplane: positives/negatives, adjusting and responding to, recognizing what is encountered—things like objects, bodies, what we call life. We are not born as blank slates. We already know things.[120]

The temporal lobes continuously update themselves from that original template. As we gain experience; as we see, hear, taste, touch, feel, smell, and do even more, the lobes expand what they can identify with—to keep the limbic and brain updated. During the early years of life (birth to just under six), kids match the basics they already had a template for with actualities (what they encountered in the physical world). This is the reason we need to read to babies and young children, take kids on field trips and to museums, go to retreats and educational centers. I suspect it is also the reason why so many who are born blind, supposedly with no concept of sight, can see and even recognize colors and patterns, during near-death states. There are a few who found sight to be foreign, uneasy, even strange; still, the majority felt a comfort with the ability, as if their knowledge-base related to things past.

IMAGERY BLUEPRINTS

Those libraries carry within them imagery/sensory blueprints—*patterns* we can associate with broad, universal themes (archetypes); designs and expectations of family and culture (stereotypes); and the specifics of becoming an individual personality (individuation).

From my research on near-death states, I came to recognize various correlations between archetypes, stereotypes, and individuation as applying to both the ages of children who had near-death episodes and the phases of change the majority of adults grappled with afterward. What I observed helps to shed

Changing Patterns in Mental Models

Archetypes	Stereotypes	Individuations
Broad, larger-than-life shapes, patterns, themes of universal import; detached (i.e., angels at a distance holding out their hands in a gesture of caring as they encircle a spiral to higher realms).	Societal engagements, structures, activities geared to environmental and societal expectations (i.e., angels holding each hand as they walk with you and talk about your life and the way you lived it, an awareness of rewards and responsibilities).	Individual assertions, relates to personal curiosities and the need to identify one's rightful place in the overall scheme of things (i.e., either challenge or co-participate with angels while exploring new options and new choices in life).
Time awareness: Now; based on immediacy or simultaneity.	Time awareness: Short term; based on shared consensus.	Time awareness: Long term; based on priorities and values.

Age Links of the Kind of Imagery Found in Children's Near-Death Episodes

Infancy	Three to just under six	Beginning with puberty

Reacculturation Process Most Adults Go Through After Near-Death Episodes

Phase One (lasts about three years)	Phase Two (lasts about four years)	Phase Three (usually after seventh year)
More cognizant of archetypes, universal themes and issues, greater realities, other worlds; impersonal, detached from ego identity/personality.	Concerned with societal interaction and interrelationships, service- and healing-oriented; realigns or alters stereotypical roles, community-oriented.	Aware of self-worth, practicality and discernment emphasized; tends toward self-governance and self-responsibility, and spiritual development.

more light on the natural process of brain development and memory formation in tandem with what forces may be at play during otherworld journeys. I make no assumptions when I state that there is a larger dynamic at work within this process than personal concerns about oneself, one's beliefs, and one's life. That dynamic seems to arrange and rearrange reality according to what is needed at any given point in our development and within the universe at large . . . while restructuring our brains and reawakening our hearts.

As we interpret our otherworld journeys, we reinterpret life's meaning and purpose. As we explore how consciousness can change, we explore creation itself and the wonder of the universe. As we find order afterward, we reorder our world and our place in it.

All of this is based on what I have seen, cross-checked, and verified. See how I would express my observations in the chart "Changing Patterns in Mental Models" on page 169.

This chart shouldn't scare you. It's just a simple way of showing how what we become aware of when very young relates to the first phase of integration we go through after a near-death state; how that clarifies the second phase of integration when we are older children and our view of ourselves in society alters; and how after puberty, the strength of confidence we achieve relates to what is possible with phase three integrations.

Take a few minutes to digest these correlations. Kids aged three to six (some begin around two) have invisible playmates, see monsters/aliens/angels/fairies, and have near-death experiences. This is the "birth of imagination," when the temporal lobes are working overtime to acculturate the limbic. Compare medieval near-death states with modern ones and you'll recognize immediately how imagery and scenarios change with the times and one's exposure to new knowledge, styles, and trends. Remember how, after Americans walked on the moon, suddenly everyone embraced the reality of "universe." Our lovely "blue marble" populated dreams and visions as if that image of earth had forever been known. Just look at reports of near-death states and traditions of otherworld journeys and how they abruptly shifted once the media sensationalized "tunnels." Yes, tunnels have always existed to some extent in our shared memories, but the image did not become popular or even a visionary artifact until *after* Raymond Moody's first book was published.

Images and the integrity of sensory input alter in tandem with how our environment changes. Our temporal lobes keep their libraries of what is real and what can be depended upon current with changing times. That's their job. Our job is to keep them stimulated.

But wait. Let's not just flit information around about mental models and imagery blueprints without "rerolling the tape on chapter 17 and things future." Hey, this is important. I'm one of those who returned with supersensitive, spongy-fat temporal lobes. They changed as I did.

Brain Development Comparison between Three- to Not-Quite-Six-Year-Olds and Brain Shift Experiencers

Three- to Not-Quite Six-Year-Olds	Brain Shift Experiencers
Temporal Lobe Development Emerging Consciousness	*Temporal Lobe Expansion* Enlarging Consciousness
Prelive the future on a regular basis, spend more time in the future than in the present.	Prelive the future on a regular basis through dream states, visions, future memory episodes.
Play with futuristic possibilities as a way of "getting ready"; rehearse in advance demands soon to be made upon them.	Pre-experience challenges and opportunities before they occur as a way of preparing for demands they will soon face.
No natural understanding of time-space states; consider "future" an aspect of "now." Gain perspective and continuity by establishing the validity of action/reaction or "future" (continuous scenery and connected wholes).	No longer restricted by a sense of time-space states; awareness of simultaneity and the importance of "now." Embrace broader dimensions of experience beyond that of "future" (unlimited perspectives held in tandem with the continuity of stable reference points).
Progress from archetypal mental models to stereotypical ones in a process of self-discovery.	Progress from stereotypical mental models to individuation processes in a journey of soul discovery.
The Birth of Imagination	**The Rebirth of Imagination**

Note that the reliability of things future signals that a person's brain is shifting in structure, function, possibly chemicals as well—a growth spurt. As part of that growth spurt, we tend to revert back to the same brain development phases we had as children; we do this, I believe, for the same reason: to re-establish continuity and order through the process of advance "rehearsals" so we can ready ourselves for the further demands of true maturity (the rediscovery of and identification with soul).

What are near-death and other related experiences? They're growth spurts.

THE "INFAMOUS" SYLVIAN FISSURE

The Sylvian fissure located in the right temporal lobe was declared the "God Spot" by researchers at Laurentian University in Montreal, Canada, a claim later denied by a Swedish team.[121] Actually, this business of a special location in one's brain where God resides began over a hundred years ago, becoming a serious issue when modern test subjects had the Sylvian fissure in their right temporal lobe stimulated by a special pulse. Those subjects reported having pleasant, heaven-like experiences that seemed similar, at least superficially, to near-death states. This type of research, on the role various parts of the brain play in spiritual and religious experiences, now has a name—neurotheology—and much of this work has focused on the right temporal lobe.

Among these new researchers are Andrew Newberg, M.D., and Eugene d'Aquili. They concluded that "spiritual experiences are the inevitable outcome of brain wiring."[122] Things like certain rhythms, rituals, and even total silence have been verified as ways for the brain to perceive self as endless, in touch with all creation—in utterly real, coherent perceptions. Even praying lights up the brain in distinctive ways, especially in the right temporal lobe.

Always true? Maybe not. Willoughby Britton, a psychology doctoral student, had a unique idea. She tested near-death experiencers in a sleep lab and found that they did indeed exhibit unusual brain waves of synchronized patterning in the left temporal lobe.[123] Epileptics who have temporal lobe seizures often report spiritual, mystical experiences during their seizures. Researchers trying to show a link between near-death states and epilepsy discovered that the spiritual and out-of-body episodes of epileptics occurred almost exclusively in the left temporal lobe.

The idea of a "God Spot" in the brain has virtually been discarded. That early research did not hold up to further testing, yet the notion that our brains are wired for things spiritual and religious has. In fact, current thinking about our temporal lobes matches what I've noticed right along, and that is: the left seems to respond more often to anything that unsettles, challenges, or is anxiety-producing or painful (active during unpleasant near-death states); the right seems to respond best to whatever uplifts, pleases, or encourages or gives relief (active in pleasant near-death states). The mistake I believe we make in assigning duties to lobes is that we skip over or fail to recognize the value of sadness *and* joy, worry *and* relief, pain *and* healing, "house cleaning" *and* inspiration, hell *and* heaven. *Both temporal lobes are purposeful and active during transformational processes.* They enable us to learn from and heal the positives and negatives in our quest for wholeness.

THE MANY WORLDS CONCEPT

Physicists have discovered that a particle can be in two places at the same time. Subatomic systems can become so entangled (interconnected) by this ability that measuring one location affects the other location, even if the two are light-years apart. Further, if one subatomic system is at a decision point, it will choose both answers, rather than either/or. This implies that a photon can have many histories and that there are many worlds co-existent in the same place at the same time.

Jeff Tollaksen, a physicist at George Mason University, said in an interview that "Something that happens now is affected by something that happens in the future." To him this "suggests that the universe has a destiny—a destiny that is out there and coming back to us from the future."[124] Cambridge physicist Stephen Hawking and his colleague Thomas Hertog are discovering the same thing when they toss aside "bottom-up" approaches to "the theory of everything" (that there is one history/one event) in favor of "top-down" models. These top-down models show that the universe did not have just one unique beginning and history, but rather a multitude of different beginnings and histories—and it has experienced them all.[125] Physicist Michio Kaku agrees: "Our universe may be but one in a multiverse."[126]

Some popular scientific theories are losing their luster because of this new work. One of them is the uncertainty principle. It states that the co-ordinates of a single physical object, such as the position and velocity of an electron, can never be accurately determined simultaneously . . . yet the many worlds concept refutes this. Physicist Daniel Sheehan put it this way: "The present is always a negotiation between the past and the future." Translation: the future can leak into the present—as any near-death experiencer already knows!

MANY WAYS TO INTERPRET OUR MANY WORLDS

We're gaining steam with this, so hold on as we roll through a few more "fresh ones" from science: *Our world as we think it exists is part of our imagination.* We have no way to know what is real. It's just a model. Our brain constructs our world from waves—we see light waves and our brain constructs a chair. In truth, we live in a matrix. Studies like those of Carl Gustav Jung and Joseph Campbell help us build a living science from symbols.[127] Experiences like near-death states give us invaluable extensions of our frames of reference as they emphasize how the world really works and who we are in the world.

Our brain is set up to see only what it is programmed to see (this protects our subconscious from being bombarded by too much external stimuli). The brain is inclined to find patterns and make associations when none exist, to transfer consciousness to inanimate objects, and to "fill in the blanks" if data is missing. The brain wants to see what is there, and it wants meaningful, complete pictures. We are pattern-oriented by nature, but awakenings "cut loose" those patterns. The perceptual prejudices our families, schools, and culture construct for us (the bias of consensus) get ripped apart or majorly challenged by sudden shocks (like losing your job, a child dying, an accident) or much more powerfully by breakthroughs in consciousness that transformational episodes initiate. We emerge from the "caterpillar chrysalis" of past brain programming to fly *beyond* what seems to limit.

We have otherworld journeys so new forms can be readied for new ways of perceiving and sensing. These "initiations" update the temporal lobe libraries—a distinct advantage in growth spurts—while uncovering the original templates and what they contained. I offer the following as a way to interpret and understand the inner territories of a psyche laid bare from such a jolt.

The Four Levels of Near-Death and Other World Imagery

Personal	Mass Mind
Images from one's own life	Images of a collective nature that reflect the human condition
Memory Fields	**Truth**
Sometimes called "false images," these are as much archetypal and evolutionary as they are primordial	That consistent, stable reality that undergirds and transcends creation and all created things

Descriptions/Definitions	
Personal Imagery	**Mass Mind Imagery (sometimes referred to as "group" or "racial" mind)**
Landscapes and environments the same or similar to one's own life, loved ones, and pets that were once part of one's world, conversations and dialogue that concern personal matters, family secrets, and intimate revelations. Awareness of physical happenings during out-of-body states that are later verified as accurate.	Landscapes and environments typical of what one could adjust to or expect from one's culture, an overriding sense of the familiar—even if particular sights seem somehow peculiar or different, dialogue with beings about the human condition and how it has evolved and where it might be heading, objective about the progression of the human family. Awareness of a mission or a job yet to be done for the betterment of one's fellows, and of how every effort counts.

continued on the next page

continued from the previous page

Memory Fields Imagery (sometimes referred to "phantom" or "false" images)	Truth Imagery
Includes access to panoramic archetypes/universal symbols of historical appeal—such as God as a man, angels as humans with wings, religious figures as loving authorities, globes of light as guardians, demons as elements of punishment, satanic figures as the personification of evil. Also applies to representative symbols, such as skull for fear, whirlpool for threat, yin/yang circles for mystical order, tree of life for continuity, tribunals for judgment. Actual visuals may harken back to primordial earth and sky phenomena such as canopies of ice crystals or comets hitting a given area. Awareness of wisdom levels, life stages as stairways, layers of thought-forms as "the twelve heavens and the twelve hells."	A sudden knowing, like a strong feeling or sense of higher knowledge and greater sources to that which is true, from regions of "The Absolute." Seldom is there much in the way of imagery except for vague or indefinite shapes and/or abstracts. Invariably, overleafs (accommodations) will form to put one at ease; once the individual relaxes, overleafs dissolve. Discovery that the Truth level overflows with unbounded joy, complete and unconditional love, total peace—an ecstatic communion with Oneness. There is no sense of doubt with Truth and no imagery that has permanence.

MANY PLANES, MANY BEINGS

Dr. Strassman, in his work with DMT and the effect it has on people, noted what many have long suspected—that all the many frequencies of the electromagnetic spectrum could be inhabited, that because we can't see such beings with regular vision or register their presence electronically doesn't mean they are not there.

Otherworld journeys have all manner of folk appear in them: both the living and the dead, animals, angels, elementals, phantoms, and "the indescribable." There has never been a shortage of beings in experiencer accounts. Some don't even have bodies but are experienced as wind, standing waves, musical sounds, coronas of light. The puzzle of what to make of this has always centered on the question of credibility. How can we accept and trust what we cannot prove is real? If you are a near-death experiencer or one who has undergone an impactful transformation of consciousness, you may not have the choice you think you have. It's enough that the otherworldly can populate your episode. But when they follow you back to conscious reality and continue to manifest? That's "over the top."

So, the crazies begin: church groups calling otherworldly episodes "counterfeit"; Eastern religions labeling them "maya" or "illusion"; wannabes worship experiencers as "masters" and "guides." I have witnessed experiencers give precise details of how other-worldly beings came to them and now lead them, channel through them, advise them. Yet the result of this continuing association can become more of a play of egos than anything profound or worthy. That's the catchy part. Proof of authenticity lies in the afterward— how you and those around you are affected over time. The beings we meet in our journeys are not always what they seem, neither are they necessarily positive.

The following chart highlights how to recognize the real source of power behind beings of spirit. Use comparisons as an aid in cross-checking motive.[128]

Discerning the Source of Spirit Beings and Voices

LESSER MIND	GREATER MIND
The Voice of Ego Personality Level	The Voice of Spirit Soul Level
flatters	informs
commands	suggests
demands	guides
tests	nudges
chooses for you	leaves choice up to you
imprisons	empowers

continued on the next page

continued from the previous page

promotes dependency	promotes independence
intrudes	respects
pushes	supports
excludes	includes
is status oriented	is free and open
insists on obedience	encourages growth and development
often claims ultimate authority	recognizes a greater power/God/Deity
offers shortcuts	offers integration
seeks personal gratification	affirms Divine Order, along with the good of all concerned

After studying thousands of cases, I can confirm that the notion of many worlds is more real than we can imagine, yet insufficient to accommodate the territory. A "frame" exists that holds everything together. We are born knowing this; it is part of the original template in our temporal lobes. That frame "holds together" by keeping in balance the fabric of space (the light and the dark of matter) with the etheric folds of mind (the light and the dark of spirit). During otherworld journeys we can slip into and be surrounded by the curve and bend of space and/or the stretchy folds of ether. Not everyone is aware of what they are experiencing, but many are. This framework can be recognized through the folds of thoughtform bands. These bands, if viewed as a panorama, look like horizontal planes that curve or bend around what exists. In and through these horizontal folds are worlds within worlds. Vertical passageways (like slits or chutes) are part of the arrangement; they enable a quicker ascension or descension through the folds. In between, filling the entire dynamic, is a state of suspension (sort of like the colloidal state) where a type of non-energetic Presence holds or releases as needed to maintain overall balance. This Presence (consciousness) maintains the frame.

Have I lost you? How else can I describe this panorama and how it applies to our otherworld journeys, what we see, the experiences we have, the beings we meet?

OTHERWORLD ENVIRONMENTS, MANIFESTATIONS, ENTITIES

Horizontal Folds: Provides the vibratory bands where time/space/matter can take on form and shape to populate and celebrate life's rhythms and possibilities. Supposedly, the Horizontal's varied folds or layers (worlds) encircle the earth and are separated by energy frequencies, with each layer representative of a particular growth cycle as consciousness advances or declines through the experience of earthlife. The twelve heavens and twelve hells are here (exact number depends on one's culture or religion).

Points of Contact from Horizontal "Worlds": voices, emanations, sounds, odors, feelings, touches, sensings, shapes, memories.

Awareness of Presence from Horizontal "Worlds": thoughtforms, emotional responses, hauntings, medium controls, elementals, imaginary friends, disincarnates, conjured apparitions, plays of light and shadow, energy surges, light balls or tubes, luminosity, "the darkness that knows."

Manifestations from Horizontal "Worlds": wee folk, guides and guardians, angels, gods and goddesses, spirit keepers, masters, demons, aliens, functional or accidental "creations," seductive enchantments, visionary visitations, ghosts, apports, "walk-ins from beyond."

The Vertical: Traditionally referred to as a "passageway" through and beyond the Horizontal Folds, as if leaving the confines of time/space/matter. Ascending the Vertical is supposedly a sign of evolution or an evolving consciousness; descending the Vertical, a sign of devolution or a devolving consciousness.

Typical Imagery: Single or dominant image of a pillar or column, hourglass, huge tree with roots and branches, ray or beam of light, upward (or downward) path/road/stairway/ladder, pairs of cones or vortexes/cyclones (one inverted over the other with spouts or points touching or nearly so). Whatever shape taken, the resulting image is always vertical and always dominates the scene, be that of a dream, painting, or visionary experience.

In Between/Suspension: Traditionally referred to as "unifying with total Oneness." Sanctity of all sanctity is said to be encountered here—a numinous experience of all knowing, all love, all joy, all peace—with the Source of All Being.

Typical Experience: Any imagery or abstracts are temporary and quickly dissolve once the experiencer is at ease—instant illumination, enlightenment, music sweeps, brilliance, God/Allah/Deity.[129]

Did this help? I hope so, because there really aren't the right words in the English language to explain how space can curve and bend and how thought-forms as a substance can fold to form layers or bands of energy. In case it isn't obvious by now, I can see these folds, and so can a lot of other experiencers.

CHAPTER TWENTY

BRAIN SHIFT: DEEP STRUCTURES

"From the very beginning, life has evolved as if there were a goal to attain, and as if this goal were the advent of the human conscience."

—LECOMTE DU NOÜY, PH.D.

The near-death phenomenon and other impactful transformations of consciousness are outplays of deep brain structures that reveal how the brain develops through patterns of culture and belief, to support the thrust of mind and soul in an advancement toward higher modes of development and evolvement.

Allow me to back up what I just said by re-examining near-death scenarios, cultural differences, heaven/hell states, temporal lobes, the limbic system, the pineal gland, sensitivity, DNA, and "things dark." There is more to be said about all of them.

DEEP STRUCTURES IN NEAR-DEATH SCENARIOS

In a paper published in the *Journal of Near-Death Studies*, Jeffrey Long, M.D., and Janice Miner Holden, Ed.D., made this statement:[130] "Virtually all NDE investigators agree that the similarities between NDEs are far more impressive than their differences . . . they affirm the 'deep structure' of NDEs that is not lost in their surface structure variations across individual developmental level, culture, and life experience. The same features reported by adult NDErs have been reported also by child NDErs." True.

They buttressed their point by comparing the fact that elements of actual scenarios always appear in a certain and same order with Noam Chomsky's discovery that the superficial diversity yet underlying uniformity of grammar worldwide is an example of deep and surface brain structures.[131]

Is it really true that elements in a near-death scenario always appear in a certain and same order like grammar does? Although the basic patterning has remained consistent over time and throughout the world, we cannot claim that *all* aspects of near-death states have been so consistent (the media hype about the Moody model, first published in 1975, altered the universality of some elements, like tunnels and judgment).

I believe that what Long and Holden are referring to is the "stereotypical" near-death experience in both popular myth and research fact, which bypasses a large number of narratives that differ. You cannot depend on questionnaires plus some interviews to supply enough data. This is why I remain distrustful of emailed cases published "as is" on websites. Since my work was never informed by the Moody model nor NDE Research Scales, my four types of patterns accommodate brief experiences of maybe one or two elements—the warmth of darkness as well as light, and scenarios that arrange themselves in varied ways. What I found is that the experiencer's conceptual level of reality provides the initial core or basics of what is accessed, experienced, and later altered by the episode. Once that conceptual level is altered, the "floor" (deep structures) of the brain changes.

Yes, language is sequential; still, elements in near-death states, although appearing linear and ordered, can be and often are experienced simultaneously.

DEEP STRUCTURES IN CULTURAL DIFFERENCES

Carol Zaleski has studied near-death accounts from medieval and modern times. She wrote: "What both critics and researchers failed to notice was the striking evidence for the cultural shaping of near-death experience. They were unaware that what we call 'near-death experience' today is nothing new. . . . [P]eople who return from death, bringing back eyewitness testimony about the other world, can be found in nearly every religious tradition; and although they have many similar features, such reports invariably portray this experience in ways that conform to cultural expectations."[132]

Consider this from Stephen E. Potthoff, Ph.D: "The profound role the NDEs of early Christian martyrs played in shaping views about the afterlife is also apparent in the construction and decoration of early Christian churches throughout the Mediterranean."[133]

America, Canada, Scandinavia, Australia, some European and South American countries, South Africa, and Israel are some of the locales from which the most uplifting and radiant near-death experience accounts originated. Cases from other countries tend to center around expectations, afterlife beliefs, and judgments/taboos of that culture (even with children). In China, for instance, experiencers are often confused by out-of-body experiences, lights, seeing the deceased, and having expanded abilities afterward. They tend to apologize for things like this, or ignore such elements. Muslims from predominately Islamic countries have been known to punish experiencers if they dare to talk about having had a near-death episode.

Allan Kellehear, Ph.D. has focused a great deal of his work on cases from Asia and the Pacific region. He's also studied Native Americans and various preliterate hunter-gatherer peoples.[134] He notes that out-of-body experiences are common throughout, as are reports of supernatural beings and many worlds; few experiencers describe anything like a tunnel; people with nonlinear beliefs do not have life reviews (e.g., for Australian Aborigines, life is like a Mobius strip—you are born and born and born—an unending wraparound); life reviews are a cultural function of individuality, reflecting one's interior self and linear concept of time (in many cultures the "collective" or group consensus predominates); and episode descriptions cannot be separated from the language used to describe them—the culture itself provides the crucial components.

Kellehear's work implies that the scenario components themselves may reflect evolutionary changes in the deeper structures of the human brain and how it functions. Other researchers disagree. One compared the accounts of English speakers with non-English speakers, using several translators. From this study he claimed that no such anomaly exists—that cases worldwide consist of the same basic elements.[135] I would argue that just because an interpreter can speak English doesn't mean he or she can *think* in English, nor does it mean that the non-English experiencer can either relate to or understand given elements in the Moody model (e.g., what has been found with the Chinese). Claiming that "everything fits" necessitates thorough, in-depth, and observational follow-ups. Questionnaires are never enough, no matter how cleverly designed.

DEEP STRUCTURES IN HEAVEN/HELL STATES

There is an undeniable longing in all of us for paradise, for a world or heaven we somehow know inside our deepest self. We have been there before and we want to go back. Mythologies and novels explore this memory. Shamans train to visit these very worlds. Religious clerics hold to revelations from sacred texts. Intertwined between such approaches are millions of people of every age who actually and personally witnessed the etheric, the spirit worlds of light and dark. Generalizations like "heaven is good" and "hell is bad" miss entirely the utter realness of what these people experienced and how that affected them. For example, the life review in near-death accounts nullifies the cultural and religious insistence that Satan is the personification of evil ("Satan" in Aramaic, the language of Jesus, actually means "crazy thinking"). What case after case make clear is that we seem more likely to be punished *by our sins* than because of them, and that we each have a part to play in what happens to us. Sterling members of society have more distressing episodes than do murderers. This implies that many of us are disconnected from our inner self, the true us. You could say that "we get what we need" because one's deeper response appears to direct much of the scope of what may be encountered during a near-death state.

I have noticed that imagery arranges itself around whatever it will take to impress, shake up, reassure, or challenge experiencers. The type of imagery is not as important as its intensity and the individual's response to that intensity. This explains, at least to me, why life reviews are mostly absent in non-industrialized societies.

Nonetheless, there is yet another angle to images of heaven and hell . . . and it focuses on the power of archetypes.

Let me say at the outset that the "need factor" in cases of near-death states is quite evident. But there are two need factors—one for the individual and one for the masses. Both can be encountered in transformational episodes of any type. The individual version of need has been addressed (the "unfinished business" of whatever we hide, deny, repress, or forget). The collective version magnifies the concerns and needs of humankind itself. Carl Jung had a name for this sense of the collective; he called it "mass mind." It is in this collective sum of human consciousness that archetypes reside.

Jung wrote that archetypes ("symbols with meaning") become energized by stress, hopes, dreams, wishes, and during transformational states. They can become so energized, wrote Jung, that they can take on a life of their own and exist outside of individual consciousness. He called them "psychoid factors,"[136] and used that term to describe a process that bridges the gap between the psychological world and objective reality. He explained how, under certain conditions, archetypes could become physically real in objective space. His examples were fairies, demons, angels, spiritual manifestations—and he explained how when a person sees a strange physical reality, the individual projects his or her fears/needs/desires onto what is seen to give it meaning. Since our eyesight takes in only a small percentage of the electromagnetic spectrum, it would not be a stretch to believe that "beings" could live in areas normally ultra or infra to our sight.

So what exists in this collective reality? Almost every religious and spiritual tradition teaches that good and evil, heaven and hell, light and darkness, Creator and Destroyer, are to be found there. By facing this, even just small bits of it, we can begin to fathom the whole of humankind—right through the journey of self to the light of revelation. Symbolic archetypes "shadow" the work ahead of us—first for self, and then for others. These meaningful symbols give us perspective and purpose at the cost of radical honesty. This second need factor and our willingness to face its ramifications give us the freedom we long for— true paradise.

This deeper structure underscores the vastness of spirit and the thought-form layers of heaven and hell. It is never just "you and me" that is revealed; it's the sum of us and our Source. Oneness can only be viable when it includes the whole.

DEEP STRUCTURES IN TEMPORAL LOBES

Little ones often lose their bonding with parents after near-death states, and imprint instead to larger strata of that which is present at core levels (the original templates of the temporal lobe libraries). Babies and toddlers initially see Deity as the archetypal father figure with an entourage of winged ones until they begin to question that image—and question they do. A deviation I found with skin tones of religious figures, however, suggests that something else might be at play.

That deviation did not seem to be one at first: child experiencers, regardless of ethnic background, tended to be accurate, at least historically, about the skin coloring of any religious or holy figure they saw (a remarkable finding)—except for Buddha. They always saw him with a yellowish cast to his skin (Oriental/Asian) rather than more Caucasian (Buddha was from India). Did I make a mistake in my sessions with them, was I careless, did I somehow influence these children with something I thought? Recently I learned that explorers have been able to trace "Bon," the Tibetan version of what we now call Buddhism, to cave drawings in China, existent thousands of years before the birth of Buddha. Were the children linking back to this ancient depiction of what Buddhists later became?

I cannot explain odd deviations, but other researchers encounter them, too. A researcher in England was puzzled by an experiencer who was greeted in the near-death state by a half-human, half-elk man. Yes, the greeter had the head of an elk. Although anomalies seldom occur, the fact that they occur at all begs the question—why?

Experiencer narratives are amazingly accurate, many verified. Deviations? Those I know about seem purposeful and serve a function—like living greeters (once the experiencer is more at ease, the living disappear, and are replaced by imagery typical of near-death states). Perhaps these are another form of psychoid factors or shadowy archetypes that invite us to ask more questions. Or, deviations may simply be examples of mind play, where the mind itself, now freed from former constraints, may experiment with other ways of utilizing the brain organ.

I'd like to think the latter is true because I have witnessed so many unique ways experiencers can now use their brain. One is parallel processing. Some experiencers are able to engage in utterly different streams of thought and reasoning simultaneously, without skipping or confusing a single detail. Examples: the entire charting system I used in Appendix III of *Future Memory*, each item a key to the basic tenets of existence and mind, life/death/eternity, was thought of and developed without any effort or desire on my part . . . while I was delivering a talk on near-death experiences to a crowd from Stiles For Relaxation Bookstore, Portland, Oregon.[137] Bill, a child experiencer, examines things and solves problems in a way that suggests that he has a parallel-processing system instead of a brain. He says most problems get broken down somewhere in his brain; the various portions of each are attacked by different subparts of his brain and the solution is integrated and put together with no conscious effort or control on his part.[138]

Remember the experiments with the Mind Mirror in chapter 17? Dowsers were searching for what the "dowsing mode" is, when they discovered a brain-wave pattern that showed the synchronization of the highest and lowest electrical outputs in the brain, suggesting that certain dowsers were fully conscious while in deep sleep states: the notion of "active rest." Near-death experiencers who "download" information or "slip" into otherworldly realms afterwards exhibit (at least from what I have seen) that same or similar brain-wave pattern. Only a few dowsers were found to be so gifted.

With experiencers, my finding that 42 percent of adults and 65 percent of children who exhibited what I saw as brain waves of "active rest" suggests that this type of patterning may be a common aftereffect of the transformational process. It will take clinical testing to verify this, of course; still, if my observation continues to hold up, we may be faced with having to redefine the temporal lobes and how they function, the limbic system, and the brain itself. The *axis mundi* or "world tree" (the archetype that separates spiritual imagery from earthly/human affairs) is rooted in the original template of the temporal lobes. As the brain alters function, so the world tree branches out to encompass farther and deeper reaches of what exists beyond the definition of what is possible.

DEEP STRUCTURES IN THE LIMBIC SYSTEM

The brain is a work in progress. Brain wiring and brain structure are malleable; one hemisphere can take over the duties of the other if there is an injury.[139] In an interview, Michael Merzenich, M.D., of the University of California, San Francisco, said: "We now know that the qualities that define us at one moment in time come from experiences that shape the physical and functional brain, and that continue to shape it as long as we live."[140]

The brain continually reorganizes itself. It is so malleable that many scientists today consider it to be a "plastic" organ. You literally create your brain from the input you receive. Doing this also creates structures of energy that enable your mind to shape the very thing that is being perceived. The idea that we create our own reality stems from this brain/mind function. The Akashic libraries don't just *contain* knowledge; they *are* knowledge. They exist as a presence. The deep structures of our temporal lobes (the original template) directly relate to mass mind while actively supporting the span of individual preference. That template reflects focused thought and intention (what we concentrate on, we give power to) as well as the wider view of collective reality (what we do to the few, we do to the many).

The brain recharges itself daily, and creates new brain cells constantly; a single idea lights up the entire brain for a brief while. Brain studies have identified a "mesolimbic pathway" deep in the emotional part of the brain that produces feel-good chemicals like serotonin and lights up whenever we seek to serve or help another, or make a positive gesture in the world around us. Guess what gets activated in near-death states? This very helper's high, with no evidence that serotonin is involved. Guess what happens to the limbic system? It accelerates and expands and deepens its functions to the extent that feelings literally become the language of the soul.

Why else do you suppose near-death narratives are so important in hospice to relieve the fear of death? Because of experiencer stories of life after death? Not hardly. That deep emotional part of our brain orders the very structure of molecules in our cells. The higher the frequency of energy present, the greater the resulting coherence . . . until the union of heartbeats prove to the dying that there is nothing to fear.

DEEP STRUCTURES IN THE PINEAL GLAND

That tiny "pinecone" in the middle of the brain and behind the eyes is the pineal gland—the master endocrine gland. It boasts the highest concentration of vitamin B-12 in the body, as well as the trace mineral cobalt. Its magnetic sensor reads the earth's magnetic pulses, solar/lunar cycles, and energy charges while acting as a valve controlling the flow of memories into consciousness. Similar to the human eye, the pineal is light-sensitive and secretes the chemical melatonin that governs our twenty-four-hour sleep/wake cycle and our sexual cycles—from puberty to menopause. Pineal melatonin levels peak at 3 AM.

In case you didn't know, melatonin, the most primitive universal pigment in living systems, directs a huge number of biochemical interactions, "eating" light as it converts light waves into other forms of energy for maintaining the evolution of matter. Melatonin is said to act like a "black hole" or "phase space" wherein the brain's holographic patterning is stored. If you consider ours "a looking glass universe," as did Karl Pribram, M.A., Ph.D, then the observer meets the observed in this holographic black hole.[141]

Let's not forget glial cells. They insulate connecting cables that carry electrochemical impulses between brain neurons. Neurons only account for 10 percent of the brain; glial cells make up the difference at 90 percent. That means that glial cells are super important. They are electrically active and, as a field, have a memory beyond what is stored in the genes. Glial cells and neuro-melatonin "dance" together throughout the limbic system and the pineal. They act as light receptors and light converters, providing an environment where enough "contrast" can be generated to enable us to recognize things. We see not just because we have eyes, but because we have biophysical conduits/backups that can translate and pick apart electrical waves. Without the contrast these conduits provide, eyesight would be of little use.

Combine the deeper functions of melatonin, glial cells, and the pineal gland—to "manufacture" the spirit molecule, DMT—and you have the perfect parties for facilitating the soul's movement in and out of the body through birth, death, and higher levels of the meditative experience.

DEEP STRUCTURES AND SENSITIVITY

Dig deep enough and you'll discover that surprises can make sense. Take pain, for instance. I've yet to find an individual who experienced pain during their near-death episode—fear maybe, or awe, horror, excitement, love, anger

... but not physical pain. Leave your body and presto, pain disappears—*but not your feelings.* You are more objective and less emotional, but, for the most part, your feelings are still intact. When this happened to me, I noticed that the presence of physical pain dissolved the instant my need for physical form ceased. I still had feelings because I still had a vivid memory of my feelings, what they were, and why they mattered. That memory identified me as me (notice limbic/pineal involvement here).

During each of my three episodes and afterward, I came to recognize "memory" as the primary mover and shaper of both physicality and personality. I saw that memory, any memory, existed first as a charge in an energetic matrix. If the charge was strong enough (with more input feeding into it), the matrix spread into a thought/memory field, perhaps enveloping other and similar fields. (How I uncovered the history of Goddess Runes is an example of how one can recognize and work with memory fields: I felt and sensed such a presence, followed where the "memory" of it led me, and was guided into research channels where I could verify realities.) I noticed this same penchant with most other experiencers: we often "know" things because we connect with the memory of them ... which can include the past as well as the future.

This sensitivity to memory (those energetic thought fields), enables experiencers to appear unusually "psychic," when in truth, their new or expanded sensitivity aligns more easily with other stratas of resonance (what vibrates together comes together).

If this sounds familiar to you, you've probably heard of Rupert Sheldrake, Ph.D. and his discovery about "morphogenic" or M-fields.[142] Sheldrake, a plant biologist, rediscovered what scientists previous to him had proved: "that memory fields, like magnetic or electrical fields, were capable of transmitting information across time." He noticed that genes alone could not explain how plants, animals, and life itself develops—but memory fields can. From this observation, he went on to suggest that living things are shaped by a sense of memory beyond that inherent in genes. That memory can be accessed through invisible morphic fields—the same way radio stations can be tuned in. Sheldrake claims that nature relies on these morphic fields to shape our entire world. A chicken is a chicken because of how sperm and egg align with the "channel" that broadcasts the information needed to direct the chicken's formation . . . same with trees, grass, and people. Everything takes its form from a memory field, a field that alters as its "members" evolve.

Each time Sheldrake's theory is tested, it works. Are M-fields tucked away in what is called the zero-point field? To consider this we need to combine DNA and things dark with the power of memory.

DEEP STRUCTURES IN DNA AND THINGS DARK

The scope of sensitivity many experiencers gain verifies for me that the memory fields we come to access, read, and interact with are layered. There are levels to them, just like broadcast channels. You enter into a frequency you can align with, hence the validity of "resonance" (vibrational integrity). Those fields contain the secret of life's ability to exist, maintain itself, and expand. Amazingly, most near-death experiencers consider this so-called secret old hat.

To quote Lynne McTaggart, author of *The Field*: "Researchers discovered that the Zero Point Field contains the blueprint for our existence. Everything and everyone is connected with one another—from man to matter—can be traced back to a collection of electric charges that are continually in contact with this endless sea of energy. Our interaction with this field determines who we are, will become, and have been. The field is the alpha and omega of our existence."[143] ("Zero-point field," incidentally, is a scientific term that refers to the fact that at absolute zero, energy can still be measured.)

Recent discoveries in vacuum physics indicate that the Akashic field has its equivalent to the zero-point field which underlies space[144] . . . that the quantum vacuum is actually the origin of mind and matter; the zero-point field its carrier of information; the material world a vortex within it. I believe that the quantum vacuum is what near-death experiencers and mystics call "the void" and is the source of "dark light." The vacuum is organized and informed, operating as a data bank for the soul.

When we speak of Akashic records, quantum field, zero-point field, quantum vacuum, and morphic field, we are in essence recognizing the necessity of "the invisible dark." Our brain functions more like a radio than a computer in the way it receives what is broadcasted from this sea of darkness that fills the in between of things and provides the fabric that interconnects everything. The in between is considered that which contains and embraces and unifies all—the realm of the superconscious mind—where everything becomes more of itself as it converges back into the collective whole. Actually devoid of color, the in between is said to be a network of luminous shimmer.

I am captured by the fact that so few experiencers have anything negative to say about things that are dark. Child experiencers sometimes call the dark or black light in their episode "the darkness that knows;" they relate to it as if it were a function of "mother" in the way the darkness cradles and guides and maintains "potential" (the illusion of structure).

Things dark: the vortex, the void, the vacuum, dark energy, dark matter, dark light, black hole. Let's give this some perspective by taking a look at what the NASA satellite known as Wilkinson Microwave Anistropy Probe (WMAP) found during its orbit in deep space. The universe is made of three things: 4 percent ordinary atoms, 23 percent dark matter (nature unknown), and 73 percent dark energy (equally mysterious whose antigravity effect is causing the speedup of our universe's expansion).[145] Scientists worldwide have noted that the constant energy exchange of all subatomic matter with "The Field" accounts for the stability of the hydrogen atom plus the stability of all matter. If "The Field" ceased to exist, the suspicion is that all matter in the universe would collapse in on itself and disappear.

Do experiencers of a transformation of consciousness really interact with "The Field"? Absolutely. The memory fields they encounter, on any level or in any layer, are alive. The transformative state itself operates like an interference beam bouncing off holographic images. The off-angle (created by the intensity of the episode) shakes us free of convention long enough so that our brain, our heart, and our memory shift into other frequencies of vibration (other fields).

The code breaker is our DNA. The coiled design of our DNA, its vibrational spin and built-in electronics, make it the perfect antenna for communication exchanges between our body, environment, universe, and the memory fields of mind and matter. DNA is a biological Internet operated by the needs and desires of consciousness. Only 3 percent of our DNA has been identified and mapped. The other 97 percent (or "junk" DNA, as it's called), constitutes the sensitivity essential for the interaction and interplay we have with "mind" (the intelligence that pervades every jot and tittle of creation). This Internet knows all the codes. What we need to learn is how to use the "mouse" better. Transformative episodes do that. They give us a glimpse of the vastness of our world, how it operates, and who we really are.

It's all consciousness.

The universe is awake. It is we who have been sleeping.

CHAPTER TWENTY-ONE

SPIRIT SHIFT: SECOND BIRTH

"You see, if matter ultimately dissolves into octaves of light, and light dissolves into octaves of consciousness, and consciousness dissolves into octaves of reality, then matter, light, consciousness, and reality are all interdependent like an ecosystem. And, like an ecosystem, if you change one element you affect the whole."

—ERNEST V. MBENKUM

Ernest Mbenkum grew up in a small tribe in West Africa, later moving to London. He told me: "I've had my own share of NDEs, and, frankly, I do not believe I will ever learn anything from any school on this planet." Like a typical experiencer, his mind quickly grasps quantum realities. He has devised systems of thinking whereby he can give sound advice to business people, design clever websites, and teach what he has found of value to others—without seeming "strange."

There are millions of near-death experiencers like Mbenkum who, in their own unique way, are making a difference in the world . . . after having discovered how to stabilize and control their own differences. What experiencers go through feels to them like a second birth. Some go as far as to change their name afterward.

I have long claimed that near-death states are both a movement through brain (head/gut) and a movement through mind (memory fields/

consciousness). They are both literal and symbolic—objectively physical while at the same time subjectively spiritual. You cannot separate this polarity from the phenomenon. To understand near-death states, you must keep them in balance with what they demonstrate and convey. Seeking only to dissect them is no more effective than preaching their glories.

In the last twenty chapters of this book I have carefully laid groundwork based on field research and study. I have deviated somewhat when I admitted I could actually see energy fields/waveforms (as many experiencers can). Now it is time for me to summarize what I have gleaned from over thirty-three years of work in near-death studies and the decade prior to that when I researched transformations of consciousness, and move the subject up to the next level. The rest of this book does that; it draws from a larger venue and the models and patterns that apply. I begin with this statement: *those who go through a transformative state truly are born again.*

ELEMENTS OF A SECOND BIRTH IN CHILDREN

Note: this is not true in all cases; presented here as a summary statement.

- Those hardly born can undergo what appears to be a second birth.

- Temporal lobe expansion can precede or accelerate natural development.

- The learning curve can reverse itself, placing abstract conceptualization before foundational understanding.

- IQ enhancements and faculty extensions can accompany heightened spatial/nonverbal/sensory-dynamic thinking, giving rise to creative problem solving.

- Sensing multiples can open up whole new worlds of possibility and new dimensions of what is real.

- Parental bonding lessens, with imprinting to the other side a likely result.

- A new or different sense of self and of origin becomes the norm.

- Brain shifts can jump-start "the engine of evolution," enabling the human species to adapt to ever-changing needs and pressures.

- Spirit shifts can advance attitudes and behaviors toward social justice and moral integrity, as compassion and caring replace the obsessions that drive greed.

A thought: advanced technology is returning increasing numbers of children from death's door, who wind up being ideally suited for . . . advanced technology.

ELEMENTS OF A SECOND BIRTH IN ADULTS

Note: this is not true in all cases; presented here as a summary statement.

- Adult experiencers can suddenly appear younger and feel reborn.

- IQ enhancements and faculty extensions can accompany heightened spatial/nonverbal/sensory-dynamic thinking, giving rise to creative problem solving and a more active sense of memory.

- An awareness of "future" can clarify the earth world of time and space by engendering "rehearsals" that provide for advance preparation in meeting life's demands.

- Sensing multiples can open up whole new worlds of possibility and new dimensions of what is real.

- Brain shifts can jump-start "the engine of evolution," enabling experiencers of any age to adapt to ever-changing needs and pressures.

- Spirit shifts can advance attitudes and behaviors toward social justice and moral integrity as compassion and caring replace the obsessions that drive greed.

- The higher mind can emerge as the higher brain develops, thanks to the structural/chemical/electrical changes that occur in the brain after a brain shift.

A thought: the more intense the shift, the less tolerance or desire one has for alcohol, tobacco, drugs, chemical products, excesses of sugar and meat.

PRE-FRONTAL LOBES IN THE BRAIN

The pre-frontal lobes (backing up the forehead and sides of the forehead) are called the "wings of the brain." They represent the highest and best in brain development throughout the human family, and comprise the seat of judgment, morals, empathy, compassion, and well-being. The pre-frontals take about nine months after a child is born to be fully formed, yet they continue to develop until the child is around seven, undergoing a "growth spurt" at puberty. These lobes are directly connected to the heart and limbic system, and unite all brain structures as if a "governor" of body systems.

They also have a direct influence on spiritual imagery and sacred symbols. Pre-frontals cannot handle more than seven items at once, plus or minus two. Strings of numbers, like social security numbers, cannot exceed seven, plus or minus two. If they did, you couldn't remember them. In a strange way this is equally true with the sacred and spiritual. Of such traditions, the "sacred seven" can be traced to this core arrangement order in our brain and in how our body formed around that ordering. All symbolic archetypes and myths are based on this.[146]

Also, many of the "new" children (those born since about 1982[147]) have prominent foreheads, some extending beyond the tip of their nose.[148] This is an indication of exceptional pre-frontal development and suggests that these children might possess higher levels of consciousness, love, altruism, and a connection to things spiritual.

There is evidence of this type of pre-frontal expansion and re-ordering, sans outward curving foreheads, among experiencers of near-death and other transformative states. This is significant. Don't confuse the "helper's high" that occurs when the chemical serotonin is produced in the mesolimbic pathway with growth spurts that change the makeup of the pre-frontal lobes. These growth spurts are really big.

Why do you suppose that universally a transformation of consciousness leads to compassion, caring, and unconditional love? When the wings of the brain open up and take flight, the second born become altruistic—and drawn to the sacred.

BIOPHYSICAL LIGHT

In a study of terminally ill patients, physicians at George Washington University observed that immediately before death the brains of the dying showed a spike in electrical activity. Some researchers pointed out that this was physiological evidence supporting the reality of near-death experiences. The study shows that despite the approach of death, the brain demonstrates a remarkable level of activity, not the simple fade-out that one might expect.[149]

Each of us possesses biophysical light. Bone, for instance, has a piezoelectric effect just like crystals. As we have seen, significant numbers of near-death experiencers display electrical sensitivity in the way their energy interferes with electrical equipment and electromagnetic fields. Science tells us that the light coming out of living things is coherent (well-ordered). Coherent light can magnify power hundreds and thousands of times over—which is why thoughts are so powerful—and why those who have undergone a transformation of consciousness exhibit brighter auras (energy fields) than most people.

Mystics point out that the Akashic field is really the ether, and as such is the fifth element (said to contain all frequency patterns and relationships to those patterns—the memory fields). Pythagoras, an ancient Greek philosopher, spoke of the same thing. This ocean of light is said to fill the universe, ourselves, and everything else. Have you ever seen a living blood cell through one of those special microscopes used for live cell analysis? I have. It is bright with light. So is every particle of us. Interestingly, the more spiritual and loving we are, the greater our light. Biophysical light expands into radiant spirit light when this happens.

SPIRIT SHIFT

We humans are programmed to evolve. We possess the exact apparatus we need to do so; when triggered it will advance that growth. The elements that constitute the pattern of a spirit shift appear as follows.

- There is a universal form of stimulation that enables the brain to be altered, shifted, and restructured: Kundalini/Ku/Christos power currents.

- There is a universal passageway through the brain that leads to pure unadulterated consciousness: the limbic system.

- There is a universal section in the brain that creates patterning (overleafs) so thoughtforms can take on familiar shapes for engaging interactions and response: temporal lobes.

- There is a universal source of light receptors and light converters in the brain that provide the environment where enough contrast can be generated to promote recognition: glial cells, neuro-melatonin.

- There is a universal switch inside the brain that can shift bodily functions and cycles to accommodate the rhythms of spirit and the reality of memory fields: the pineal gland.

- There is a universal place in the brain where healing and becoming more loving and altruistic takes wing: the pre-frontal lobes.

- There is a universal condition affecting the brain with enough magnitude and strength to ensure the expansion and enhancement of consciousness itself: a light flash.

- There is a universal phenomenon that transcends the human experience and reveals the soul's experience: enlightenment.

As we have the physical endowments we need to assure the continuance of life (procreation, birth), we also have the physical endowments we need to assure the evolution of life (renewal, rebirth).

None of this is imaginary.

Spirituality is real.

CHAPTER TWENTY-TWO

SPIRIT SHIFT: BIOLOGICAL IMPERATIVE

"Evolution is the emergence of that which already is in form, in an ever-upward spiraling. The whole process of evolution is to produce a being who can consciously co-operate with the Evolutionary Principle, which is Pure Spirit."

—ERNEST HOLMES

We are forever seeking an ecstatic high because of our subconscious drive to advance the species . . . just as we are forever seeking an orgasmic high because of a subconscious need to procreate the species. The high of sex and the high of enlightenment activate energy surges and bodily systems that seem similar, yet are vastly different.

The brain is hard-wired to have otherworldly mystical and religious/spiritual experiences. We have all of the physical equipment needed to produce these ecstatic states. But this equipment is not causal. It is auxiliary. So is the procreative system. Our sex organs do not cause procreation of themselves. Only when stimulated do they respond accordingly.

Brain shifts serve to accelerate evolutionary advancements in the human family. They stimulate increased brain capacity and access to mind. Geometric images in natural patternings (visions, dreams, art), if radiant or luminous, are often signs or signals of the higher brain/higher mind in mutual reception.

Evolution is not just adaptation to changing needs and environments. True evolution is geared toward improving and perfecting form so powerful bioelectrical currents can be accessed and utilized without harm. That which underlies Creation is a force that stretches, pops, shimmers, and hums as it moves, alters, changes, transforms, mutates—from the particle to the wave and back again—the same and yet different . . . ever spiraling as if "The Movement of God's Thought." There are near-death experiencers who claimed that once on the other side of death they felt as if they were inside a giant brain processing thought, as if we were all projections of that thought, and so too were planets, asteroids, solar systems, and the universe itself. These testimonies and others like them imply that Creation is *exactly* designed to produce a consciousness capable of participating in its own creation.

There is a biological imperative for life to exist and to continuously evolve in form, capacity, and intellect—towards ever-higher order.

The law of chaos explains how this imperative works: when existing systems become disordered, an underlying order that appears as randomness emerges as a new order.

THE BIOLOGICAL IMPERATIVE BEHIND TRANSFORMATIVE STATES

We are not here by accident. The vast majority of near-death experiencers and those like them return convinced of that—that there is a "plan." Most call it "God's Plan" or that of Deity. Whether or not you agree with what this implies, the work I have done over the decades has shown me that the lens through which we view transformative states is much too small.

Forgive me for repeating, but I intend to do a lot of that in this chapter, as I want to make certain you recognize the patterns that form from the various details I have been giving you. It's the patterns that tell us the larger story, unveiling one surprise after another. Transformations of consciousness are not what you think they are. They are more.

Look again at how these experiences happen: *suddenly or under turbulent conditions* ("baptisms of the holy spirit," near-death episodes, shamanic vision quests, kundalini/ku breakthroughs, from certain types of head trauma or being hit by lightning) *or from slower, more tranquil means* (spiritual or religious disciplines, rituals/worship, meditation, mindfulness techniques, or, because in a prayerful and sincere state of mind, an individual desires to become a better person).

Look again at the universal patterning that spreads out from them: "Initial," few elements, more of an introduction for the individual to other ways of perceiving reality (a stimulus); "Unpleasant or Hellish," distressing, as if a confrontation with distortions in one's own attitudes and beliefs (a healing); "Pleasant or Heavenly," loving, as if a realization of how important life is and how every effort that one makes, counts (a validation); and "Transcendent," luminous, as if an encounter with Oneness and the collective whole of humankind (enlightenment).

Look again at the mosaic of physiological and psychological aftereffects which evidence not only changes that follow, but the possibility of transmutation. The end result of integration can be spectacular: more intelligent, healthier, able to heal, more patient and loving, happier, wiser, more spiritual and spiritually guided, self-governing, creative, innovative, highly intuitive with unusual sensitivities, service-oriented, open-minded, possess a certain calmness with rapid change and the coming of death. These traits lie in stark contrast to what most societies consider to be "normal" behavior.

Mull over what you have just read in light of this very big surprise: *the physiological and psychological traits that many experiencers develop may be and often are passed on to future generations.*

Earlier in my work I disagreed with this notion. I even found cases where, in my estimation, such an idea had no truth in fact; I said so in several of my books. Then I started to discover the opposite: children of experiencers who must have inherited their parents' unique characteristics because such traits were not present in older generations of the family. In many of these cases, those same traits also passed from that child to grandchildren (again, the only link being the older grandparent who had had a transformative experience).

Admittedly, DNA is altered by the intensity of unusual or unique experiences. Yet, thanks to scientists like Emma Whitelaw (who worked with mice), findings now show that a child's DNA can bear the physical "marks" of a parent's experience **plus** the consequences of that experience. Adaptation can actually occur in **a single generation,** making it hereditary.[150] This finding puts transformative experiences squarely in the lap of evolutionary processes that advance the human species . . . and in ways we may not have previously recognized.

Hold on to this thought as we explore broad sweeps of time, searching for repeating patterns that mimic the transformative process—individually and culturally.

EVOLUTION'S UPS AND DOWNS

Some years ago I hunkered down in a library (there really are people who do that sort of thing), curious to see if any important historical figures might have had a near-death experience as a child. This is what I looked for: a serious illness or accident between birth and age fifteen that nearly claimed the individual's life; marked differences in behavior afterward; the effect of aftereffects (especially bouts of depression intermingled with brilliance, sensitivity to sound/sun/medications, robust health yet complaints about digestion/allergies, hunger for learning, creative/intuitive, abstract at young ages); and an almost obsessive drive to accomplish a particular task or project.[151]

In that week I found evidence that Abraham Lincoln, Albert Einstein, Queen Elizabeth I, Edward de Vere the 17th Earl of Oxford (whom I now believe to be the real Shakespeare), Wolfgang Amadeus Mozart, Winston Churchill, Black Elk, Walter Russell, and Valerie Hunt all might have had near-death episodes. My sense from this exercise, and what I keep finding elsewhere, is that most of those who made a significant difference in their society, and in the world, had a near-death or transformative episode as a child that inspired their life's work.

You may get bogged down trying to search through historical data about wet/dry/hot/cold weather cycles, earth changes, and pole reversals. With all the sociopolitical unrest versus improvement that occurred, you may begin to wonder if the human family actually spent more time devolving than evolving.[152] But don't stop there. Notice the incredible number of breakout periods of invention and creativity that criss-crossed our planet in wave after wave of upliftment, such as what happened during the Golden Age of Greece. Each major region on earth had its "Culture Bearer," an enlightened and charismatic genius, who brought reason and justice, industry and philosophy to the populace, enabling the refinements of culture to occur (Example:

Huang ti; the legendary "Yellow Emperor" of China[153]). Notice that all the world's great religions formed within the same basic time frame because of Great Lights who taught a better way to live.

Include in this search what we can know of ancient peoples, intelligent habitations, dating back millions of years, and the cyclic rise and fall of great cities and empires. The Mayan Calendar illustrates this, not as some "end of the world" cosmic clock, but rather as a device used to track the development of consciousness on this planet.[154] Esoteric traditions underscore these early claims, as do researchers who have discovered actual relics that predate current conclusions—relics that have repeatedly been tossed off as "mistakes" or "anomalies" by scientists unwilling to study them.[155]

Please note as you glance across the historical landscape "of record" (which must include oral histories, myths, dream recall, and "memories" to be complete), that whenever the human family was at its lowest ebb and seemed to be enveloped in "darkness," "new lights" entered in the form of great teachers, leaders, and messiahs. Were they all suited to their role because they were "Chosen of God" or possessed of a "Divine Destiny," or, because as children or as an adult they were transformed by an experience of "the numinous"? History points to the latter.

The miracle is . . . each transformed individual, adult or child-turned-adult, taught others how to be like them, or to be as if "born again," or as if to have "the new face" of what it means to live in accordance with Higher Truth.

Even more of a miracle is . . . thanks to the modern conveniences of film, books, newspapers, and television, anyone can be exposed to experiencers of transformative states and their personal narratives. This exposure alone can alter and uplift the consciousness of others . . . and it is doing just that.

My research has shown me that near-death and transformative states of consciousness comprise the vehicle that advances the human species. This advancement is a biological imperative. No other form of adaptation or pressure can compare to the power unleashed by a consciousness freed to know Itself.

What I have just said may seem excessively speculative, an unnecessary stretch, that does nothing to advance the point of this book. Au contraire, this is exactly where my research has led me. I now believe this is why we have transformations of consciousness, why we crave them, and what they are for.

THE HEART

When I stated that "no other form of adaptation or pressure can compare with the power unleashed by a consciousness freed to know Itself," I want to also state that the unleashing of that power gains its momentum from the harmonics of the human heart.

In many important ways, the heart is like a fifth brain. Between 60 and 65 percent of all heart cells are neural cells. The heart is the major glandular structure in the body, with an electromagnetic field five thousand times more powerful than that of the brain organ. Shaped like a torus donut, the heart field busily converts one form of energy to another as it generates an infinite number of harmonic waves. These harmonics run throughout all bodily systems and are so sensitive that *they react to conditions four to five minutes before actual occurrence.* This futuristic awareness tells the heart if what's coming is positive or negative so it can prepare. First the heart feels the coming event, then the brain is aware of it, then the eye sees it.[156]

These harmonic waves come into coherence when you feel good, are in love, experience happiness, have bonded with someone in a positive way, or are in a supportive relationship. When the heart's energy coheres, it taps higher energy fields to empower itself, while emoting feelings of love and connectedness. This feeling sense operates like a thinking mind with an unbelievable memory, as the medical community is now discovering with heart transplants: the history of the donor can infuse, even overshadow, the life of the organ recipient.[157] Although cellular memory is true of every cell and body part, a heart transplant can seem as if a "brain transplant."

Heart harmonics entwine worldwide. Our spiritual traditions claim this is so because our heart is the center of our soul. A soul set free by these harmonics serves. The universal law of love translates "Treat others as you would like to be treated." This Golden Rule is the real measure of behavior between peoples. Love propels us, shapes us, heals us, designs our very being, and determines how we evolve. Charles Darwin wrote in his second book that the power of love and moral sensitivity were more important in evolutionary processes than the survival of the fittest and natural selection.[158]

Love, or the lack of it, dominates near-death scenarios. You see the lack of love in unpleasant states (where people are distressed or confused by what they find) and in rueful life reviews. But the fullness of love, being loved, and discovering the power of love layers the overall effect near-death states have on experiencers, their significant others, and anyone who hears about them. It is no exaggeration to say that the majority of near-death experiencers return "in love with love." The love they were bathed in provides the momentum that pushes them over the edge. That love, beyond the descriptions we give it, connects us to All That Is . . . God/Allah/Deity. For just a few seconds or minutes, you were one with The One. That experience of love beyond measure pales anything less. It is challenging for experiencers to "step it down" a few degrees after their episode so as not to freak people out.

The heart's code is love: love of Source, love of others, love of self. Yet we understand the power of love best when we see what it can do through the magic of empathy and compassion. To talk about near-death experiences and transformative states of consciousness is to talk about the heart's ability to expand, embrace, and include the fullness of waveform harmonics—which we recognize as altruism.

CONSCIOUSNESS

Just ask experiencers. They'll tell you that everything they saw, be it bird, flower, grass, rock, river, or mountain. Every swirl of color, every speck of darkness, every skeleton, storm, rage of wind—was alive, full alive, totally conscious and aware of that consciousness. Everything! Nothing is inert.

Scientists are beginning to agree that the universe is looking less like a great machine than a great thought. The consciousness of that thought comprises the full spectrum of visible and invisible realities, the very fabric that underlies vibration, pulse, plasma, and the harmonics of the universal heart becoming aware of itself as it, too, evolves and expands.

As we move closer to a sense of oneness within ourselves, others, and our world, we move into a natural vibratory rhythm of forty cycles per second—a little fast for us now, but we're getting there. In transformative states, and especially in the research now being conducted, we are learning that each human being contains the organizing intelligence of the universe. The structure of how our brain/mind assembly works follows the blueprint of how our universe works. Even cellular biology reveals the mechanisms that bridge mind/body connections, providing us with a molecular basis for consciousness and evolution. There are master switches in our physical body that create the conditions of our body and shift with our changing place in the world. We are continually affected by consciousness, eternally co-existing with all beings in the timeless moment of "now." What is known to one mind is knowable to all minds.

We seem to think that "potential" is dream stuff. I challenge that assessment. My work has shown me that potential is functional. Potential is what causes the shimmer in the Void. It is a pre-energetic, a sense of presence that appears in advance of manifestation. Potential is that functional thought-stream that partners the creative process in actual creation. Without the presence that defines it, creation would lack the energy it needs to order what is intended into directional force fields.

If you don't understand a word I've just said, remember this: potential is a thing, a function—what exists just before consciousness stretches, pops, shimmers, and hums along in its journey from the particle to the wave and back again. Without potential, light waves would never become dense enough to form matter. Potential obeys the need for consciousness, through intention, to reflect Creation's core intelligence.

In near-death and transformative states we become aware of our own and the world's potential. We discover that everything is twice created: first in mind, then in form.

CHAPTER TWENTY-THREE

SPIRIT SHIFT: A NEW MODEL OF EXISTENCE

"Everything you can imagine is real."

—Picasso

Do the math: The global population is about 6.6 billion people. Using the current estimate that 5 percent of persons have had a near-death episode, you wind up with around 330 million experiencers worldwide. Beverly Brodsky, who had such an experience as a child, asks: "Could those of us in this wave be the majority or at least the norm for humans alive on this planet today?"[159]

As if to answer Beverly's question, a study done in the United States, and released in 2009 reported that 49 percent of the population had undergone a sudden awakening—through a near-death state or because of a transcendent, mystical, religious, or spiritual experience—that completely changed the way they viewed life. Changes in physiology were reported as well (i.e., brain function, intuitive ability, quick to heal), and being more altruistic and deeply loving of God/Allah/ Deity. Aftereffects were said to be continuous, as if making new choices based on a new vision was enough to start the process of becoming new.[160]

What is happening to people, especially those influenced or changed by near-death states, is making a tremendous difference in how death is viewed. For instance, information about the phenomenon, along with experiencer narratives, enables the dying to prepare for death, while reassuring loved ones that in some incredible way life does indeed continue.[161] Research on the human biofield affirms this by showing that our field does not dissipate at death; it continues on in a lucid and present form.[162] This encourages the injured, diseased, or confused to prepare for new life through the transformation of self, not the ending of self.

Transformational awakenings, all of them, give us models, new models of how to live, how to think, what to believe. We are made to have these experiences—to become new.

NEW BEHAVIORS

I've talked before about how experiencers change after a transformative episode. This time, I want to be much more specific and focus on what seems to be emerging as a new model of behavior—that is surprisingly consistent. This is no small thing, since millions of people are involved.

Behavior traits:

Glow of some kind—usually to eyes, skin, face

Sensitivity to light and sound

Highly intuitive, know things

Comfortable with things future—future knowing, future memory

Waking up around 3 AM for no reason, and/or, having vivid dreams

Less concerned about privacy

Prefer open windows, open doors—same with closets, curtains, cupboards

Comfortable with silence, often prefer it

Acutely aware of injustice, of people hurting—want to pitch in and help

Animals, birds, and children attracted to them

Dilemmas with money and telling time—prefer "natural clock"

Challenged by contracts, criteria, rules—more open and trusting

Ecumenical, usually at home in any religion—one family, one God

Electrical sensitivity to some degree

Sensitivity to pharmaceuticals, prefer natural/alternative healing methods

Change of eating habits and food preferences—lower blood pressure

More allergies, sensitive to smells and barometric pressure changes

Can slip into depressive states, frustration, anger—yet quickly recover

Use language differently—new interests, new words, new ideas

Smarter, more curious, a hunger for learning

Affinity for nature and ecology, simple things

More loving, while challenged to make and maintain loving relationships

Hear music when no sound is present—the music of existence

Walks and talks with Divine Beings, God/Allah/Deity

Expansive views, more universal in outlook

More detached, less boredom or need to compete

Don't kid yourself. Transformative states are not magic. Aftereffects, although remarkable, take some getting used to. Carmel Bell, who had her near-death experience in 2009 (chapter 14), has this to say about what comes next: "Expect anger. Look for it. Here it comes. Don't think *you* escaped— because you didn't . . . and just to be sure—duck! Everyone expects me to be pleased, amazed, and privileged for having gone through this. I joke and tell my husband that the only reason I don't kill myself is that I would have to talk to *them* again. I am not afraid of dying. I am afraid of being unreasonably annoyed with [spirit] beings who set me an impossible task and then walked away, leaving me to manage it. And people! So many people have changed towards me."

Carmel is new at this. Give her a few more years and she'll catch on ... that transformative states are not magic, nor is there any guarantee with integration. Awakenings, breakthroughs, transformations of consciousness can be tricky. The ego is still involved to some degree. But taken as an overall model of how we can change, the process is extraordinary. We can become living examples of a happier, healthier, more creative individual.

WHY ARE THERE SO MANY OF US?

Millions upon millions of people is a whole lot of folks. We are not just seeing individuals transformed. Today, we are witness to a large segment of the human family switching directions; generations born since around 1982 are born changed similar to near-death kids and the traits they come to display.[163] Mass mind is shifting. We are evolving as a species. So is our planet and our universe.

Some people have likened what is happening to a global near-death experience. Palden Jenkins calls it a "soulquake."[164] He reminds us that the Black Death of the 1340s began a historic shift that eventually evolved into the modern world. The Lisbon earthquake of 1755 is said to have sparked the European Enlightenment. The Tangshan earthquake of 1976 brought an end to the Maoist era in China. Each cataclysm led to unparalleled progress and gains because of how people changed. Who's to say how many had near-death experiences? What will the 2004 Indonesian tsunami, the 2005 Katrina hurricane, and the 2010 Haitian earthquake teach us? New models? Already the human family is focusing on how best to engage locals in cleanup, enforce stricter building codes, reform traditions, support psychological and spiritual assistance, and redesign infrastructure.

Large-scale "soulquakes" are quickening. Astrologers call the "energy punch" of 2010 through 2012 "the perfect storm." We have nothing to compare these energetics with, except maybe in fossil records and memory fields. Hubble just photographed Pluto changing its colors and planets brightening as activity on them increased. Astrophysicists tell us we are at the very beginning of a new cycle of magnetic storms (sunspots) that are due to peak in 2012—with an intensity 30 to 50 percent greater than any of the previous cycles—simultaneously with a galactic alignment that occurs once every 25,920 years. Back up your computer records. Our earth's magnetic field has weakened to the point that a magnetic reversal could occur any day. Are changes this massive cyclical? Of course they are. But not the current lineup of "heavies" populations and technologies must now face. The stage is set for a universal awakening.

You want to know what else is hitting in 2012? The full impact of governments and municipalities being unable to collect needed taxes for basic services during the economic downturn of 2008 and 2009. The Mayan Calendar predicted this time of upheaval. Sounds like a colloidal condition, doesn't it?

History shows us that huge clusters and waves of people expand in consciousness at times when all seems lost and life overwhelms. (When our "nest" is spoiled, we get a chance to rebuild and start anew.) Evolutionary spirals move on the energetics of upswings and downswings. This one is up. So what's happening? A whole lot of folks are transforming into change agents, ready to make a difference. They self-organize easily, as if possessing a collective vision.

I love the title of Paul Hawken's book: *Blessed Unrest: How the Largest Movement in the World Came Into Being and Why No One Saw It Coming.*[165] This "movement" is exactly what I refer to . . . no leaders, no managers in the traditional sense, just people who want to democratize opportunity and knowledge. (Wikipedia is an example of this: a self-organizing Internet database that exceeds the ability of published encyclopedias to update rapidly and accurately.)

When we move into a larger picture of who we are and what really exists in the world around us, we automatically begin to live in accord with self-governance, self-responsibility, and self-awareness. The key word here is *automatically.*

Also, the bioelectrical field of the human brain is in sync with the geomagnetic field of the earth. Whenever the planet's energy shifts, *corresponding transformations usually occur throughout the human family* (implying that a biological imperative on a global basis is presently underway[166]).

Why are there so many of us? We're here to help facilitate "the changes."

REMODELING OUR FUTURE

Your beginner's guide to society's makeover should be Gregg Easterbrook's *Sonic Boom: Globalization at Mach Speed.*[167] It gives Easterbrook's keen perspective on how far we have progressed in just the last generation. Because world economies are linked technologically, transformations on every level of society, everywhere, occur each and every day. Easterbrook paints a bright future as we learn how to shift into the realities of climate change, the evolving economy, and changes in education, gender roles, militarism, and much more.

Still, if you feel as if everything is falling apart and no one is in charge, you're right. This "collapse anxiety" always precedes terrific, innovative opportunities (the chaos theory at full-throttle). To quote Easterbrook: "A chaotic, raucous, unpredictable, stress-inducing, free, prosperous, well-informed future is coming. It will be a Sonic Boom." Can we handle this? You bet we can . . . with better models.

READY—SET—GO

Seventy percent of the human race will be living in cities by 2050. Lay new sidewalks linking residential areas with schools and shopping centers. Form "walking school buses" (groups) to escort kids to school. Build recreational pathways wherever possible, turning vacant lots/roofs/window sills into gardens. Encourage restaurants to create better menus; schools to ban soft drinks and salty/fat snacks, and to stop selling candy for fundraisers. Entice families to toss supersized plates and take classes in healthy cooking. Provide short-rail trains for inner-city travel and bullet trains for long distance. Have recreational, sports, creative, and educational areas reasonably placed—competitive arenas, too.

The brain itself is social—we are wired to connect with others. Use vacant halls, rooms, buildings for social activity centers, including for after-school programs and exercise/game routines. Provide opportunities for social connections, low-cost trips, life-long learning, self-improvement, new adventures, public speaking, Internet use/training, and social networking. Promote the exchange of spiritual/religious information and ecumenical gatherings, parades, celebrations, fairs, and musical opportunities (drumming, voice, dance, concerts). Encourage mentorships (adults with teens, the elderly with babies, animals with shut-ins and children, birds with prison inmates).

Finances and business management reinvent capitalism.
Bring back the concept of "spiritual capitalism" from the eighteenth century.[168] Shift toward self-governance, individual rights. Balance solutions that arise from collaboration/consensus—the new boss is you.[169] Use the book *Natural Capitalism* as the text for sustainable management and the "Green" M.B.A.[170]

Make it a point to learn about "the other party"—be that a country, culture, people, tradition, language, environment, or social expectation. Also make it a point for management to work entry-level and mid-level positions occasionally to ensure quality improvement. Learn how to listen. Investigate new innovations, like acoustic farming, where plant genes can be activated by sound (suggesting that sound could be an alternative to light as a gene regulator.)[171] Be prepared to make new investments and business adjustments on a regular basis, including the education and integration of immigrants. Compete with patience, clever tactics, and the willingness to admit and correct mistakes. Inspire entrepreneurship and micro-loans ("banking" to aid others yields higher dividends than savings accounts). Expect fluctuations as economic power continues to shift internationally.

The body electric and energy medicine.
Acknowledge that the body is an energy system and its aches and pains are signals of energy imbalance. Convert to body/mind exercises, visualization, healing touch therapies, alternative remedies (such as homeopathy), prayer, meditation (whether active or passive)—for daily or as-needed use. Learn as many healing techniques as possible, especially laying-on-of-hands, Reiki, and home versions of first aid for self and others. Emphasize illness prevention, healthy foods, spiritual/religious renewal, and positive lifestyle changes. Stay away from pharmaceuticals whenever possible and sweeteners like aspartame. Accept personal responsibility for your state of mental/physical/emotional/spiritual health. Know that inexpensive, safe, workable

healthcare systems already exist (another could result from the discovery of a "Genesis Phase" in water, a phase which, when concentrated, forms a double-helix like that of DNA; may well explain things like homeopathy[172]).

Multi-dimensional knowing and intuition.
Develop a comfort level with psychic/intuitive abilities and skills. Be willing to test yourself, take classes, improve, read informative books, attend seminars/conferences/study groups. Know that 90 percent of all Nobel Prize winners got their ideas from sudden insights that came in visions, dreams, and metaphors. Plumb the depths of the inner self and the range of multiple dimensions with creative imagining. Realize that all minds are entangled (connected) with each other, and respond to emotional events that affect the human family. Be respectful, as no one has the right to invade another's mind. Avoid accepting psychic/intuitive guidance from anyone, including yourself, until the source of what was offered has been questioned and verified to the degree possible. Pay attention to sudden inner promptings, though, that "feel right," as these can be time-savers, truth detectors, cautions, informative aids. Choose the ideals you want to live by and know why you chose them, to ensure sensory input that is beneficial and richly textured.

Primary perception and intelligence exist on all levels.
Communicate with plants, animals, cells, all manner of existence and expect a response—usually in the form of sensations, feelings, sounds, imagery. Use basic cautions, yet know that life responds to life—what lights up brain cells for self also lights up the same brain cells when others are also affected: personal consciousness actually reflects shared consciousness.[173] Knowing in advance is commonplace through all kingdoms—humans, animals, insects, plants, elements. Understand that nature knows ahead of time what's coming and sends out signals—like sounds, smells, feelings, sensations—that alert the various kingdoms (e.g., birds automatically lay fewer eggs and produce fewer young if a dry year is sensed).

Accept what science has shown, that animals are capable of sympathy, shame, and compassion; many can use tools, self-medicate to some degree, and engage in social rituals (whale songs rhyme and have meter). Recognize the telepathic ability of DNA strands to communicate at a distance, recognize each other, congregate, join, and self-organize—instantaneously—and in ways that seem like magic. Learn how to participate in this world of mutuality: build structures and lifestyles that honor the ebb and flow of climate/weather conditions and the beauty of sacred geometry (based on the golden ratios of harmony[174]). Realize that conscious awareness exists throughout Creation and all created things.

A Surprise from History

All major progressive social movements in the Northern Hemisphere were originated by Quakers. All major progressive social movements throughout the world and throughout history were originated by small groups of people, like Quakers, who had undergone an awakening and were possessed of a new consciousness.

CHAPTER TWENTY-FOUR

SPIRIT SHIFT:
A NEW CHRISTOLOGY

*When asked if he believed that Jesus was a genuine histori-
cal figure: "Unquestionably! No one can read the Gospels
without feeling the actual presence of Jesus. His personality
pulsates in every word. No myth is filled with such life."*

—ALBERT EINSTEIN

Here the consistency of near-death patterning hits a wall. Or, at least
it seems to. Unequivocally, experiencers return convinced of God/
Allah/Deity as Source and of the personal relationship they now have with
Source. Some come back adamant that the teachings of religious canon are
indeed God's Word because of specific revelations given to them. Others,
equally "struck" by powerful truths they encountered during their experience, are now absolutely certain that infinity is not bound by the concepts of
individuals looking at it—and neither is God.

It is impossible to explain how the near-death experience, for that matter
any impactful transformation of consciousness, jiggles your heart and turns
your brain around. The incident is so real that you feel as if your very soul is
laid bare. You basked in the numinous. You! Words fail. Only the gushing
fumble of oohs and ahs relay the struggle you have in telling your story—
what you saw, felt, heard, touched, tasted. Revelation, a little or a lot, overwhelms.

And, oh, those stories. A Buddhist in Bangkok names the spirit greeters "Yamatoots" and receives strict instructions for future behavior, perhaps in a court trial. A Native American meets riders of the wind who serve the Grandfathers, and is taken on a journey through sky worlds. A devoted Christian stands in awe of heavenly hosts who unveil the real gospels and speak in diverse tongues. A child sees the dead as alive and hears songs and sees colors and smells scents not of earth. A corporate executive recognizes that the consequences of our actions determine our fate, not God. A stained-glass cutter uncovers the purpose of war.

Today's climate of "expectancy" (that end of the world stuff) puts a lot of pressure on adult and child experiencers of any type of "transformation in light" to fess up. Christians expect news about the Second Coming; Buddhists want to know when the Maitreya returns; Shia Muslims strain for word of the 12th Imam; UFO folk await the date for a landing of aliens on the White House lawn. The books that sell best on near-death topics are those that tell people what they want to hear. Don't believe me? Just compare sales stats with buyer profiles. For instance: Mormons tend to buy books bankrolled by Mormons; Pentecostals, the ones on physical resurrections; Catholics, healing miracles; Baptists, prophecy in the Lord's Name; New Agers, spirit-based nuance sans hell; Scientists, what they can replicate.

The most common question asked of researchers: "Experiencer stories conflict with each other when it comes to religion. One says one thing, another something else. What do I believe?"

WHERE ARE WE AS A PEOPLE?

On December 9, 2009, the Associated Press printed a story entitled "Religious Expression Repressed in Third of Nations." According to the article, of the world's most populous countries, citizens in Iran, Egypt, Indonesia, Pakistan, and India live with the most restrictions. The United States, Brazil, Japan, Italy, South Africa, and the United Kingdom have the least of restrictions on religious freedom. High or very high government restrictions affect 57 percent of the world's population. In practice, only about a quarter of the world's countries implement constitutional language protecting religious freedom.

The Pew Research Center's Forum on Religion & Public Life found that in the United States, 28 percent of American adults have left the faith in which they were raised for another religion, or have no religion at all; 44 percent of adults have either switched religious affiliation, moved from being unaffiliated with any religion to being affiliated, or dropped any connection to a specific religious tradition. Among Americans ages 18–29, one in four reports not being affiliated with any particular religion.

Approximately 33 percent of today's people are Christian, 21 percent Muslim, 16 percent profess to being nonreligious, 14 percent are Hindus, 6 percent are Buddhists, 6 percent Chinese traditional religionists, 6 percent Primitive/Indigenous, .36 percent Sikhs, .22 percent Jewish.

And we are still fighting wars in the name of religion. On March 9, 2010, two hundred Christians were slaughtered in Dogo Nahawa, Nigeria, after the horrific killing of three hundred Muslims two months before. Tit for tat. And insanity in the name of religion still continues . . . On November 21, 1996, in Virginia Beach, Virginia, a lovely garden dedicated to one of Westwood Hill Baptist Church's most beloved and devoted Sunday School teachers was viciously destroyed by the Church pastor and a group of parishioners after they learned the man was a member of the Masonic Lodge. And this: Harvard University's distaste for religion is well known—yet the school was founded in 1636 as a training ground for Christian ministers. Tilt.

Obviously, we need to take another look at our religious traditions and the contradictions we so easily overlook or deny. Near-death states reflect this core paradox in stunningly undeniable testimony.

WHAT IS IT WE SAY WE BELIEVE?

The beliefs we have, what we cling to and, for some, willing to die for, are seldom grounded in anything that can be construed as fact—or even verifiable. Near-death scenarios and transformative narrations often reflect this conundrum. What can we rely on? Not as much as we think. Follow me, as we re-examine two of the world's greatest religions and the holy scriptures that uphold them. Both are still awash in unsolvable controversy; their traditions sometimes in conflict with the direct spiritual perception that accompanies transformational states.

The Holy Qur'an of Islam is a collection of divine revelations given to Muhammad during the twenty-three years as he wandered about. He went into seizures when each revelation came, convincing those of his time that either he was a soothsayer, mentally deranged, or a messenger of God/Allah/Deity. These teachings were not put into book form until after his death. The full range of his writings were later destroyed when a standardized version was decided upon and adopted. The Qur'an is best spoken or chanted as if a poem (Muhammad's preference). Islam does not have a central authority; thus, the interpretation of individual clerics and scholars assigns meaning and specificity to religious practice. Because so few Muslims read or understand the Qur'an, tradition outweighs scripture (e.g., the mistreatment of women is not part of the Qur'an, neither are the extremes of sharia laws). Muhammad himself warned about the great corruption that would come to Islam from an area in what is now Saudi Arabia. Wahhab was born there. A rigid extremist, he and his followers destroyed many of Islam's holiest shrines in an effort to establish Wahhabism as a purer form of Islam. Wahhabism is the progenitor of what became Muslim terrorism. Over time, the countless interpretations and translations of the Qur'an have deviated from the original Arabic. Because this is true, the faith itself is in need of reformation.

The Holy Bible and Christianity did not develop as the masses are taught. The Sinai Bible (the oldest known) contains the first mention of Jesus, beginning when he was 30 years of age. When the New Testament of the Sinai Bible is compared with modern-day versions, 14,800 editorial alterations can be identified. Paul was actually Apollonius of Tyana, a first-century wandering sage (the Latin version of "Apollonius" is Paulus). Restructured writings of Apollonius became the Epistles of Paul in AD 397.[175] Early Gospels never mentioned a virgin birth. Christ's suffering, the crucifixion and the resurrection, did not appear in the Gospels until the 12th century—coinciding with the upsurge in Christian militarism and the beginning of the Dark Ages. The Gospels themselves are questionable. According to the *Catholic Encyclopedia*, Mark was written first, with the scribes of both Matthew and Luke dependent upon Mark as a source and framework for their own writings. Well known in biblical scholarship are facts about "The Great Insertion" and "The Great Omission." The Great Omission is the crucifixion/resurrection story. The Great Insertion is the final chapters of the Book of John that detail this story.[176] Warnings about an "Anti-Christ" were never given credence until the Reformation of 1517, when the reigning Pope was declared the Anti-Christ by Martin Luther. A common complaint of scholars concerns the man Jesus. Did he ever exist? They point to the First Council of Nicaea, 325 AD, when Constantine, emperor of the Roman Empire, sought to unite all religious factions of his day under one deity. As a compromise, attending churchmen agreed to link Hesus (a Druid god) with Krishna (Sanskrit for Christ) to create Hesus Krishna or "Jesus Christ."[177] The Second Council of Nicaea in 786–87 AD denounced the first one yet kept the name Jesus Christ, and set about creating the Holy Bible. Discoveries of the *Dead Sea Scrolls* and *Codex Sinaiticus* challenge this work, revealing writings and gospels previously unknown.

Are you screaming yet? You will—if you dig further into the varied histories related to the origins of religious sects/edicts/revelations.

Karen Armstrong, an expert on religious history, puts into perspective any misgivings about who or what to believe, when she states: "Jews, Christians, and Muslims all knew that revealed truth was symbolic, that scripture could not be interpreted literally, and that sacred texts had multiple meanings, and could lead to entirely fresh insights. Revelation was not an event that had happened once in the distant past, but was an ongoing, creative process."[178]

Thanks to Wikipedia and the Internet, anyone can search out facts, forgeries, inventions, political and power maneuverings, behind the existence of each of the world's great religions, their scriptures, and what they teach. Secrets are now passé. Scientifically, we know that fear tends to overrule reason (the brain is wired to flinch first and ask questions later). This explains why religious hierarchies that ruled by fear devolved over time into authoritarianisms that emphasized "church" over "relationship." That type of control bred corruption, turning original blessings into sins.

The hunger for revelation is soul deep. Yet, no matter the urge, how much we muck up or mess up, the "Power of Spirit" ever guides us, uplifts and remakes us, and has since time immemorial.

You think I'm kidding? Get this: experts tell us that Gobekli Tepe, the world's oldest religious temple and complex city uncovered in southeastern Turkey, was built 11,500 years ago. This discovery establishes that the desire to live in *relationship with Source* (God/Allah/Deity) brought people together in urban settings replete with agriculture, animal husbandry, art/pottery/sculpture/architecture, and specialized labor—*seven thousand years before the pyramids, before Stonehenge, even before the Neolithic breakout.* So startling is this find that it can now be said: *man's first house was a house of worship.*[179]

Who knows? With research of near-death states suggesting that religion itself began when experiencers "preached the gospel" of what they had learned from their episode . . . this theory may explain Gobekli Tepe. Today, clerics can be fired from their position if they dare to base a sermon on the near-death experience or admit that they had one. Why? Because near-death episodes validate *and challenge* every religious institution and the beliefs they profess.

SO, WHAT ABOUT JESUS?

There is no question in my mind but that the Holy Bible is inspired text. Irrespective of how it came to be, the end result is filled with archetypal stories that model the human condition in ways that still apply. I consider the Qur'an an inspired and insightful work, as well. We can learn a lot from both books.

Jesus, though, deserves another look. The image or sense of Jesus or of a Jesus-type figure appears in the majority of near-death and other transformative states worldwide, even if experiencers are not Christian. The question is . . . why? Stick with me as I attempt to offer an answer.

There are dead ringers (love that phrase!) for the biblical story of Jesus in earlier writings about Messianic figures; and they all follow the same basic story line—as if that were somehow a "requirement" to prove Messiah-hood. The most detailed and specific, from birth to death (making the Jesus story seem like a mere copy) is that of Mithra, a Persian deity. Even so, claims that the man we know as Jesus is just another legend, fall flat. The Sinai Bible covers his ministry; *The Lost Books of the Bible and the Forgotten Books of Eden* detail his childhood and early years[180]; three letters written while he was still alive describe his physical appearance.[181]

His original name was Yeshua (Yehoshua), and he was tossed off at the time as little more than an independent rabbi who sought to establish an apocalyptic movement for Jewish restoration. Far from being an apocalyptic rabble-rouser, however, he spoke instead of how God was loving and forgiving and that death did not end life, that the pathway to God lay within each individual.

What did he look like? Although differing slightly, the three letters basically agree that he was quite tall and had a swarthy complexion, hair the color of new wine or sunburned gold, and soft blue or gray eyes. Authorities who were informed of his unique physical appearance could easily identify him in any crowd. It is for this purpose that the three letters were written.

The Holy Shroud of Turin, Italy (said to be the burial cloth of Jesus after he was crucified) illustrates what could have been his actual body size, thanks to positive/negative formats of photographs taken of the physical imprint on the Shroud.[182] The clincher is that the imprint itself, detail for detail, exactly matches the body of a crucified man, killed in the manner the Book of John states, with the cloth itself dating back to that general time frame. Scientific studies of the Shroud that discounted this have since been rendered false, as the fragment they studied turned out to be contaminated. Further testing has yet to occur.

The biggest clincher is how such an exact imprint could ever have been created to begin with. Of the ways investigated, only a flash photolysis (the breakdown of materials under the influence of intense light) could explain it. All living things emit light. But, at death, that light (radiation) flares in strength as if a "deathflash." This light/radiation contains information about the organism that just released it. Testimony from attendees at the deathbed mention this, that as death takes hold the dying begin to glow from an inner light that brightens with last breath.

Did Yeshua/Jesus emit enough radiation at death to imprint his image and wounds on his burial cloth? Or . . . was it Christ who accomplished this feat?

CHRIST

What are we to make of Albert Einstein's comments at the start of this chapter? Or, about the "Thomas Jefferson Bible," created by our third president, when he snipped out from the King James edition what he considered to be the authentic accounts and sayings of Jesus and threw the rest of the book away? Or, the translator Stephen Mitchell when he gave us *The Gospel According to Jesus: A New Translation and Guide to His Essential Teachings for Believers and Unbelievers?*[183] Legends abound of a man identical to Yeshua/Jesus who (after his death), visited and taught in the Americas, and in many other countries.[184] Countless millions have been moved by his visage in dreams, visions, near-death and other transformative states . . . not really of the man and his appearance, per se, but of the "Presence" he emanates. He is powerful because of what he became.

Yeshua/Jesus was not born Christed. "Christ" is a state of consciousness one attains. The term "Christ" variously means "the annointed one," "savior," "great teacher," "avatar." Yeshua/Jesus, from what we know in the Bible, never claimed to be the "Son of God" (as misquoted in modern translations); rather he referred to himself as the "Son of Man." Again and again, he made it plain that anyone could attain the Christhood, that we are all "gods in the making" capable of doing what he did "and more also." He presented himself as a model for individual empowerment and the expansion of consciousness, and he never wavered from such teachings. It is only in conservative sects that he is regarded as the "great exception," instead of the "great example" he sought to convey.

An interesting thing about consciousness, once it expands it can keep on expanding. If coherent (well ordered, balanced, guided by higher intent), it can magnify in power hundreds of thousands of times . . . enough to reach a state of superfluidity where it cannot be contained. Those who expand in this manner transcend individual beliefs, cultural ideologies, and religious dictums.

A NEW CHRISTOLOGY

Jesus became the Christ, and, in so doing, passed on the template of what this is, why it is a preferred state of consciousness, and where it can lead. His teachings apply to every religion, every nation, every peoples, every timeframe, every experiencer of a transformative state of consciousness.

The Template

Template Basics: Characteristics that lead to expanded consciousness (whether achieved over time or suddenly in near-death or transformative states).

Know thyself (be self-actualized and free as the soul you are).

Open your mind (awaken to broader insights).

Welcome change (only in change is growth possible).

Learn from opposition (we attract what we dislike to become better).

Pray often and without hesitation (there is a power greater than you).

Breathe in gratitude (that greater power loves you).

Treat others as you wish to be treated (pass the love on).

Acknowledge intelligence in all things (everything is interconnected).

Communicate respectfully (service boomerangs).

Accept tragedy as well as success (sacred intervention comes in disguises).

Bless what you achieve (a positive mind expands even more).

Forgive all hurts (you become whatever it is you cannot forgive).

Allow passion to be egoless (surrender to a Higher Power).

Template Activation: Linkups that operate in tandem (brain shift/spirit shift).

Bodymind level—heart, emotions, smell, immune system, temporal lobes, prefrontal lobes, survival instinct, memory.

Spirit level—love, ecstasy, integrity of memory, upliftment, otherworldly realities, empathy, awareness that life continues, knowing.

Template Cautions: Mess-ups that can jettison the creativity of a free soul.

Evil that grows as a cancer. Cause—*lack of empathy*. Solution—put yourself in another's place; care about that person's feelings, needs, wants; recognize that he or she is a part of you, and what you do to each one you do in some manner to yourself.

Violence that begets violence. Cause—*kundalini misused*. Solution—spiritual power can backfire without guidance; engage in service projects, volunteerism, helping others; learn about intention and how to redirect your mind from "me first" to "us in relationship."

Yearnings for a Golden Age. Cause—*control issues*. Solution—wake up to the trap inherent in feeling "chosen," or following another who claims to be; double-check your feelings and drives to see what motivates you, as the distinction between "will" and "willfulness" is a fine line.

Template Spread: As consciousness expands, it spreads through deep structures. The core of what it means to be human and alive in your own body radically shifts—to an awareness of perfection on every level—the universe, memory fields, darkness and light, DNA's biological internet.

Percentage of spread from the individual to the masses—based on study of flow states and fluid dynamics as applied to traffic, crowd behavior, animal migrations, ideas "whose time has come," trends, fashions: **the shift/spread figure is 4 to 5 percent.** That's all it takes to change a pattern, muck up or straighten out any activity (external or internal as relates to the greater whole), start or stop something new.

Percentage of population worldwide reporting near-death experiences and transformations of consciousness: **4 to 5 percent.**

A NEW MIND . . . there is a Presence that breathes through us, feels through our heart, thinks through our mind, hears through our ears, speaks through our mouth, touches through our skin. When we are aligned with this Presence, we are healthier, happier, more alive than we could possibly imagine or describe. This Presence is a subtle, quiet force that possesses great power and sets "afire" an ego-less passion waiting within to be set free.

A NEW REALITY . . . we live in a giant hologram that reflects back to us One God, One People, One Family, One Existence, One Law—Love, One Commandment—Service, One Solution—Forgiveness.

A NEW CHRISTOLOGY . . . the template Jesus taught for expanding our consciousness is a biological imperative for the advancement of the human family. Transformative states reflect this. To whatever degree we manage to transform, it is the sum of the whole that tips the scales. And we are there: the tipping point has been reached.

CHAPTER TWENTY-FIVE

FINAL WORDS ABOUT SCIENCE

"A new scientific truth does not triumph by convincing its opponents and making them see the light, but rather because its opponents eventually die and a new generation grows up that is familiar with it."

—MAX PLANCK, PH.D.

Science is now shifting from a matter-based understanding of the world to the recognition that consciousness is primary. This presents a real conundrum about objectivity: how can anyone discover, define, or research consciousness when all of us are inside of it? *We can switch to a model based on the unified field theory.* You cannot use linear models to describe what energy does. We don't really "attract things;" we shift wave forms in varied field arrays to allow deeper connections to what already exists. What already exists? An underlying sea of quantum light. Evidence suggests that the very laws of nature may be but "habits" that reflect a type of mass mind process to growth and learning.[185]

The tension this shift is causing runs smack into real "heavies" like money for grants, recognition and awards, political values, social pressure, betrayals between colleagues, "fudging" on findings, protecting one's reputation.[186] In medicine, for instance, neurosurgeon John L. Turner recalled: "I remember a doctor in Ashville, North Carolina, saying that some lawyers, at the behest of drug companies, were threatening to pull physicians' medical licenses if they practiced non-traditional medicine."[187]

This tension has bred "pseudo-skeptics:" those who practice *scientism* (an authoritative view that refuses to consider alternative explanations even when substantial proof exists to back up those explanations). Stated Eugene F. Mallove, Sc.D., before he was killed, supposedly during a robbery: "'Accepted Wisdom' in science, I was to learn, was a most unreliable guide. I now believe that the central issue in science is the war for its very soul, the battle of true science (Science with a capital 'S') against its tyrannical antagonist, Scientism."[188]

Forgotten in this uproar is the simple fact that if it weren't for the principles of matter, truth, and reason laid out by philosophers, there would be no science. The real conflict here is the philosophical difference that grew over time between science and spirituality—*a philosophy that originally gave Western cultures a distinct advantage and supported freedom of choice.*

ENTER "NEAR-DEATH"

How has this affected the field of near-death studies? Rune Amundsen of Norway shares a familiar story: "As a graduate student of psychology back in 1979, I wrote my thesis on the near-death experience. The grand old man of parapsychology in Norway, Professor of Biology Georg HygEn, told me at the time—'You are jeopardizing your professional career.' I could not believe him. The essence of science was to me the open and free inquiry. Phenomena, either of this world or any other, are not 'unscientific.' Well, to make a long story short, I have found Mr. HygEn's remark to be sadly accurate. Within the domain of the so-called 'paranormal,' I claim that science is literally dead. The physicalistic bias within the scientific community is massive and is seriously hampering scientific progress within the fields of psychology and psychiatry. And scientists pursuing a serious interest in 'the inner man' are becoming more and more an endangered species within the scientific community. Being an intrinsic optimist, I will seek rebirth within the spirit of science."[189]

Between near-death researchers there are also challenges aplenty. Kenneth Ring, in his 1980 classic,[190] set about the verify that there is a "core" pattern to near-death scenarios:

1. An experience of peace, well-being, an absence of pain;

2. A sense of detachment from the physical body and progressing to an out-of-body experience;

3. Entering darkness, a tunnel experience with panoramic memory usually of a positive nature;

4. An experience of bright, warm, attractive light; and

5. Entering the light, meeting persons or figures.

During the same years he was amassing his research, however, I was doing the same thing, and discovered as I did four distinctive types of scenarios—not just one. My argument afterward, even with Ken, was how can all researchers compare their work to what is now termed the "classical model" when it doesn't hold up in broad-based studies? How valid can what we think is valid be?

On the psychiatric front, Bruce Greyson, M.D., examined the similarities and differences between near-death experiencers and those who are mentally ill. He recognized that dissociation (feeling detached from yourself, depersonalization) is actually a very common response to any trauma or extreme change; that post-traumatic stress disorder (intrusive thoughts, flashbacks, amnesia-like symptoms) is not at all like the positive, uplifting near-death scenarios that can continue to inspire years later; that absorption (fantasy proneness) does not test out with experiencers as any kind of fantasy; and other psychotic disorders lack the complexity and sophistication of the phenomenon. Greyson was impressed that near-death states can actually be mentally therapeutic, while significantly lowering distress and death anxiety. He found that experiencers are more likely to see themselves as part of something greater than themselves.[191] His work silenced a lot of naysayers.

CHALLENGES FROM THE MEDIA

We have an opportunity, through the study of the near-death phenomenon, to see how brain, body, and spirit might operate to fulfill agendas beyond that of personality or place. What downplays valid work done by serious researchers is the way media sources continue to headline piecemeal experiments from those who want to disprove near-death states.

Herein follows the truth behind some of the headlines.

Media Headline, *Out-of-Body Experiences are all in the Brain.* Came from a report in *Science Journal,* August 24, 2007, describing a lab experiment where the illusion of being in a virtual body outside one's own was created by disturbing the visual input of volunteers wearing virtual-reality goggles connected to video cameras. What they really induced was the "doppelganger" effect, a general misplacement of body image while the individual remains body-oriented. The making of "phantom" bodies is part of regular shamanistic practice, both in ritual work and to increase the spread of information coming to them through the phantom (about their environment). This image supposedly confuses enemies as well, or "signals" that a shaman is present. Superficial at best, doppelgangers have no relation to genuine out-of-body states or near-death experiences.

Media Headline, *Hit the Spot for Out-of-Body.* Most major newspapers in September of 2002 had a field day with this one: a forty-three-year-old woman undergoing treatment for epilepsy in her brain's right hemisphere experienced what seemed to be a near-death scenario when electrodes were implanted in her right angular gyrus of her brain. From this singular episode the assumption was made that a misfiring brain causes near-death experiences. No one seemed to notice that what the woman described were superficial images and feelings that do not match the depth of true near-death states, nor did she exhibit any pattern of aftereffects.

Media Headline, *'Near-Death' Survivors Show Brain-Wave Abnormality.* Various news sources in 2006 focused on a study done by a neurologist in Kentucky, who claimed that 22 percent of near-death experiencers showed a rare brain-wave pattern known as "synchronized brain activity" in the left temporal lobe (a simultaneous firing of neurons similar to an "electrical storm"). He also found that experiencers had a significantly higher rate of a sleep disorder known as rapid eye movement, or REM intrusion. This study was flawed at the get-go: the control group consisted mostly of the researcher's friends and colleagues; it was based on four yes or no questions; previous medical research on REM intrusions showed that experiencers have about the same amount of these as unselected samples from the general population; and—get this—*there was no attempt made to do "before" and "after" testing.*

In other words, they could not tell if this so-called "brain abnormality" was present with experiencers before their near-death state, *or was the result of it.*

Wilder Penfield, M.D. was a neurosurgeon who did groundbreaking research with electrical probes while his patients were conscious during brain surgery. He reported that one patient experienced every trait of the near-death experience during a probe of the Sylvian fissure in the right temporal lobe. This gave rise to unsubstantiated claims that the Sylvian fissure was the "God Spot" and that all near-death experiences were simply an illusion. The media loved this one—even though that one person made no mention of deceased loved ones or a life review, or the type of intensity and depth of lifelong aftereffects.

As a followup, Michael Persinger, Ph.D., a cognitive expert in neuroscience, created the "God Helmet" (a helmet wired to stimulate the brain with fluctuating magnetic fields). This did produce feelings of a "presence" in volunteers, but any reported imagery was fragmentary, incoherent, and lacking in any overall scenario or message (and no aftereffects pattern). Swiss researchers, while attempting to duplicate Penfield, stimulated the region next to the Sylvian fissure, which produced replays of symphonic orchestra music. Does that prove all symphonic orchestra music is an illusion? Does the God Helmet prove near-death states are an illusion?

SPEAKING OF VERIDICAL PERCEPTION

No experiment involving probes or stimulation of the brain has ever reproduced genuine near-death states, the patterns of aftereffects, or "veridical perception." With "observable information gained when experiencers were outside their body or without vital signs," I know of only a few cases that should have been verified but weren't. The rest were. Those who say that revelations of this type in near-death states are phony are either those who refute verification obtained by others out-of-hand or those who come back decades later demanding to interview all parties when most by then have either moved away or died. The majority of those who made such claims in my work did have third party/objective validation of what they heard, smelled, or felt. Some of these cases were eventually published. Here are some examples of my cases with veridical perception.

Carroll Gray,[192] who while still in the uterus "saw" her mother being beaten by her drunken father. When she was two and a half years old, she told her parents and relatives everything she saw and heard during that beating. Every detail. And she was correct. In a subsequent episode, she was met by a kind man (who turned out to be her predeceased grandfather) who showed her a stopwatch and pen knife, saying both were hers. Her exact description of these items and designs on them were stunning, and eventually caused problems in the family when she insisted they were hers. Twenty years later, her mother was cleaning out boxes and discovered the grandfather's will—which explicitly instructed that the pen knife and stopwatch be given to his namesake and granddaughter. At the time of his death he had no granddaughter or namesake.

Rand Jameson Shields[193]—had a past-life recall during a near-death episode. He later drew the scene of that recall, detailing the city and his life there. It turned out to be accurate. Merla Ianello—saw what was happening to her body when her parents tried to save her, as her baby brother watched (not the one in the high chair, but another brother who wasn't conceived until the following year).[194] She knew him by sight and name. Steven B. Ridenhour—whose episode was verified on television by the woman who experienced an almost identical scenario to his, as they both nearly drowned—same time, same place—yet had never discussed what they saw.[195] Mellen-Thomas Benedict—whose miraculous healing of the brain tumor that killed him was recorded on X-rays (which I saw), and reconfirmed by his mother (whom I spoke with).[196]

George Rodonaia—of many "impossible" revelations in his account, I was able to verify with his wife Nino about the time when she stood at the grave where he was to be buried, going over in her mind a list of men who might be her future husband.[197] Although his body was stored in a freezer vault in the morgue at that moment, "he" was actually "inside" his wife's head and witnessed her exercise. I asked Nino why she wouldn't have anything to do with George for a year after he revived. Her reply: "I had no privacy. I couldn't live with him knowing he could see my every thought and what I was doing."

Margaret Fields Kean—her daughter affirmed that right after Margaret was resuscitated, she somehow "floated" out of her body and out of intensive care into a closed-off room where she "sat" on the bed of a dying boy burned black in a fire, and counseled him not to fear death, that he and his parents would be okay.[198] Months later, while still in recovery and in a wheelchair, Margaret attended a horse show that her daughter won. Parents of the boy, hearing the name of the winner, searched for and found Margaret and thanked her for what she had done for their son. They knew of her because she had told the boy her name.

The most spectacular I have run across was not my case but that of Arvin S. Gibson, who personally verified the account. It was that of a crew of 20 "hotshots" (people who fight forest fires), who all suffocated when trapped by an unexpected flare-up.[199] In the hospital, each crew member was interviewed separately by investigators before they could talk with each other. The investigators discovered that each one shared in basically the same near-death experience: they saw each other leave their bodies, and pointed that out to each other while out-of-body. They each remembered what they said, the other's reply, and other details as well.

ON THE ATTACK

Attacks from doctors who say near-death experiences are all in the mind don't wash with facts. Claims that neuroscience has proven that the soul is the activity of the brain are untrue. No such proof exists. Just because a researcher doesn't find something doesn't mean it didn't happen. Data based on website questionnaires broadens the global experiencer base and is important, yet lacks measures to assess details such as who knew what and when. Connections between ecstasy, epilepsy, and near-death states remain unproven and invalid.

Those who have worked in this field have faced censure, loss of tenure, an array of threats and insults, and outright attacks—and from every source you can imagine and a few you probably can't. It seems like the greater the praise and attention researchers receive for what they discover, the greater the backlash. Recently, Pim van Lommel, M.D., the Dutch cardiologist whose study and follow ups made *Lancet* medical journal in December 15, 2001, faced the same relentless criticism even though his book, *Consciousness Beyond*

Life: The Science of the Near-Death Experience, was a bestseller in Europe.[200] The English translation is now available.

Negativity aimed at me began in the early eighties and has been ongoing. I rather suspect that the main reason for this is because I use a different protocol than other researchers, and that renders me suspect. In March 2010 I was labeled a "dangerous influence" by a fellow researcher. He begged me to stop destroying the research he is so passionate about. His gripe? I don't do double-blind studies with a control group, and I dare to broach topics such as shamanism. I've said this before and I'll say it again: I am not a scientist. I am an observer and analyst who specializes in fieldwork (and that includes significant others whenever possible). My protocol is that of a police investigator. I cross-check my findings with different people in different parts of our country at different times. Since over 70 percent of the medical procedures used today came from professionals who work as I do, I never once hesitated in the strength and purpose of my mission [validation of my research style by Raymond A. Reynolds, a professional in law enforcement, can be found in the back matter of this book].

By the way, the technique of double-blind studies with a control group has only been around about one hundred years. It evolved for studying the effect of a single agent acting upon a single illness that had a unique cause. It can be and has been helpful in near-death studies; still, the protocol is basically useless for in-depth work, deeper issues, the range of consciousness, otherworldly involvements, and the ability to see and interact with varied frequencies either infra or ultra to the physical senses.

WHAT'S COMING—FUTURE RESEARCH

While I strive for perspective, that context undergirding phenomena that might explain it, my peers strive for details that can be listed, compared, tested, and duplicated. I believe that both methods are not only necessary but crucial. As science turns more and more to the study of consciousness as primary, the need for broader skill-sets will demand that people such as shamans, bioengineers, DNA experts, psychics, musicians, electrical and plasma experts, dowsers, kinesiologists, symbologists, historians, philosophers, energy medicine practitioners, and ministers come forward to work side by side in cooperative projects. The days of the individualist, pioneering researchers of grit and stubborn determination are coming to an end. Team studies linking people of multiple disciplines is the way of the future.

For those who prefer pure science, here are two books not to be missed: *Irreducible Mind: Toward a Psychology for the 21st Century*; and *The Handbook of Near-Death Experiences: Thirty Years of Investigation.*[201] Besides these two, I have listed five others of exceptional worth in with this same footnote.

The three great mysteries facing science are: What is consciousness? What is time? What is free will? Human evolution cannot explain self-awareness. Intelligent design misses the point. In-depth research, on near-death and other transformative states may finally open the door to the real mystery and the power of direct perception. Who knows? Maybe someday my work will be celebrated for its insight, not labeled as dangerous by naysayers.

CHAPTER TWENTY-SIX

VOICES

"I wanted to wrap this book up in a neat package. Now I've learned that some poems don't rhyme. Some stories don't have a clear beginning, middle, and end."

—GILDA RADNER

A man in Portland, Oregon was out driving north of town. It was around midnight, the dark of the moon, late October. A sudden temperature drop had created black ice on the road. The road had tight switch-backs. He missed one and crashed head-on into a large tree.

"I floated up that tree," he told me. "I was up on top looking down, and I saw my body. An arm was gone and there was blood everywhere—the car in pieces. I wanted to save my body. I really wanted to save it so I looked around for help. Nothing, no houses. Then up on a hill I saw a house. The second floor window, the one to the right, had a light on. I floated over to the window and started jumping up and down, screaming as loud as I could: 'There's been an accident. Call the police.' I repeated this, over and over."

"The guy inside told the police: "There was this jumping fog outside my window. Fog doesn't jump up and down. I just stared at that fog and then heard a loud voice in my ear, "There's been an accident. Call the police." So I called, then I grabbed a flashlight and went downstairs. It took me a while to find the wreck.'

"I was blinded from the impact. The doctors and nurses thought I was hallucinating when I talked about what happened, about being on top of the tree, floating over to the house, jumping up and down, yelling for help. They couldn't shut me up, so they called the guy. He and the police came and confirmed my story—mostly the guy did. Everything is in the accident report. Two months later my sight came back. I used to be a professional artist. My right hand was gone, so I used my left. I said, 'get me pencil and paper.' I drew the accident scene, every detail. They called the police and the guy back. They looked at my drawing and said it was totally accurate. People were shocked. It was so dark that night that even a sighted person couldn't have seen the details I did. No one could explain it. Some years have passed but I can't stop drawing that scene. It haunts me."

Teri Csanady saw the English landscapes painted by Michael John Hill and exclaimed, "You have been there! You have captured the light on the other side." Michael asked, "Where?" Teri answered, "You have had a near-death experience [like I did]." "Yeah, I was run over by a truck when I was nine, but I don't recall much of the experience." Michael's sister Laurie added, "I can remember Michael at age two drawing pictures of our mother at the ironing board. Even then, he was driven." After he was hit by the truck, painting became an obsession—trees—barren of leaves, along a river or near water, with a light that speaks to the very heart of one's soul, even to his own soul as if awaiting rebirth.

"It is my opinion," said Teri, "that Michael has been living with the aftereffects since childhood. One afternoon he called me and asked if I wanted to go to church with him. I said no, but I would love to take him to Baha'i Temple in Wilmette. After climbing the stairs to the Temple, together we walked in a circle, reading inscriptions over the doors. Over one set of doors, facing East, we paused to read, 'Ye are the fruits of one tree and the leaves of one branch.' I looked up at Michael as tears welled in his eyes. I could feel his pain and frustration. It was the kind of frustration that comes with the knowledge of having crossed over, of having been 'there,' of having returned from the threshold of death carrying his message for mankind with a remote memory of 'the other side.'"

Michael John Hill has recently been injured in an accident that rendered him blind. He is awaiting surgery, hopefully to restore his sight. He speaks little but admitted that "I dream an awful lot in vivid color, and I paint pictures in my dreams." Some of his inspiring work is displayed on gallery websites.[202]

Kim Kregel tells this story about her daughter Kelsea. "I am the mother of an 11-year-old who had a near-death experience when she fell into a hot tub when she was two and nearly drowned. She had no memory of the experience, but prior to her fall she was terrified of water. My attention from her was distracted when I started tending to my eight-month-old son. During that time she silently fell in. When we realized she was no longer by my side, eating pizza, I turned around and saw her lying face down at the bottom of the hot tub. We jumped in, my friend performed CPR, and I ran for a phone. We PRAYED. We prayed to God; we prayed to Mom and Grandmother who had passed that if they saw Kelsea to send her back. I rode in the ambulance. Doctors were not sure of her prognosis. Three days later she was discharged. Her first sentence to me was, 'Mommy, I came back! Mommy was crying, Tanner was crying, and Kristen was crying.' I told her, 'Honey, I know you did, and thank you!' I didn't ask her any more questions after that. I was afraid to know, but now I regret it. Amazingly, after her near-death experience, she was no longer afraid of water. Nine years later I have this amazing child. She is so gifted and charismatic. She was writing at three, reading short stories at four, and is a high achiever [with a high intelligence]."

In the seventh grade, Kelsea had a class assignment to write a 55-word story. This is what she wrote: "Dead. I am dead. I jumped into the pool waiting for what seemed like a lifetime. Voices crowded me in my mind. A person lifts me out of the water, crying. They said I am dead. Soon, I don't know where I am at. It's pitch white and I hear cheerful cheers and cries. I'm alive." Her Mom said: "What she meant by 'I'm alive' is that she was alive in heaven."

David King explains: "I have been going through a process of recall this last decade. Most of my spiritual insights were buried after my 1988 NDE. This had to be done with my consent. I retained memories of many things for a few weeks, and then I had a ceremonial process in Hawaii where I put 'spirits' in charge of my vast memories pertaining to the 'spiritual insights' of my past—including all my 'afterlife' experiences. I have a long history of NDEs dating back to childhood. I can testify there is a vast difference in the way the 'afterlife' is perceived through the mind of a child. As children, we don't have all the knowledge imposed on us from the world. It is a more pure 'reflection' on the spiritual realm.

"I had a massive near-death experience in 1978 when I was a teenager at the age of 18. I was telling my doctors about the 'trip into the light' and many of the mystical happenings around me in the aftermath. I was able to prove various things to my family, friends, and the professionals. One of the extraordinary feats I could accomplish was 'future memory.' I couldn't access my childhood memories, but if I concentrated on memory, then flashes of future events would appear in my mind. I was instructed to 'read' headlines well into the future. I followed the advice of many people and completed the task, and then I buried the memories. My Grandfather warned me to NEVER take advantage of that 'foresight' and profit financially. He felt the gift had been given for spiritual purposes, and if the headlines contained loss, suffering, or pain, then people would look down on me for turning a profit. The decade of predictions was from 2000 to 2010. Every major headline in the news [thus far] had been successfully predicted.

"I feel we all have so much of a mystery hidden within us. The world seems to blind us to that 'glorious' light. If half the world could tap into that 'gold mine' hidden within, and utilize it to its fullest, I feel the world will be twice better for it."

My name is Granit Nikq and I am a Muslim, and I am not afraid to use my full name. I was eight years and I had an NDE. My mother and I came from a visit of my father. It was first day after new year, and in Holland almost everyone lights up fireworks theirself. I found a very huge and illegal firework on the ground, and when I lighted it, exploded in my hand. I do not remember the explosion because at the same time I was in a tunnel. The tunnel rotated and was just like a cloud. In the cloud-like tunnel were millions of other lights—red, green, and much more. Just like a Christmas tree, little sparkling lights. In the end of the tunnel was a Sun-like light, but I could look into it. Also classic-like music I was hearing. At that moment I was flying through the tunnel and felt no pain, very good. The flying was not very fast. I looked around and I talked 'with thoughts,' and remember like yesterday the following two phrases: Where am I? Wow, it is beautiful here. After those two phrases I remember myself back in my body. My sight came back to me very slow, and I heard a big bleep in my ears. I told my mother I was with God. But she said I just imagined it. As a big wonder, I had not even a scratch on my hand. Very strange, a little bit of blood only.

"I remembered whole my life this experience. I always had a good feeling in Church and Bible teachings. Then after 9/11, I heard that I was different, that I was a Muslim. After three years of searching, I became very depressed with lots of scary nights and a dark man encounter that would take my breath away. I thought God was going to punish me in hell. This is now a year ago, and I'm taking pills for depression. Sometimes I have doubts, but I read an NDE story and I feel better again. I don't know why I am an NDEr with doubts. Many of my fellow NDErs have no doubt. I just hope the depression and doubt will fade away. No way what I saw an illusion. I think life compared to the NDE is an illusion."

Steven McFadden wrote an article about Grandfather Secatero's story.[203] He gave me permission to carry some of it here. Grandfather is a Native American elder, highly respected, and honored throughout the Navajo Nation.

"While Leon Secatero was teaching at a conference in early February, he experienced a stroke. He eventually lost consciousness and found himself on the other side. He found himself among an assembly of Wind Walkers— the spirits of the many elders and medicine people he has known over the decades of his life. The Wind Walkers had knowings they wanted to share. Their communications helped illuminate Leon's understandings about the sacred path leading into the next five hundred years.

"Leon told me that when he journeyed to the other side, he saw the Wind Walkers sitting in circles. As far out as he could see, the Wind Walkers sat grouped in progressively larger concentric circles. There were clouds of light, like a dome, stretching over all of these circles. Leon saw many recently deceased Navajo elders, as well as the spirits of people who had died years ago. He saw also the spirits of elders and medicine people from all the different cultures and spiritual pathways around the world.

"'Many people talk about seeing the other side,' he said. 'I know this was the other side. The things I saw were very beautiful. I saw the glass world, the crystal world, and many different colors of light.' Leon told me he saw the Wind Walkers take corn pollen in their mouths to bless their words before they spoke to him. 'The elders talked about positive things, focusing on the positive to make things happen, to bring in good energy so that life will continue. They said to use song, prayer, dance to focus on positive thought, and to help us go forward on the path to the future in a good way, in a sacred way. Put your concentration on the positive. That's how it's done.'"

Michael Hutchison was a leader in the AVS (Audio/Visual Stimulation) light and sound industry for many years and authored three books,[204] mostly about stimulating brain power. Then he got hit by a quadruple whammy: a house fire where he almost died from smoke inhalation; when he fell head over heels into a rocky river bed after slipping on ice while crossing a foot bridge; lay paralyzed in icy water with a broken spine after the fall; almost died of pneumonia in the hospital. Although he never experienced the near-death phenomenon, he did undergo a soul-deep transformation of consciousness that lead to a complete surrender of will. Doctors expected total paralysis, yet he's in a wheelchair and able to do more than what is typical for a quadriplegic. In losing everything, he discovered what is real.

"I had this sensation of bliss or consciousness as just being some transparent, invisible, all pervasive substance that surrounded and permeated and interpenetrated everything in the world, and I was swimming in it. We all are—all the time—even though we don't know it. Everything that happened in that bliss was totally effortless. I found that my actions became effortless, too. When I lifted up my hand, for example, it wasn't me lifting my hand, it was just this Consciousness or bliss acting through me. I realized that I wasn't 'doing' my life, but that I was being lived through by Consciousness. I wasn't breathing, but I was being breathed through. I wasn't thinking, I was being thought through. I wasn't seeing, I was being seen through. When you look at it this way, everything is happening just the way it is. Everything is perfect, just the way it is. There's no need to worry about anything, because whatever is going to happen, happens. There's nothing you can do about it, so just sit back, and let it happen, because it's all going to, anyway." Fatalistic? Not hardly.

Linda Seay-Skaggs was tormented by a near-death-like experience where she was yanked out by force. "It felt like something beyond 'me' did this. And at this point, I felt it was God showing me my anger at Him. When I had my experience there was no one to turn to for help. Being human, unable to talk to anyone, then reading about wonderful, loving NDEs created confusion . . . let alone wondering with great heartache and dismay of why and how I could be so angry at God. When I came back I felt raw, [like I had] a spiritual scrubbing. It's taken the last few months of reading and writing and as objectively as possible to go over my life review, to understand. I am still working on it.

"For years I called what I saw a 'monk,' because it resembled that in appearance. Please believe me. I am not making this up! It was dressed in a long black robe with long sleeves and a hood. This Angel of Death showed me his face. It was a bleached white skull 'grinning' at me, looking at me through empty eye sockets. I was mortified and horrified beyond words. I cried out, 'Lord Jesus. Please, have mercy on me.' What came from my lips did not come from my heart: I woke up absolutely shocked I was alive, then more shocked at what happened next. After having to start my day for over 15 years taking allergy medication and nasal spray, suddenly I was healed! I can breathe! Wow!

"What I feel happened was due to the culmination of all I had lived, being rejected and not loved or wanted—then feeling God had not protected me. For me that was the ultimate betrayal, not loved enough. I asked God to heal me; He did."

Kathy Forti, a clinical psychologist in the Los Angeles area, had a near-death experience in the spring of 2003 that turned her into a quantum inventor. "I was leaving my office one evening and suddenly I felt like something had been physically removed from my body. My clinical training immediately kicked in and I looked inward to see if there was any depression component to this feeling, but I knew that wasn't the case. Yet for some reason I felt like my work on earth as I knew it was completed. Was I getting ready to die? I went home pondering what to do about this dilemna."

Within hours after the exodus of her old guidance, Forti found herself drawn into a swirling vortex, then into a tunnel, horizontal, feet first, moving at a tremendous speed. "I could see Light at the end of the tunnel, and I knew with all certainty that it was 'The Tunnel' everyone had been talking about. Before I could reach the Light, I was stopped in the tunnel and just hovered there. I tried to make myself go forward, but I couldn't. Suddenly, I was spun around with great intentional force and sent back the same way I came. There were voices in my head saying, 'Breathe, Kathy, breathe.'" Forti found herself back in her physical body, but her whole left side was paralyzed. A voice in her head told her to relax, not to worry, that all would be okay. Within a short time she regained feeling, 24 hours later she became obsessed with quantum physics. "I was getting up every morning between 3:00–4:00 AM to do internet research on everything from scalar potentials to DNA sequencing. It felt like I was getting a crash course in quantum mechanics. The Guides wanted *me* to do it. It was supposed to be *my* mission. It wasn't until I finally accepted this that information really started to come to me in the form of data stream downloads, insights, pictures, and concepts I'd never heard before. What they wanted to bring to our world was a method by which to re-awaken our DNA. It was all based on mathematical and algorithmic code, which they called 'the language of the universe and man.'" In December of 2008, after many years of pain-staking development, the device that Forti has received guidance on was finally ready to be born. It's called Trinfinity8. Forti says that Trinfinity8 is a spiritual tool for positive vibrational change and has been referred to by many intuitives as an "Ascension" device to help an individual shift into a higher energy state. "It looks like I signed on for the long-haul," Forti says.[205]

Andrea Arrowsmith remembers her own birth, coming down the canal and laying on a steel table watching doctors care for her mother, who almost died. "I remember before birth, seeing three possible ways to incarnate. I was helped and guided by beings with diadems (crowns) to choose which one would be best. In my teens I remember all nature turned to light fire-flame around me and I was joy/love only.

"I have had a near-death experience as an adult. I went to a HUGE light and was taken to various realms and know the secret to the music of the spheres that supports all creation. I have seen the creation of music and light and know how the music works from the big spectrum to the smallest. I create music CDs and soul songs to clear the atmosphere for all to feel the spirit, God, and also their own souls."[206]

In 1991, Dan Rhema survived a near-death experience caused by the multiple brain infections of dengue fever (breakbone fever) and spinal meningitis. During his recuperation, Dan began to compulsively create multimedia collages, sculptures, and masks from found objects. He also began to paint, capturing the images flowing through him in a unique three-dimensional style. It soon became apparent to Dan that these acts of creation were healing and re-creating him. He has taken this realization and made it the focus of his art; trauma can awaken creativity and, through creativity, healing can begin.

"The near-death experience," explains Dan, "brought me to a place where I no longer need to seek answers to all the big questions - I am content to let the mystery be. In my life, the difference between reality and unreality has become permanently blurred. I now experience a Zen-like existence living right here, right now only in the present moment.

"The sensation of floating began during my near-death experience and I have continued floating ever since. One night, I had a dream that I was gazing out from within the sculpture I had just completed. At that moment I understood that I had not been reborn as an artist—I had been reborn as the art."[207]

Here is some of Callaghan Grant's story. "In 1977 I was killed being kicked in the face by a horse. I sustained serious brain damage and did not begin to recover my short-term memory for 18 months. While I was dead, this is the exchange that occurred between my Self and a being I called Michael. Please remember as you read this that the language of this exchange was not verbal. Complex understandings were passed directly from his awareness to mine in a sequential manner that our brains understand as language.

Self: 'Perfect.' I sighed within myself at the moment I shed my body. I felt light and utterly free. A beneficent darkness enveloped me. 'I am perfect! NOTHING can EVER hurt me again.' I rejoiced. Suddenly I became aware that someone was there with me.

Michael: 'Nothing could have ever hurt you to begin with. You are an eternal Being.' He answered matter-of-factly, and yet I KNEW Him.

Self: 'That being so, and I know it is, then why was it all so scary?'

Michael: 'It was necessary that your experience be intensified by the belief in your own mortality, or YOU would have never taken the exercise seriously, and you would not have learned what you went there to learn. Nor would you have done what you went there to do.'

Self: 'Which was?'

Michael: 'You went to learn to summon your WILL.'

Self: 'What? I went through all of that just to learn what I want?'

Michael: 'You do not understand what I mean by WILL.' A cascade of memories tumbled through my awareness. I was a child, screaming in horror and kicking, trying desperately to shed my first pair of shoes at the age of two. Then I was a four-year-old struggling to escape my pedophile great uncle, leaving my body and watching from a distance, and then I was lifted up into the clouds where I met a flock of jeweled birds that flew around me, calling in happy recognition. Then I was shrieking as my father blistered my bum. He held me by the arm as I ran circles around him while he wore a switch out on my legs. Then I was free again and again as abuse after abuse vaulted me out and out and away into the clouds to visit my birds. Then a screened door is opened, and I smelled the pie, still warm in a napkin, as my mother handed it to me through the back door. And I felt love, all forgiving love, love that knew that all of it had not mattered EXCEPT THE LOVE, because love had taught me that all suffering is redeemed by love—LOVE that forgives in a way that made it all worthwhile, so long as you found the LOVE. I laughed as I remembered that this figmentary 'self' was not real at all. I had but put on a body that could suffer so that I could learn to forgive all things—forgive them because they were not real. It was a hysterical joke Michael showed me: the world was a dream and nothing more. It was a jest: the Son of God made captive by the very world He created! And it was only LOVE that could undo the spell of believing in that terribly poignant, terribly beautiful, and yet silly dream."

All these stories are as real as the people who told them. So is this book.

SPECIAL TRIBUTE

To the thousands and thousands of people who have crowded my years, I say thank you!

There is no way I can contact you personally. In most cases you never knew my name and I did not know yours. Where you live now or if you are still alive is unknown to me. But, just in case you might read this book, please know I am grateful we met and shared time together. Actually, grateful is not enough to say. I am honored and humbled to have crossed paths with you and to have been your "sounding board," someone safe you could talk to and cry with and share in the wonder of special moments when life turned upside down. Seldom did I talk about what happened to me. It was YOU; you were my moment's gift.

How many of you were there?

Between 1966 and 1976, I estimate maybe three thousand—mostly in groups and classes and workshops, usually under the heading of Inner Forum. Then headquartered in Boise, Idaho, I would also include the Northwest. Those were the days when I couldn't find enough material on altered states of consciousness, psychic phenomena, mysticism, and the transformative process that I felt I could trust, so I created a mechanism whereby thousands could benefit from this learning, not just me.

Between 1978 and 2010, I estimate that I have had sessions with, spoken to, phoned, written to nearly four thousand adult and child experiencers of near-death states. The primary numbers were found in the Central, Northeastern, and Southern states—many came from other countries.

This was intensive work, personal, intimate, deep, even with significant others and health-care providers. To say I was obsessed would be an understatement. I had no guidelines, only the instincts of a cop's kid.

Again, to each and every one of you, thanks!

INTERNATIONAL ASSOCIATION FOR NEAR-DEATH STUDIES— IANDS

The International Association for Near-Death Studies (IANDS) exists to impart knowledge about and operate as a clearing house for information about near-death experiences and their implications, to encourage and support research and related phenomena, and to aid people in starting local groups that wish to explore the subject.

They have numerous publications, among them the scholarly *Journal of Near-Death Studies*, a general-interest newsletter entitled *Vital Signs*, various brochures and materials, a CD-ROM that indexes all *Journal* articles, and CEU courses for medical, mental, and spiritual health-care providers. More such programs are in the offing. Membership in this nonprofit organization is *open to anyone*; dues are annual and include various benefits.

Donations to cover operating expenses are always needed and always welcome, especially for the NDE Research Fund. CDs and some DVDs of IANDS conference speakers are available.

For more information, contact:
International Association for Near-Death Studies (IANDS)
2741 Campus Walk Avenue, #500
Durham, NC 27705–8878
(919) 383–7940 voice/fax
services@iands.org
www.iands.org

NOTE

S ince my protocol is different from others in the field of near-death studies, it is fair and appropriate that a Criminal Justice Instructor and career
law enforcement officer comment on my research style. I am humbled by
what Raymond A. Reynolds had to say about what I have done. Here is a
presentation of his opinion.

APPLICABILITY OF POLICE SCIENCE INTERVIEW/INQUIRY TECHNIQUES IN RESEARCH OF NON-LAW ENFORCEMENT MATTERS

I have had the pleasure of being acquainted with P. M. H. Atwater and her research for a number of years, having first met her at an event where she was a presenter regarding her research and findings on near-death experiences. After hearing her presentation, I inquired of her if she had training and experience in the police science of observation and interviewing, as that portion of her methodology sounded very familiar. She shared with me that her father had been in law enforcement, and she had received substantial training and experience in that activity through observation and discussions with her father. I have read most of her publications and had discussions with her as to the research protocols she uses, those being primarily Clinical, Narrative Collection, and Observational (police science). The following comments relate primarily with the technique of interviewing willing participants (Observational).

After learning of P. M. H. Atwater's techniques through discussions and disclosures in her publications, I am of the opinion that she does indeed use well established and successful law enforcement methodology in the Observational protocol in interviewing subjects in her research.

This generally entails observation of the person's sensory mode, such as sight, hearing, or touch (feeling), and establishing rapport with them on that level. This is so, whether the subject of discussion is something the person has experienced of a sad, exciting, frightening, or overwhelming nature. Here we are speaking of the interviewer being careful to use non-threatening body language, rather, probably being somewhat reflective if we encourage the person with an informal atmosphere and through relevant open-ended questions, acknowledging comments, and encouraging them to continue with such comments as, "oh, please do continue," "really," "oh," "uh-huh," etc., information continues to flow.

It is my opinion after being taught these highly refined techniques and many years of utilizing them successfully, teaching them and seeing positive results in law enforcement work, that they do indeed have value outside of that venue. I think this is obvious in the results realized in the work of P. M. H. Atwater, as there is clearly a consistency in her methodology and that used in law enforcement.

Raymond A. Reynolds

Experience/credentials of Raymond A. Reynolds:

I am retired from a career in law enforcement encompassing service as a Military Police Officer, State Police Officer, and Federal Criminal Investigator, the latter extending from field investigative work to executive level management. Additionally, after retirement, I participated in Criminal Justice Training as a Training Coordinator/Instructor for approximately 10 years.

NOTES

1. Moody, Raymond, Jr. *Life After Life*. Covington, GA: Mockingbird Books, 1975.
2. Ring, Kenneth. *Life at Death*. New York, NY: Coward, McCain & Geoghegan, 1980.
3. *I Died Three Times in 1977* was a self-published piece I did in 1980. Only fifty copies were ever printed (that's all the money I had at the time). It still exists as an e-book on my website. This small book is only a compilation of four articles I wrote for *Many Smokes Magazine* published by The Bear Tribe (Sun Bear). A fuller account is now available as an e-book on *Amazon.com,* entitled *I Died Three Times in 1977—The Complete Story.* It is out in Russia as a print book through Stigmarion Publishers.
4. I was deeply involved then in a *Search for God* Study Group, as part of the Association for Research and Enlightenment (ARE), and in the psychic readings of the late Edgar Cayce. As an adjunct, I explored Huna, hypnosis, reincarnation, numerology, astrology, divination, ghostly hauntings, mediumship, biblical translations, esoteric teachings, prayer, laying-on-of-hands healing, meditation, various other healing modalities, mysticism, and psychic phenomena. I took part in numerous experiments (local, regional, national), and became professional in astrology, numerology, earth energy and sensitivity training, ghost dehaunting, healing, dream interpreting. The death of a dear friend (Margaret Matthews) led me to create "Inner Forum," Idaho's first non-profit metaphysical corporation. I wrote and edited the *Inner Forum Mini-Magazine*, started the Northwest's first metaphysical speakers bureau, and produced monthly programs and workshops, so the public could see for themselves the difference between valid phenomena and psychic/spiritual experiences of a beneficial nature and those of egotistical fantasy and self-promotion. After six years of this, a board of directors was formed and I stepped down. The organization folded one year later. Most of the memorabilia from those days have long since been lost, although you may be able to locate some newspaper articles about this in the archives of the *Idaho Statesman Newspaper* in Boise, Idaho.
5. The place was Twin Falls, Idaho. The Station House was the Twin Falls Police Department. Police Chief throughout my growing years was Howard Gillette. My

Dad, Kenneth L. Johnston, when interviewed by a *Times News* reporter (after my first book came out, and when asked why he raised me this way), said there was a spate of child abductions at the time and he wanted me to be alert. He tossed the "observation exercises" he held me accountable for as a game we played. Not so to me. He was the fifth man I had called "father" in my young life, and I took everything seriously. I was incapable of "gamesmanship."

6. Among the studies that have verified some of my findings is the paper entitled "Near-Death Experience in Survivors Of Cardiac Arrest: A Prospective Study In The Netherlands.". It was authored by Pim van Lommel, Ruud van Wees, Vincent Meyers, and Ingrid Elfferich, and published in *Lancet* medical journal 12–15–01. Another was "A Comparative Study of Near-Death Experience Outcomes in 56 Survivors of Clinical Death," by Richard J. Bonenfant, Ph.D., published in *Journal of Near-Death Studies*, Vol. 22, No. 3, Spring 2004.

7. The International Association for Near-Death Studies (IANDS) exists to impart knowledge concerning the near-death phenomenon, to encourage and support research dealing with the experience and related phenomena, and to aid people in starting local groups that wish to explore the subject.

8. Details about this groundbreaking discovery appear in the May 7, 2007 issue of *Newsweek Magazine*, in the article "Docs Change the Way They Think about Death" by Jerry Adler.

9. The man I am referring to is George Rodonaia. He was assassinated by the KGB (run over twice by a car driven by an agent) in Tbilisi, Georgia, in 1976. Because he was a vocal communist dissident, his case was highly political, necessitating an autopsy on the third day of his corpse being stored in a freezer vault. (Unfortunately, the actual temperature of that freezer vault cannot be verified.) He revived while a team of doctors were cutting open his torso, much to the utter shock of those present (his own uncle was one of the doctors). His story is detailed in *Beyond the Light: What Isn't Being Said About The Near-Death Experience*. This book has now been reissued through Transpersonal Publishing, Kill Devil Hills, NC, 2009. The original was through Birch Lane Press, New York City, 1994. Rodonaia is now deceased.

10. For a discussion on 2007 estimates of people having had a near-death experience, refer to my book, *The Big Book of Near-Death Experiences,* Charlottesville, VA: Hampton Roads, 2007.

    A 1995 study done in Germany about this was conducted by Hubert Knoblauch from the University of Zurich, Ina Schmied from the IGPP in Freiburg, and Bernt Schnettler from the University of Konstanz. Entitled "Different Kinds of Near-Death Experience: A Report on a Survey of Near-Death Experiences in Germany," it was published in *Journal of Near-Death Studies*, Vol. 20, No 1, Fall 2001.

    Also refer to IANDS' website, research section, *www.iands.org.* And: *Adventures in Immortality*, George Gallup. New York, NY: McGraw-Hill, 1982.

11. Melvin Morse, M.D. with Paul Perry. *Closer to the Light: Learning from Children's Near-Death Experiences*. New York, NY: Villard Books, 1990.

12. Elisabeth Kübler-Ross, M.D. was a pioneer in the fields of death and dying and hospice care. Her seminal work is *On Death and Dying*.

13. *Children of the New Millennium*. New York: Three Rivers Press, 1999. This book "died" an almost instant death after I refused to drag near-death kids from one television talk show to another. Nearly two-thirds of the book was gutted by my publisher after the company was taken over in a buy-out. The new crew preferred a "fluff" piece, geared more to entertainment than groundbreaking research. *The New Children and Near-Death Experiences*. Rochester, VT; Bear & Co. (Inner Traditions), 2003. I credit Stephany Evans, my agent then, with saving my research of children's near-death experiences. She found Inner Traditions, a publisher willing to pick up the pieces from *Children of the NewMillennium*. With their help, I was able to put most of the deleted material back, although a complete rewrite was not possible due to the time factor.

14. A full discussion of electrical sensitivity can be found in *Beyond the Light*, Transpersonal Publishing, Kill Devil Hills, NC, 2009. Refer to "Research Methodology" appendix.

15. Eadie, Betty. *Embraced by the Light*. Placerville, CA: Gold Leaf Press, 1992.

16. Brinkley, Dannion with Paul Perry. *Saved by the Light*. New York, NY: Villard Books, 1994.

17. Moody, Raymond E, Jr. *Life After Life*. Covington, GA: Mockingbird Books, 1975.

18. A longer version of Rich Borutta's story, including his computer simulation of the feathery spirits that accompanied him into the light, appears in *The Big Book of Near-Death Experiences*. Charlottesville, VA: Hampton Roads, 2007.

19. For more details about the Jimmy John story, check out *The New Children and Near-Death Experiences*. Rochester, VT: Bear & Co., 2003.

20. Retired Col. Diane Corcoran is now an advocate for veterans who have had a near-death experience. For more information, contact her at 2705 Montcastle Court, Durham, NC 27705; (919) 624–0547; diane.corcoran@kapa.net.

21. Refer to *The Fingerprints of God*, Arvin S. Gibson. Bountful, UT: Horizon, 1999. I mentioned this case in two of my books—*The Complete Idiot's Guide to Near-Death Experiences* and *The Big Book of Near-Death Experiences*.

22. *The New Children and Near-Death Experiences*. Rochester, VT: Bear & Co., 2003. Margaret Evans, page 139. Merla Ianello, pages 142–144.

23. *Beyond the Light*. New York, NY: Birch Lane Press, 1994. Ricky Bradshaw, pages 15–16.

24. Mellen-Thomas Benedict—no book at this time. Refer to *Beyond the Light*, pages 75–79, and my website—*www.pmhatwater.com*. An update was posted there of what was revealed to him at death.

25. Brinkley, Dannion with Paul Perry. *Saved by the Light*. New York, NY: Villard Books, 1994.

26. Sawyer, Tom (yes, that's his real name) with Sidney Saylor Farr. *What Tom Sawyer Learned from Dying*. Norfolk, VA: Hampton Roads, 1993.

27. Dougherty, Ned. *Fast Lane to Heaven*. Charlottesville, VA: Hampton Roads, 2001.

28. My website is *www.pmhatwater.com*.

29. This is the case of Haisley Long, pages 93–94 in *Beyond the Light*. New York, NY: Birch Lane Press, 1994.

30. Nancy Clark is the woman involved here. Her case can be found on pages 94–98 in *Beyond the Light*. New York, NY: Birch Lane Press, 1994. She wrote *Hear His Voice: The True Story of a Modern Day Mystical Encounter with God,* Publish America, P. O. Box 151, Frederick, MD, 21705.

31. Refer to *The Curtain Torn* by Larry Buttram. Manassas Park, VA: New Virginia Publications, 2009. To reach Buttram directly, e-mail him at lab1949@ verizon.net.

32. This and many other such historical accounts are covered in Carol Zaleski's book, *Otherworld Journeys: Accounts of Near-Death Experiences in Medieval and Modern Times*. New York, NY: Oxford University Press, 1987.

33. The article "An Old NDE" by Donald R. Morse, DDS, Ph.D., appeared in Vol. 31, No. 3, July 2008 of *Journal of Spirituality and Paranormal Studies*. Dr. Morse can be reached at dentpsych@aol.com. I thank him for his kindness in allowing me to quote from his article.

34. This quote came from an article written by Phyllis Galde entitled "Interview with J Z Knight: Channeling Ramtha." The article was published in the January 2009 issue of *Fate Magazine*, pages 12–20. Thank you, Phyllis, for permission to quote.

35. Refer to *Beyond the Light*, the Anomalies chapter, pages 108–111.

36. For an in-depth discussion of the "alien factor," refer to *The New Children and Near-Death Experiences*, the Alien Existences chapter, pages 152–166.

37. Thank you to Khurram Aziz of Amsterdam, the Netherlands, for sharing Ramana's story with me.

38. Refer to *The New Children and Near-Death Experiences*, the Cases from History chapter, pages 123–132. Far more is detailed about Edward de Vere in Appendix V, *Future Memory*, pages 264–273. Charlottesville, VA: Hampton Roads, 1999.

39. For more information about "Embracing a Birth Affliction," turn to page 136 of *The New Children and Near-Death Experiences*.

40. Todd Murphy, a fellow researcher; taken from personal correspondence dated April 5, 2006. Todd is the one who has done so much work with child experiencers from Thailand. His website is *www.spiritualbrain.com*.

41. For the case of George Rodonaia, refer to *Beyond the Light*, pages 16–17 and 79–83.

42. The story of Robert C. Warth and the finding about tonsillectomies are on pages 48–49 of *The New Children and Near-Death Experiences*.

43. This video was available on YouTube: http://www.youtube.com/watch?v=-np13 EPq10w.

44. *Rachel's Magic Swing* is a fictionalized version of a child's near-death experience, and is based on Kathryn's own. At my insistence she finally wrote her own story, *The Day I Almost Drowned: A Child's Near-Death Experience*. Both books are self-published. To obtain copies, access *www.rachelsmagicswing.com*.

45. A great resource for physiological/medical differences between males/ females and what that might mean is the work of Leonard Shlain, M.D. His book, *Art and Physics: Parallel Visions in Space, Time, and Light* (HarperCollins, New York City, 1991) is revolutionary.

46. A good book about the surprising ebb and flow of that eco-system called the human body is: *Sex, Sleep, Eat, Drink, Dream: A Day in the Life of Your Body*, Jennifer Acker-

man. New York, NY: Houghton Mifflin, 2007. The "Hour of the Wolf" is in Chapter 13, page 186.

47. A surprising book by Gavin de Becker examines intuition and the limbic system in a way few people do. Really valuable information: *The Gift of Fear*. New York, NY: Dell, 1999.

48. Read *Sixth Sense: Unlocking Your Ultimate Mind Power*, Laurie Nadel, Ph.D., New York, NY: ASJA Press/iUniverse, 2006.

49. Check out *The End of Time: The Next Revolution in Physics*, Julian Barbour. New York, NY: Oxford University Press, 2001.

50. Gilles Bedard can best be reached via e-mail at info@inerson.com. His website is *www.inerson.com*. His programs on "After the Darkness Dawns a New Light" are outstanding. The neuroscientist he works in collaboration with is Mario Beauregard, author with Denyse O'Leary of *The Spiritual Brain: A Neuroscientist's Case for the Existence of the Soul*. New York, NY: HarperOne, 2008.

51. I found this announcement in the "Pyramid Research Center Newsletter," Vol. 2, No. 4, 1988.

52. Narby, Jeremy. *The Cosmic Serpent: DNA and the Origins of Knowledge*. United Kingdom: Phoenix (The Orion Publishing Group), 1999.

53. Begin by becoming familiar with the American Society of Dowsers. They offer excellent conferences, classes, plus a well-stocked bookstore on the subject. Contact: American Society of Dowsers, P.O. Box 24, Danville, VT 05828; (802) 684–4317; asd@dowsers.org; *www.dowsers.org*. I am a life member, having joined a few years after I "died" in 1977. My "strong suits" are deviceless dowsing and earth energy sensing.

54. This quote is from the article "Spirituality Legitimized . . . Almost" by Rev. Karen E. Herrick, Ph.D, LCSW, LMSW, CADC. This article was published in *Journal of Spirituality and Paranormal Studies*, Vol. 29, No. 4, October 2006, pages 227–236. The actual quote is on page 235. Additional source for the last few words in the quote is: Peterson, E.A., Nelson, K. "How to Meet your Clients' Spiritual Need." *Journal of Psychosocial Nursing*, Vol. 25, No. 5, pages 34–39. Should you wish to contact Dr. Herrick, you may do so at keherrick@aol.com; P. O. Box 8640, Red Bank, NJ, 07701.

55. Peterson, Christopher and Martin Seligman. *Character Strengths and Virtues: A Handbook and Classification*. New York, NY: Oxford University Press, 2004.

56. Try these websites to better understand the assault against natural health products and the right of individuals to choose their own health care practitioners and remedies: *www.naturalnews.com/023121.html* (about what happened in Canada); *www.codexalimentarius.net/web/index_en.jsp*.

57. American Center for the Integration of Spiritually Transformative Experiences (ACISTE) can be contacted at: ACISTE, P. O. Box 1472, Alpine, CA 91903; *www.aciste.org*; info@aciste.org; (619) 445–4443.

58. *The New Children and Near-Death Experiences* and *Beyond the Light*.

59. Refer to the article, "Different Kinds of Near-Death Experiences: A Report on a Survey of Near-Death Experiences in Germany," by Dr. Hubert Knoblauch, Ina Schmied, and Bernt Schnettler. *Journal of Near-Death Studies*, Vol. 20, No. 1, Fall, 2001. No

fieldwork or followup was conducted after this survey, nor were "significant others" contacted.

60. James, William. *The Varieties of Religious Experience*. New York, NY: Routledge, 2002. Orginally published in 1902.

61. "The Varieties of Religious Experience," page 228.

62. This list of elements from the work of William James was arranged by Karen E. Herrick as she studied for her Ph.D. To obtain the various footnotes she made, or to inquire about the class she took in "Psychology and Spiritual Experiences," contact her directly at keherrick@aol.com; P.O. Box 8640, Red Bank, NJ 07701. Thank you, Dr. Herrick, for the hours went spent discussing this.

63. "The Varieties of Religious Experience," page 175.

64. Huston Smith has taught religion and philosophy at M.I.T., Washington University, Syracuse University, and the University of California at Berkeley. He is the author of many books, including the classic *The World's Religions* (HarperCollins, New York City, 1991); and *Why Religion Matters*. New York, NY: HarperOne, 2001. His latest is *Tales of Wonder: Adventures Chasing the Divine, an Autobiography*. New York, NY: HarperOne, 2009.

65. Bennet, Sage. *Wisdom Walk: Nine Practices for Creating Peace and Balance from the World's Spiritual Traditions*. Novato, CA: New World Library, 2007.

66. The story of Walter Russell is detailed in *The New Children and Near-Death Experiences*, pages 128–130. To avail yourself of his voluminous articles, books, artwork, and research, contact: University of Science and Philosophy, P. O. Box 520, Waynesboro, VA 22980; (800) 882–5683; *www.philosophy.org*.

67. An excerpt from *The Universal One*, Walter Russell, University of Science and Philosophy, Swannanoa, Waynesboro, VA 1926, page 8.

68. Nassim Haramein is the Director of Research at The Resonance Project Foundation, and is currently seeking funding for more extensive lab facilities. Contact him at (808) 327–9630; haramein@theresonanceproject.org; *www.theresonanceproject.org*. A DVD of the talk I attended of his, when he was the Keynote Speaker for "Homecoming" (the first time he came), is available through Center of the One Heart, P. O. Box 511, Culpeper, VA 22701. Actually, there are two DVDs—one of his talk and one for questions and answers. Both are excellent, but I would especially recommend the Q&A.

69. "Spiritual Retreat for NDErs" may become bi-annual as demand increases. Operated by experiencers Linda Jacquin (founder), David Bennett, and Bill Taylor, the Retreat is held at Mercy Center, St. Louis, Missouri. Check out their website, *www.neardeathexperiencers.org* for more information. They have special features on YouTube.

70. *Life After Life*, Raymond E. Moody, Jr., M.D. Covington, GA; Mockingbird Books, 1975.

71. Kenneth Ring, Ph.D., has written many incredible books about his research of near-death states. Among them are:
    Life at Death. New York, NY; Coward, McCann and Geoghegan, 1980.
    Heading Toward Omega. New York, NY; William Morrow, 1984.

Lessons from the Light: What We Can Learn from the Near-Death Experience, with Evelyn Elsaessar-Valarino. New York, NY; Insight Books, 1998.

Mindsight: Near-Death and Out-of-Body Experiences in the Blind, with Sharon Cooper. Palo Alto, CA; Institute of Transpersonal Psychology, 1999.

His eulogy for Tom Sawyer entitled "The Death and Posthumous Life of Tom Sawyer: A Case Study of Apparent After-Death Communications," was published in *Journal of Near-Death Studies,* Vol. 27, No. 2, Winter 2008, pages 111–133.

72. Sawyer, Tom and Sidney Saylor Farr. *What Tom Sawyer Learned from Dying.* Norfolk, VA: Hampton Roads, 1993. Farr, Sidney Saylor. *Tom Sawyer & The Spiritual Whirlwind.* Berea, KY: Ochamois, 2000.

73. The problem with biblical translations is that most of them originated from the Greek, rather than going back to Aramaic, the language of the Bible. "Gmeerah" wound up as "perfect," when in Aramaic the word has a range of meanings, most notably "inclusive." For more information about more direct translations, refer to the writings of Rocco Errico, Th.D., Ph.D. Contact: The Noohra Foundation, 4480 South Cobb Drive, Suite H, PMB 343, Smyrna, GA 30080–6989; (678) 945–4006; *www.noohra.com*; info@noohra.com.

74. From *Future Memory,* P.M.H. Atwater, L.H.D. Charlottesville, VA: Hampton Roads, 1999. Pages 107–108.

75. Peter Russell is the author of many books and producer of three films on consciousness. Check out his website at *www.peterussell.com.*

76. "Afterward: Making Meaning After a Frightening Near-Death Experience," by Nancy Evans Bush, MA. *Journal of Near-Death Studies,* Vol. 21, No. 2, Winter 2002, pages 99–133. This article, by the way, conveys the best way I've yet come across to regard and integrate frightening or hellish near-death experiences.

77. You can check out this news story online at http://whitehorse-leader.whereilive.com.au/news/story/a-feared-call-save-result/. The date is May 30, 2009. Carmel later wrote a book about her experience entitled *When All Else Fails* (Bookpal, Brisbane, Queensland, Australia, 2010.) It's available through Bookpal at *www.bookpal.com.au.*

78. Arcangel's survey results were published in the *Journal of Near-Death Studies,* Vol. 26, No. 4, Summer 2008, pages 303–306. Dianne Arcangel wrote *Afterlife Encounters: Ordinary People, Extraordinary Experiences.* Charlottesville, VA: Hampton Roads, 2005.

78a. An article most people have forgotten is coming back into focus because of its relevance to the natural rotation of most spiral galaxies and molecular spin of all living things on earth. Refer to: "Left-Handed Universe" by Malcolm W. Browne. It was published in "The New York times," November 25, 1986, and can be read online at: *www.nytimes.com/1986/11-25/science/left-handed-universe.html.*

79. I highly recommend this article: "A Projective Geometry for Separation Experiences," F. Gordon Greene. *Journal of Near-Death Studies,* Vol. 17, No. 3, Spring 1999, pages 151–191. His drawings show what might be happening with the geometry of leaving the body and then looking back.

80. Meek, George W. *After We Die, What Then?* Franklin, NC: MetaScience Corporation, 1980. Reissued in 1987 by Ariel Press, 4255 Trotters Way, 13A, Alpharetta, GA, 30004.

81. Tricia Nickel is also a professional astrologer. These seven points appeared in her article, "Oh Neptune . . . You Illusive Butterfly." This was originally published in *Welcome to Planet Earth Magazine* in Summer, 1992, page 23.

82. Richard Maurice Bucke, M.D., presented his research paper on "Cosmic Consciousness" in 1894 at the annual meeting of the American Medico-Psychological Association. He later authored a book by the same name, first published in 1901. While admiring the stars on a winter's night in 1902, he slipped on the ice and died instantly. His book became the seminal reference work on the enlightenment process and its universal pattern of aftereffects, and remains so today. Continuous printing by Citadel Press.

83. Please read the entire discussion on "Son of Man," page 981 in Harper's Bible Dictionary. Paul J. Achtemeier, with the Society of Biblical Literature. San Francisco, CA: Harper & Row, 1985. Jesus' preference for the title "Son of Man" is well known. Only the modern biblical translations refer to him as "Son of God." This switch in titles was accomplished by voice vote, not by biblical verification.

84. Refer to *The Daily Progress Newspaper*, February 29, 2000, both front page and in section B-4 for the article "Body and Soul" by Claudia Pinto, Staff Writer, Charlottesville, Virginia.

85. For stats on electrical sensitivity and what I discovered with a particular questionnaire I used to explore this aftereffect, refer to my book, *Beyond the Light* (now out through Transpersonal Publishing, Kill Devil Hills, NC 27948). You want to read the Appendix entitled "Research Methodology," pages 264–272.

86. "Peritraumatic dissociation" was discussed at length in the *Journal of Near-Death Studies*, Vol. 26, No. 3, Spring 2008. Look for the article "The Acute Dying Experience" by Michael B. Sabom, M.D., pages 181–218.

87. For a more in-depth study of colloidal conditions, the transformation of consciousness, and the larger story of evolutionary factors, read chapter 13, "The Innerworkings of Creation and Consciousness," in my book *Future Memory*. I first learned of the power of colloidal conditions in respect to water by reading about the work of Viktor Schauberger, a natural scientist, inventor, and philosopher. The information he learned from studying forests, soil, water, spiral movements, implosions, flow forms, and vortices was simply extraordinary. By the way, his were the first successful "flying saucers" ever made (he was forced into doing this by Hitler himself during World War II). I suggest reading the small book, *Living Water: Viktor Schauberger and the Secrets of Natural Energy*, by Olof Alexandersson, Gateway Books, Bath, England, 1976; and *The Great Tradition*, Lower Lake, CA, 1976, revised in 1990. The New Energy Movement carries material about him. Access their website at *www.newenergymovement.ca*, and look for "Schauberger's Legacy." There is now a DVD on him and his son Walter available from: *Atlantis Rising Magazine*, P.O. Box 441, Livingston, MT 59047; (406) 222-0875; 1-800-228-8381; *www.AtlantisRising.com*.

88. Arthur Rubinstein said this during intermission of the PBS television special *Arthur Rubinstein at 90* (aired in the mid-seventies). Although I had seen this television special myself, it took a friend to jiggle my memory about the surprising intermission story told by Arthur Rubinstein.

89. "Why We Believe—Belief in the Paranormal Reflects Normal Brain Activity Carried to the Extreme," an article by Sharon Begley. *Newsweek Magazine*, November 3, 2008, pages 56–60.

90. Refer to the paper "Brain Activity in Near-Death Experiencers During a Meditative State," by Mario Beauregard, Jerome Courtemanche, and Vincent Paquette. *Resuscitation Journal*, 80, 2009, pages 1006–1010.

91. There is an article about this experiment, including an update, in *American Dowser Quarterly Digest*, Vol. 37, No. 4, Fall 1997, pages 43–58. It is entitled "Brain Patterns Characteristic of Dowsers, As Measured on the Mind Mirror," by Edith M. Jurka, M.D. I was not part of Dr. Jurka's study; rather I participated in a separate contingent conducted in Charlottesville, Virginia. My job was to witness some of the experiments and to study charts. I am a lifetime member of the American Society of Dowsers. Their contact info: P.O. Box 24, Danville, VT 05828–0024; (802) 684–4317; asd@dowsers.org; *www.dowsers.org.*

    To better understand the art of dowsing, refer to these two books: *The Divining Hand,* Christopher Bird. Black Mountain, NC: New Age Press, 1985; *The Divining Mind,* Edward Ross and Richard D. Wright. Rochester, VT: Destiny Books, 1990.

92. Wise, Anna. *The High Performance Mind.* New York, NY: Tarcher, 1997.

93. Dean Radin tangled with this possibility scientifically in his book, *Entangled Minds: Extrasensory Experiences in a Quantum Reality.* New York, NY: Paraview Pocket Books, 2006.

94. This is discussed in-depth in my book, *Future Memory.* Charlottesville, VA: Hampton Roads, 1999.

95. Bird, Christopher. *The Divining Hand.* Black Mountain, NC: New Age Press, 1985.

96. Article, "Unconscious Decisions in the Brain" by Staff Writers, Leipzig, Germany (SPX), April 15, 2008. Refer to *www.terradaily.com/reports/unconscious_Decisions_In_The_Brain_999.html.* Sent to me by John Chenault and Glenn Mingo.

97. For details of these experiments and the results, see *The Parapsychology Revolution: A Concise Anthology of Paranormal and Psychical Research*, Robert M. Schoch and Logan Yonavjak. New York, NY: Tarcher, 2008.

98. James E. Beichler, Ph.D., is also the Editor of *Yggdrasil: The Journal of Paraphysics*, and often presents papers at annual meetings of the Academy of Spirituality and Paranormal Studies (P. O. Box 614, Bloomfield, CT, 06002–0614). To reach Dr. Beichler directly, write to him at: P. O. Box 624, Belpre, OH, 45714; jebco1st@aol.com. Ask him about his new book, *To Die For: The Living Book of Death.* The material I quoted was taken from notes I took of a talk he gave, cross-checked against several of his articles—one of them "Life and Death in the Big City: The Geometrical Structure of Dying," pages 6–7, published in *Yggdrasil: The Journal of Paraphysics*, 2000. The rest came from his talk at the Fourth International New Science Symposium, held in Seoul, South Korea, September, 2000, sponsored by the Minaisa Club. His talk was "Single Field Unification and Consciousness."

    A funny story about how I met Dr. Beichler: his talk about a single field of unification was given in Seoul, South Korea. I was there too, giving an update on my research of the near-death phenomenon. We stayed in the same hotel; my room was directly below his. When I get excited, my electrical sensitivity tends to disrupt all manner of gidgets and gadgets, as it did in his room, to the point that he had hotel staff running up and down all night trying to fix what broke. We never actually met until presentation time at the Sejong Cultural Center. While awaiting our turn, we discovered that we were both near-death experiencers and lived only a few hours apart back in the States, and that meeting each other could make a difference in the development of our theories. The fact that we had to go half-way around the world to get together when we actually lived so close, struck us both the same way—synchronicity strikes again!

99. Einstein matches all the criteria for and characteristics of a child near-death experiencer. I examine this possibility in my book *The New Children and Near-Death Experiences,* pages 125–126.

100. The incredible synchronicity of events presaging Einstein's formulation of his relativity theory is contained in an article written by J. Timothy Green, a clinical psychologist and near-death researcher. Entitled "Did Near-Death Experiences Play a Seminal Role in the Formulation of Einstein's Theory of Relativity?" it was published, at least in part, as a "Letter to the Editor" in *Journal of Near-Death Studies,* Vol. 20, No. 1, Fall, 2001. Joe sent me his full article in February, 2003.

   For information about what happened to Einstein as a child and how it changed him, refer to *The New Children and Near-Death Experiences,* pages 125–126.

101. Read up about flow states in Mihaly Csikszentmihalyi's book, *Flow: The Psychology of Optimal Experience.* New York, NY: Harper & Row, 1990.

102. *Future Memory* was reissued by Hampton Roads in 1999. See pages 76–86. Originally published by Birch Lane Press, New York, NY, 1996.

103. Refer to footnote 66. Walter Russell had his first near-death experience at the age of seven, then again every seven years thereafter, culminating in his cosmic illumination at the age of forty-nine.

104. "Our cerebral hemispheres were originally buds from olfactory stalks. We think because we smelled," says Diane Ackerman, author of *A Natural History of the Senses.* New York, NY: Random House, 1990. Interestingly, the olfactory bulb for our sense of smell is located just above the brainstem, close to the limbic.

105. Goleman, Daniel. *Emotional Intelligence.* New York, NY: Bantam Books, 1995.

106. Irene Klotz's article in *Discovery News* was based on a paper published in the October 2009 issue of *Journal of Palliative Medicine.* Her article is entitled, "Brain Waves Surge Moments Before Death."

107. Look at pages 141–142, *Coming Back to Life* (originally published in 1988, since reissued by Transpersonal Publishing).

108. Refer to footnote [XREF].

109. So many books have been written about the Shroud, it would be best to consult Wikipedia for a thumbnail account. Research done over a decade ago, that overturned the Shroud's age, has now of itself been overturned—and reversed. Check out http://en.wikipedia.org/wiki/Shroud_of_Turin.

110. All authentic crop circles around the world form during this same timeframe. Check out this book: Sylva, Freddy. *Secrets in the Field: The Science and Mysticism of Crop Circles.* Charlottesville, VA: Hampton Roads, 2002.

111. Quoted from article, "A New Lease on Life," by Tijn Touber, *Ode Magazine*, October, 2005, page 27.

112. Karl H. Pribram, MA, Ph.D., has done so much and written so broadly, that it would be best to skim his work for whatever you wish to focus on, and then proceed from there. Access *http://en.wikipedia.org/wiki/Karl_H._Pribram*.

113. To check out The Global Consciousness Project, refer to *http://noosphere.princeton.edu/gcpintro.html*. Don't forget to click on "Current Results" from the home page.

114. Siegel, Ronald K. *Intoxication: The Universal Drive for Mind-Altering Substances*. Rochester, VT: Park Street Press, 2005.

115. The International Congress on Ecstatic States was held in the Medical Conclave of Hannover, Germany, May, 2008. One of the speakers, Dr. John H. Halpern, presented trial results using the drug ecstasy in palliative care. The film he showed focused on before and after changes. To learn more about his programs, access "Hallucinogens and Ecstasy (MDMA): Harms, Possibilities, and Research" at *http://evidence.no/en/halpern*.

116. Excellent books on drugs and the need for more honesty in learning about their history and usage:

   The Secret Teachings of Plants: The Intelligence of the Heart in the Direct Perception of Nature, Stephen Harrod Buhner. Rochester, VT: Bear & Co., 2004.

   Visionary Plant Consciousness: The Shamanic Teachings of the Plant World, edited by J. P. Harpignies. Rochester, VT: Park Street Press, 2007.

   Sacred Plant Medicine, Stephen Harrod Buhner. Rochester, VT: Inner Traditions, 2006.

   LSD: Doorway to the Numinous: The Groundbreaking Psychedelic Research into Realms of the Human Unconscious, Stanislav Grof, M.D. Rochester, VT: Park Street Press, 2009.

117. Strassman, Rick. *DMT: The Spirit Molecule: A Doctor's Revolutionary Research into the Biology of Near-Death and Mystical Experiences*. Rochester, VT: Park Street Press, 2001.

118. Jawer, Michael A. with Marc S. Micozzi. *The Spiritual Anatomy of Emotion: How Feelings Link the Brain, the Body, and the Sixth Sense*. Rochester, VT: Park Street Press, 2009. Check out pages 232–281. Also check out Jawer's website, *www.emotiongateway.com*.

119. I met Bethe Hagens at one of the annual meetups for the American Society of Dowsers. She had done quite a bit of scholarly research on goddess cultures 30,000 to 20,000 years ago, and was intrigued at the exact similarity between animal brains, the human limbic system, and goddess carvings of that era. She wrote a number of papers on her research. I have two of them: "Venuses, Turtles, and Other Hand-Held Cosmic Models" (published November 11, 1993 by Presto Graphics); and "Venus Figurines and Spiritual Technology in the Upper Paleolithic" (originally published by *The Ley Hunter*, P. O. Box 5, Brecon, Powys, LD3 7AA, Wales, U.K.). I do not know if any of her papers were accepted by scholarly journals.

120. In mid-September, 2004, Alan Slater, a developmental psychologist at the University of Exeter, presented work showing that babies as young as five hours old "Know a pretty face when they see one." His presentation was at the British Association

Festival of Science. His was not the first such discovery about babies and what they are capable of responding to. There have been many others, all of them indicating that babies are born already knowing things . . . beyond mere instinct.

121. The original research on this was done by Michael Persinger at Laurentian University, Montreal, Canada. Refer to his book, *Neuropsychological Bases of God Beliefs*. Westport, CT: Praeger, 1987. The challenge from Swedish researchers was published in *Neuroscience Letters*, December 2004, and *Science & Technology*, February 2005 (*www.stnews.org*).

122. Newberg, Andrew and Eugene Aquili. *Why God Won't Go Away: Brain Science and the Biology of Belief*. New York, NY: Ballantine Books, 2002.

123. Willoughby Britton worked at UA Sleep Research Lab, University of Arizona, for six years when she did this study of near-death experiencer brainwaves. Refer to *Arizona Daily Wildcat Newspaper*, online article, "UA Lab Hopes to Help with Sleepless Night," by Georgeanne Barett, November 24, 2004. (*http://wildcat.arizona.edu/papers/98/66/01_4.html*). Britton's work was also covered in *Arizona Daily Star*, June 6, 2004, in an article by Carla McClain entitled "Near-Death Survivors Show Brain-Wave Abnormality Study Finds" (*www.dailystar.com/dailystar/dailystar/24289.php*). Britton's finding contradicts to some extent what was discovered in the dowsing community with the use of the Mind Mirror. For that reason, I hope she changes her protocol somewhat to see what else she can find.

124. The "many worlds" concept is discussed in depth in *Cosmic Jackpot: Why Our Universe is Just Right for Life*, Paul Davies. New York, NY: Houghton Mifflin Harcourt, 2007.

125. From the "Physics Web" and an article entitled "From the Present to the Past." Find at *http://physicsweb.org/articles/news/10/6/16/l*.

126. Kaku, Michio. *Parallel Worlds: A Journey through Creation, Higher Dimensions, and the Future of the Cosmos*. New York, NY: Anchor, 2006.

127. Giants in the study of symbols are: Carl Gustav Jung (*Man and His Symbols*, New York, NY: Dell 1968—in continuous printings); and Joseph Campbell (*The Power of Myth*, New York, NY: Broadway Books, 1988—in continuous printings).

128. This chart originally came from my book, *Goddess Runes* (New York, NY: Avon Books, 1996), but now appears in *Runes of the Goddess* book and kit from Galde Press, Lakeville, MN, 2007.

129. For a more in-depth chart of the beings themselves and the planes they tend to operate from, see pages 77–78 in *We Live Forever: The Real Truth about Death*. Virginia Beach, VA; A.R.E. Press, 2004.

130. Paper entitled "Does the Arousal System Contribute to Near-Death and Out-of-Body Experiences? A Summary and Response," by Jeffrey Long, M.D., and Janice Miner Holden, Ed.D., published in *Journal of Near-Death Studies*, Vol. 25, No. 3, Spring, 2007.

131. Chomsky's work is referenced in the paper discussed in the previous endnote. For further research, check out Noam Chomsky (1969), "Deep Structure, Surface Structure, and Semantic Interpretation." Bloomington, IN: Indiana University Linguistics Club.

132. This quote from Carol Zaleski appears in an article entitled "The Death Journey of a Hopi Indian: A Case Study," by J. Timothy Green, Ph.D., published in *Journal of*

Near-Death Studies, Vol. 26, No. 4, Summer 2008. Zaleski's words actually came from "Death and Near-Death Today," published in J. J. Collins and M. Fishbane's *Death, Ecstasy, and Other Worldly Journeys*. Albany, NY: State University of New York Press, 1995.

133. Paper entitled "Refreshment and Reunion in Paradise: Near-Death Experiences in Early North African Christianity," by Stephen E. Potthoff, Ph.D. *Journal of Near-Death Studies*, Vol. 27, No. 3, Spring 2009.

134. Refer to:

Kellehear, A. (1993). "Culture, Biology, and the Near-Death Experience: A Reappraisal." *Journal of Nervous & Mental Disease*, no. 181, 2003, pages 148–156.

Kellehear, A. (2007). "Culture and the near-death experience: Comments on Keith Augustine's 'Psychophysiological and cultural correlates undermining a survivalist interpretation of near-death experiences.'" *Journal of Near-Death Studies*, Vol. 26, No. 2, pages 147–153.

Kellehear, A. (2008). "Census of non-Western near-death experiences to 2005: Overview of the current data." *Journal of Near-Death Studies*, Vol. 26, No. 4, pages 249–265.

135. This is a study by Jeffrey Long, M.D., of 1,600 cases. Details in *Evidence of the Afterlife: The Science of Near-Death Experiences*, Jeffrey Long and Paul Perry. New York, NY: HarperCollins, 2010. His website is *www.nderf.org*.

136. Jung, Carl. *On the Nature of the Psyche*. San Rafael, CA; R. F. Hull and G. Adler (Amber-Allen Publishing), 1996.

137. Appendix III, pages 250–257, *Future Memory*. Charlottesville, VA: Hampton Roads, 1999 (originally published by Birch Lane Press, New York, NY, 1996).

138. The story of Bill from Atlanta, Georgia, is on pages 55–56 of *The New Children and Near-Death Experiences*.

139. Doidge, Norman. *The Brain That Changes Itself*. New York, NY: Penguin, 2007.

140. Quote appears on page 63 of the article "When Does Your Brain Stop Making New Neurons?" by Sharon Begley, appearing in *Newsweek Magazine*, July 9, 2007.

141. For more about Karl H. Pribram, M.A., Ph.D., and his theories about the "holographic brain," refer to Wikipedia at http://en.wikipedia.org/wiki/Karl_H._Pribram.

142. Refer to *A New Science of Life*, Rupert Sheldrake, Ph.D. Rochester, VT: Park Street Press, 1995. You can access his website at *www.sheldrake.org*. Also acquaint yourself with the work of Harold Saxton Burr with Burr's book, *Blueprint for Immortality*, originally published in 1972, again in 2004, by C. W. Daniel Company, Ltd., United Kingdom.

143. McTaggart, Lynne. *The Field: The Quest for the Secret Force of the Universe*. New York, NY: Harper Paperbacks, 2008.

144. Laszlo, Ervin. *Science and the Akashic Field: An Integral Theory of Everything*. Rochester, VT: Inner Traditions, 2004.

145. Press Release No. 03–064 from NASA Headquarters, 2-11-03. Access it at http://map.gsfc.nasa.gov/news/PressRelease_03–064.html.

146. A fascinating book that explores things like this is *How We Decide*, Jonathan Blair. New York, NY: Houghton Mifflin Co., 2009.

147. Refer to my book, *Beyond the Indigo Children: The New Children and the Coming of the Fifth World*. Rochester, VT: Bear & Co., 2005.

148. For an actual picture of this protrusion check out page 251 in *The Biology of Transcendence: A Blueprint of the Human Spirit*, Joseph Chilton Pearce. Rochester, VT: Park Street Press, 2002. Pearce is, in my opinion, the best interpreter of the human brain and how it develops.

149. The study at George Washington University was published in *Journal of Palliative Medicine*, Vol. 12, Issue 12, December 8, 2009. This duplicates the work of Janusz Slawinski, a Polish physicist and member of the faculty of the Agricultural University at Wojska Polskiego in Poznan. He discovered the same thing, calling it a "death-flash," and said all living organisms display the same phenomenon at death. Refer to page 141 in my book, *Coming Back to Life* (reissued by Transpersonal Publishing, Kill Devil Hills, NC, 2008).

150. Jean-Baptiste Lamarck (1744–1829) was a French naturalist who argued that traits acquired in life by parents could be passed on to their offspring (in violation of Darwin and his theory of natural selection). He was discredited for this, even though his research verified his theory.

   Today, scientists are finding that DNA can be physically "marked" by a parent's experience, and the consequences of that experience—and his or her child can be born with that trait. Called "Lamarckism," people like Emma Whitelaw of Queensland Institute of Medical Research are finding that "the experience of parents can be visited upon their children and grandchildren, and become hereditary." Refer to: ww.qimr.edu.au/research/labs/emmaw/index.html.

151. For more details regarding this criteria, check page 124 in *The New Children and Near-Death Experiences*. In fact, read the whole chapter on "Cases from History," pages 123–132.

152. A mind-blower of a book on this is *Saharasia: The 4000 BCE Origins of Child Abuse, Sex-Repression, Warfare, and Social Violence in the Deserts of the Old World*, James DeMeo, Ph.D. Published by Orgone Biophysical Research Lab in 1998, it contains meticulous details, photos, and charts on the effects of desertification and weather patterns, effects still evident today, in numerous countries. DeMeo was a student of Wilhelm Reich. To obtain the book, contact: Orgone Biophysical Research Lab, P.O. Box 1148, Ashland, OR 97520; demeo@mind.net.

153. Refer to http://en.wikipedia.org/wiki/Yellow_Emperor. There are said to have been twelve "Culture Bearers" like Huang-ti (also spelled Huang-di), who brought the arts and sciences to that portion of the world where they lived. Because of them, societies of learning and invention have continued to flourish throughout time—irrespective of weather cycles and earth changes.

154. There are only a few researchers dedicated to the study of the Mayan Calendar, who are in sync with the teachings of Mayan Elders. One of these, and the easiest to understand, is Carl Johan Calleman, Ph.D. Two of his books are of special import:
   The Mayan Calendar and the Transformation of Consciousness. Rochester, VT: Bear & Co., 2004.

The Purposeful Universe: How Quantum Theory and Mayan Cosmology Explain the Origin and Evolution of Life. Rochester, VT: Bear & Co., 2009.

155. References: *Forbidden Science*, Edited by J. Douglas Kenyon. Rochester, VT; Bear & Co., 2008. *Forbidden History*, Edited by J. Douglas Kenyon. Rochester, VT; Bear & Co., 2005. *Forbidden Archeology*, Michael A. Cremo and Richard L. Thompson. Los Angeles, CA; Bhaktivedanta Book Publishing, 1998.

156. Although many institutes and medical facilities are doing advanced research on the heart, I still recommend HeartMath as a source of current, understandable information. Contact: HeartMath Institute, Research Division, P. O. Box 1463, Boulder Creek, CA 95006; 1–800–450–9111; *www.heartmath.org*. You may want to inquire about their Global Coherence Monitoring Project, now underway, that attempts to measure advance changes in the electromagnetic fields of people across the planet, if a future event is sufficiently important, novel, or immediate, to activate the heart.

157. Refer to Paul Pearsall's book, *The Heart's Code: Tapping into the Wisdom and Power of Our Heart Energy*. New York, NY: Broadway Books, 1998. You might also refer to the paper, "Changes in Heart Transplant Recipients that Parallel the Personalities of Their Donors," by Paul Pearsall, Ph.D., Gary E. R. Schwartz, Ph.D., Linda G. S. Russek, Ph.D. *Journal of Near-Death Studies*, Vol. 20, No. 3, Spring 2002, pages 191–206.

158. *Darwin's Lost Theory of Love* by David Loye shows us that the famed naturalist contradicted himself during his later years by emphasizing the importance of love and caring in the evolution of humans. Loye's book came out in 1998 and was published by "to Excel," and is available on *www.thedarwinproject.com/revolution/revolution .html* and, *www.thedarwinproject.com/library/library2.htm*. Publisher credit given is Pacific Grove, CA: The Darwin Project 2000. This edition will eventually be replaced by *Darwin's Unfolding Revolution*.

159. Refer to the case of Beverly Brodsky in *The New Children and Near-Death Experiences*, pages 52 and 194–195.

160. This study was done by the Pew Research Center's Forum on Religion & Public Life in 2009. It focuses on religious beliefs and practices that do not fit neatly in to conventional categories.

161. Long, Jeffrey with Paul Perry. *Evidence of the Afterlife: The Science of Near-Death Experiences*. New York, NY: HarperOne, 2010.

162. McTaggert, Lynne. *The Field: The Quest for the Secret Force of the Universe*. New York, NY: Harper Paperbacks, 2008. Updated Version.

163. My book about this is *Beyond the Indigo Children: The New Children and the Coming of the Fifth World*. I will be doing a sequel to this book in late 2010.

164. Palden Jenkins of Glastonbury, England, writes occasional articles. This one, entitled "Soulquakes," is dated 1–7–05, and is available on his website at *www.palden.co.uk*.

165. Hawken, Paul. *Blessed Unrest: How the Largest Movement in the World Came Into Being and Why No One Saw It Coming*. New York, NY: Viking, 2007. *Ode Magazine* featured an excellent article on this in their May 2007 magazine. Entitled "The Power of Many," it is by Marco Visscher, pages 34–45.

166. An excerpt from the article, "Is Our Planet a Crystal?," by historian Joseph Robert Jochmans, Lit.D., appeared in Issue 78 of *Atlantis Rising Magazine*, pages

39, 66–67. Jochmans has done an outstanding job showing the interrelationships and resulting movements in evolutionary spirals between the human species and planet earth. To purchase his full report, and others he has authored, access *www.forgottenagesresearch.com*.

167. Gregg Easterbrook, *Sonic Boom: Globalization at Mach Speed*. New York, NY: Random House, 2009.

168. Refer to *The Wealth of Nations*, Adam Smith. Boston, MA: Digireads.com, 2009. This was originally published over a century ago. Combine these ideas about self-interest with *Business and the Buddha: Doing Well by Doing Good*, Lloyd Field. Somerville, MA: Wisdom Publications, 2007.

169. Refer to *The Next Form of Democracy*, Matt Leighninger. Nashville, TN: Vanderbilt University Press, 2006.

170. *Natural Capitalism: Creating the Next Industrial Revolution*, Paul Hawken, Amory Lovins, L. Hunter Lovins. New York, NY: Back Bay Books, 2008.

171. For a discussion about acoustic farming, read the article, "They're All Ears," by Jurriaan Kamp, and published by *Ode Magazine*, December 2007, pages 74–75. To understand the power of sound, acquaint yourself with the work of Dr. Hans Jenny and his book, *Cymatics: A Study of Wave Phenomena & Vibration*. Newmarket, NH: Macromedia Press, 2001.

172. Refer to *Double-Helix Water*, David Gann and Dr. Shui-Yin Lo. Purchase a copy through White Bear Sacred Medicinals, LLC, at whitebearsacmed@me.com, as it is not yet on bookstore shelves. The contact website is *www.doublehelixwater.com*.

173. The best referral on this is *Primary Perception: Biocommunication with Plants, Living Foods, and Human Cells*, Cleve Backster. Anza, CA; White Rose Millennium Press, 2003.

174. Learn all you can about sacred geometry and the importance of golden ratios (the relationship between two numbers where the sum of the two is to the larger, as the larger is to the smaller). Geometric forms that correspond to the golden ratio are found everywhere and define beauty, harmony, spiritual imagination, and lasting value. Sacred geometry is literally the architecture of creation.

Three books on the subject: *How the World Is Made: The Story of Creation, According to Sacred Geometry*, John Michell, with Allan Brown. Rochester, VT; Inner Traditions, 2009. And, *The Power of Limits: Proportional Harmonies in Nature, Art & Architecture*, Gyorgy Doczi. Boston, MA; Shambhala, 1985. *The Golden Section: Nature's Greatest Secret*, Scott A. Olsen. New York, NY: Wooden Books, Walker & Co., 2006.

Sacred Geometry School, run by Robert J. Gilbert, Ph.D., consists of a regular curriculum, seminars, classes, publications. Inquire at The Vesica Institute, 1011 Tunnel Road, Asheville, NC 28805; (828) 298–7007; *www.vesica.org*. I have attended some of their seminars and took a few classes, and found the opportunity very rewarding.

175. The story about John Chrysostom restructuring the writings of Apollonius of Tyana to become the "Epistles of Paul," can be found in *Secrets of the Christian Fathers*, Bishop J. W. Sergerus (a 1685–1897 reprint of what John, the "golden-mouthed," is

said to have done in 397). The Catholic Church considers the "Epistles of Paul" forgeries with this statement, "Even the genuine Epistles were greatly interpolated to lend weight to the personal views of their authors" (*Catholic Encyclopedia*, Farley, editor, Vol. VII, page 645). There are other declarations similar to this (see "The Letters of Jerome," *Library of the Fathers*, Oxford Movement, 1833–45, Vol. V, page 445). The more you start digging around in Christian history, the more surprising things get.

176. References to parts of the Book of John being "The Great Insertion" in the Bible are: *Catholic Encyclopedia*, Farley, editor, Vol. VII, pages 441–442. *New Catholic Encyclopedia (NCE)*, "Gospel of John," page 1080. Also, NCE Vol. VII, page 407.

For more facts about the Bible's history and that of the Christian religion, refer to the article, "What the Church Doesn't Want You to Know," by Tony Bushby, and appearing in *Nexus Magazine*, Vol. 14, No. 4, June-July 2007. Also refer to the book, *Saving Paradise: How Christianity Traded Love of This World for Crucifixion and Empire*, Rita Nakashima and Rebecca Ann Parker. Boston, MA; Beacon Press, 2009. *Reading Judas: The Gospel of Judas and the Shaping of Christianity*, Elaine Pagels and Karen L. King. New York, NY; Penguin, 2008.

Also refer to: *Truth: About the Five Primary Religions & The Seven Rules of Any Good Religion*, The Oracle Institute. Hamilton, VA: The Oracle Institute Press, LLC, 2005. *The Sins of Scripture: Exposing the Bible's Texts of Hate to Reveal the God of Love*, Bishop John Shelby Spong. New York, NY; HarperOne, 2006. *Eternal Life: A New Vision: Beyond Religion, Beyond Theism, Beyond Heaven and Hell*, Bishop John Shelby Spong. New York, NY; HarperCollins, 2010. *God's Scripture: A Faithful Comparison—What Jews, Christians, and Muslims Must Know,* Nader Pourhassan, Ph.D. Bloomington, IL: iUniverse, 2009.

177. Refer again to Tony Bushby's article, along with the specific references he gives from the *Catholic Encyclopedia*, for both First and Second Councils of Nicaea and what came after—including the agreement among churchmen to call the "Savior of Christianity," Hesus Krishna. The allusions he makes, however, that there is no record of an actual Jesus are wrong, as explained in this chapter. He actually contradicts himself in this regard in a discussion about the Sinai Bible, the oldest known.

For a more in-depth treatment of this time in history and questions about Yeshua/Jesus, read *Jesus: The Explosive Story of the 30 Lost Years and the Ancient Mystery Religions,* Tricia McCannon. Charlottesville, VA: Hampton, Roads, 2010.

178. *The Case for God*, Karen Armstrong. New York, NY; Knopf, 2009.

179. I learned of Gobekli Tepe through a *Newsweek Magazine* article entitled, "History in the Making," by Patrick Symmes, dated 3–1–10, pages 46–48.

180. *The Lost Books of the Bible and the Forgotten Books of Eden*, Rutherford H. Platt, editor. Berkeley, CA; Apocryphile Press, 2005.

181. I read about these letters on page 245 of the book, *Portrait of Jesus?*, by Frank C. Tribbe. It may still be available through The Holy Shroud Guild, 294 East 150th Street, Bronx, NY 10451. The book was originally published by Stein & Day, 1983.

One of the letters was written by Publius Lentulus, Governor of Judea, and sent to the Roman Senate and to Tiberius Caesar. The second was a report by Gamaliel, teacher of Saul of Tarsus, addressed to the Sanhedrin, and quoting the philosopher,

Massalian. And the other was a report by Pilate to the Emperor. All three stated that Jesus was quite tall and had a swarthy complexion, hair the color of new wine or sunburned gold, and soft blue or gray eyes.

182. There have been many books written about The Holy Shroud of Turin, Italy. The best way to learn about it is to access the website, *www.shroud.com/*. Previous attempts to prove it is a forgery have all failed, including the scientific study done a while ago. Serious mistakes were made by the team of scientists, necessitating that another study be conducted at a future date.

183. *The Gospel According to Jesus: A New Translation and Guide to His Essential Teachings for Believers and Unbelievers*, Stephen Mitchell. New York, NY; HarperCollins, 1991.

184. Read *He Walked the Americas*, L. Taylor Hansen. Amherst, WI; Amherst Press, 1963.

185. One who has done amazing research on the Laws of Nature is Rupert Sheldrake. He has written several books exploring various aspects of this topic. Start with *Morphic Resonance: The Nature of Formative Causation*. Rochester, VT: Park Street Press, 2009.

186. Unfortunately, scientific fraud is fairly common. In *Public Library of Science Journal*, 2009 (*www.plos.prg/journals/index.php*), they reported that in twenty-one scientific misconduct surveys, two-thirds of the researchers knew colleagues whose work was questionable. A particularly egregious case of betrayal was concerning the first scientist to figure out the math of black holes—Subrahmanyan Chandrasekhar—who was denied both recognition and reward for his triumph by a hateful colleague, Arthur Eddington. Refer to *Empire of Stars: Obsession, Friendship, and Betrayal in the Quest for Black Holes*, Arthur I. Miller. New York, NY: Houghton Mifflin, 2005.

187. Turner, John L. *Medicine, Miracles, and Manifestations: A Doctor's Journey Through the Worlds of Divine Intervention, Near-Death Experiences, and Universal Energy*. Franklin Lakes, NJ: New Page Books, 2009.

188. Called "the new heretic" (also the name of a column he once wrote for *Atlantis Rising Magazine*), Eugene F. Mallove, Sc.D., was an expert in alternative energy sources, and was a "torch-bearer" for cold fusion. He, along with Gregory L. Matloff, wrote, *The Starflight Handbook: A Pioneer's Guide to Interstellar Travel*. Hoboken, NJ; John Wiley & Sons, 1989. Mallove also wrote, *Fire from Ice: Searching for the Truth Behind the Cold Fusion Furor*. Hoboken, NJ; John Wiley & Sons, 1991.

189. Rune Amundsen and I have been friends for many years. This quote from a talk he gave was sent to me by Liv Evensen. Rune authored a book about his research of near-death experiences in Norway, but it was never translated into languages other than Norwegian. The title is *Livets Magiske Vev*, and it was published by En Kilde Forlag, Floro, Norway, 1993.

190. Ring, Kenneth. *Life at Death: A Scientific Investigation of the Near-Death Experience*. New York, NY: Coward, McCann and Geoghegan, 1980.

191. This brief synopsis of some of Dr. Bruce Greyson's work was taken from the article "Are Near-Death Experiencers Out of Their Bodies or Out of Their Minds?," by Bruce J. Horacek, Ph.D. It appeared in Vol. 20, No. 3, page 4, of *Vital Signs Newsletter*, a publication of IANDS.

192. Carroll Gray—refer to pages 64–67, *The New Children and Near-Death Experiences*.

193. Rand Jameson Shields— refer to pages 140–141, *The New Children and Near-Death Experiences*.

194. Merla Ianello—refer to pages 142–143, *The New Children and Near-Death Experiences*.

195. Steven B. Ridenhour - refer to pages 164–165, *The Complete Idiot's Guide to Near-Death Experiences*, with David Morgan. Indianapolis, IN; Alpha Books, 2000.

196. Mellen-Thomas Benedict - refer to pages 75–78, *Beyond the Light*.

197. George Rodonaia - refer to pages 79–83, *Beyond the Light*.

198. Margaret Fields Kean - refer to pages 83–88, *Beyond the Light*.

199. Arvin S. Gibson's "Hotshots in Hell" - refer to pages 169–171, *The Big Book of Near-Death Experiences*. Charlottesville, VA: Hampton Roads, 2007.

200. van Lommel, Pim. *Endless Consciousness*. New York, NY: HarperOne, 2010.

201. Two main books:

   Irreducible Mind: Toward a Psychology for the 21st Century, Edward F. Kelly, Emily Williams Kelly, Adam Crabtree, Alan Gauld, Michael Grosso, and Bruce Greyson. Blue Ridge Summit, PA: Rowman & Littlefield, 2007.

   The Handbook of Near-Death Experiences: Thirty Years of Investigation, edited by Janice Miner Holden, Ed.D., Bruce Greyson, M.D., and Debbie James, RN/MSN. Santa Barbara, CA: Praeger Publishers, 2009.

   Seven additional renderings:

   Scientific Literacy and the Myth of the Scientific Method, Henry H. Bauer. Urbana, IL: University of Illinois Press, 1992.

   The Fundamentalist Mind: How Polarized Thinking Imperils Us All, Stephen Larsen, Ph.D. Wheaton, IL: Quest Books, 2007

   Extraordinary Knowing: Science, Skepticism and the Inexplicable Powers of the Human Mind, Elizabeth Lloyd Mayer. New York, NY: Bantam Books, 2008.

   The End of Materialism: How Evidence of the Paranormal Is Bringing Science and Spirit Together, Charles T. Tart, Ph.D. Oakland, CA: New Harbinger Publications, 2009.

   A New Science of the Paranormal, Lawrence LeShan, Ph.D. Wheaton, IL: Quest Books, 2009.

   The ESP Enigma: The Scientific Case for Psychic Phenomena, Diane Hennacy, Ph.D. New York, NY: Walker & Co., 2008.

   The Parapsychology Revolution: A Concise Anthology of Paranormal and Psychical Research, Robert M. Schoch, Ph.D. and Logan Yonavijak. New York; NY: Tarcher/Penguin, 2009.

   Three important websites:

   About pseudo-skeptics: *www.debunkingskeptics.com*.

   Archives of Scientists' Transcendent Experiences: *http://psychology.ucdavis.edu/tart/taste/*.

   The work of Rhea White and "Exceptional Human Experiences": *www.psi-mart.com* (look for EHE publications).

202. To view some of the incredible paintings of English landscape artist Michael John Hill, access:

www.kavanaughgallery.com/Michael_J_Hill.html.
www.hallmarkgallery.com/gal/.../Michael-John-14–14.html.
www.atlasgalleries.com/.
www.askart.com/.../michael_john_hill/michael_john_hill.aspx
www.shortnorth.com/LizKathryn2006.html.

203. The full story of Grandfather Leon Secatero is in the article, "Journey Among the Wind Walkers: Grandfather Secatero Recovers from Stroke," written by Steven McFadden and copyrighted in April of 2007. To read it, access *www.8thfire.net* or *www.chiron-communications.com*. Should you have any difficulty finding it, contact McFadden directly at Chiron Communications, P. O. Box 29662, Santa Fe, NM 87592.

204. Michael Hutchison's three books:

    Book of Floating: Exploring the Private Sea. Nevada City, CA: Gateway Books & Tapes, 2003.

    Mega Brain Power: Transform Your Life with Mind Machines and Brain Nutrients. New York, NY: Hyperion Books, 1994.

    Megabrain: New Tools & Techniques for Brain Growth & Mind Expansion. New York, NY: Ballantine Books, 1996.

    Two interviews of him are in the *AVS Journal*. Access *www.mindmachines.com/AvsJournal/article-AnE-InterviewMichaelHutchinson.htm*. Michael has just written another book. Details unavailable at this writing.

205. Many of you will remember the name Kathy J. Forti from my book *Future Memory*. She had a near-death experience as a teenager, which covered some scenes from her future—a future that later occurred. She wrote a child's book about a boy who had a near-death experience, called *The Door to the Secret City*. This book is now available free of charge by downloading it from: *www.scribd.com/doc/13120024/The-Door-to-the-Secret-City-Book-1-of-Freddie-Brenners-Mysitcal-Adventure-Series*.

    What she shares with us this time is her adult near-death episode that led to the creation of a device called "Trinfinity8." This device is amazing everyone who uses it for upliftment and energizing they receive—as if "custom made" for each person's needs. You can view the device on *www.trinfinity8.com*. Contact: Caramente Health Products—Trinfinity8, 1158–26th Street, PMB 486, Santa Monica, CA 90403; (310) 451–4534; Kathy@trinfinity8.com.

206. To reach Andrea Arrowsmith, contact: Inner Sounds of Light Institute, P. O. Box 613, Glorieta, NM 87535; (505) 757–3364. Her websites are *www.healingsoulsongs.com* and *www.soulsongs.gaia.com*.

207. Dan Rhema's case previously appeared in *The Complete Idiot's Guide to Near-Death Experiences* and *The Big Book of Near-Death Experiences*. I carry his voice here because of how he has changed since then, an individual who glows with a peace so distinctive; he has become unforgettable to those who have touched his life. Although he still deals with healing issues, he has gone on to author children's books, and is now finishing a book about his near-death experience that is the most elegantly powerful I have yet seen. Contact: Dan Rhema, P. O. Box 17513, Louisville, KY 40207; (502) 635–2457; dan@danrhema.com; *www.danrhema.com*.

INDEX

money problems, 92–93

Moody, Raymond, 5–6, 36, 107, 170, 182, 184

morphic fields (M-fields), 190–191

Morse, Donald R., 46

Morse, Melvin, 5

Mother light, 21

Mulligan (personal account), 29–31

multiples, 38–40

Murphy, Todd, 57

music, 80–81

Narby, Jeremy, 81

Natural Capitalism (Hawken et al.), 215

natural health products, 99

NDE Research Scales, 182

near-death experiences
    definitions of, 2–3
    length of, 15
    patterns of, 14–15, 232–233
    personal accounts of, 25–34, 61–69, 108, 119–120, 241–251
    precursors to, 139–140
    truth of, 12–14
    types of, 17–19

near-death states, patterns of, 129–133

near-death-like experiences, 44–45

negative/positive labels, 19

The New Children and Near-Death Experiences (Atwater), 40, 55, 99

Newberg, Andres, 172

Nickel, Tricia, 127

Nikq, Granit, 244–245

"non" experience, 18

Nurss, Dolores J., 121

O'Hara, Robin, 67–68

Ohno, Susumu, 81

other world imagery, 175–176

otherworld environments, 179–180

otherworldly beings, 176–178

out-of-body experiences
    as common element, 20
    cultural differences and, 183
    description of, 21
    media and, 234
    personal accounts of, 63, 64, 65–66, 68–69

oxygen, cell death and, 3–4

oxytocin, 163

Pacana, Mark, 65–66

pain, life reviews and, 23

parallel processing, 186–187

Paul (apostle), 44–45, 222

pediatric temporal lobe epilepsy, 57

Penfield, Wilder, 235

perception, 111–115, 235–237

perennial philosophy, 104

peritraumatic dissociation, 144

Persinger, Michael, 235

personal imagery, 175

personality patterns, 15

pets, as greeters, 22

peyote, 163

pharmaceuticals, sensitivity to, 72, 76, 86, 89, 211

pineal gland, 188–189

pleasant experience. *see* heavenly (pleasant) experience

positive/negative labels, 19, 116

potential, 208

Potthoff, Stephen E., 183

power punch, 142

precognition, 79–80, 95

pre-frontal lobes, 198–199

prejudice/preference, perceptual, 112–113, 174–175

previews, 40–42

Pribram, Karl H., 162, 189

Primary light, 21

ABOUT THE AUTHOR

Visit the author at *www.pmhatwater.com.* Atwater's website exists as a cyber-library of her research with near-death states, the spiritual approach to life, the positive use of intuitive abilities, and information about the "new children." Changes are made from time to time, especially regarding her travel schedule.

Other features include a section for actual near-death cases, reference lists for educational opportunities; holistic therapies; charts and fliers; and The Marketplace. The Marketplace of NDE-Related Items of Interest is a treasure trove of offerings from a host of near-death experiencers and those like them. It is offered as a public service. The purpose is to help people connect with inspired work, while enabling experiencers to have a way of promoting what they do. The Marketplace exists nowhere else. Take advantage of it.

To subscribe to Atwater's free "infrequent" newsletter, sign up at the bottom of her website home page. Newsy and free-ranging, each newsletter is unique.

The story of Atwater's three near-death experiences is now available as an electronic book. Look for *I Died Three Times in 1977—The Complete Story* on *Amazon.com.*

Atwater's blog: *http://www.pmhatwater.blogspot.com*

HAMPTON ROADS PUBLISHING COMPANY
. . . FOR THE EVOLVING HUMAN SPIRIT

Hampton Roads Publishing Company publishes books on a variety of subjects, including spirituality, health, and other related topics.

For a copy of our latest trade catalog, call 978-465-0504 or visit our website at *www.hrpub.com*